IN THE VALE OF CASHMERE

Who has not heard of the Vale of Cashmere,
  with its roses the brightest that earth ever gave,
Its temples, and grottos, and fountains as clear
  As the love-lighted eyes that hung over their wave?

- Thomas Moore

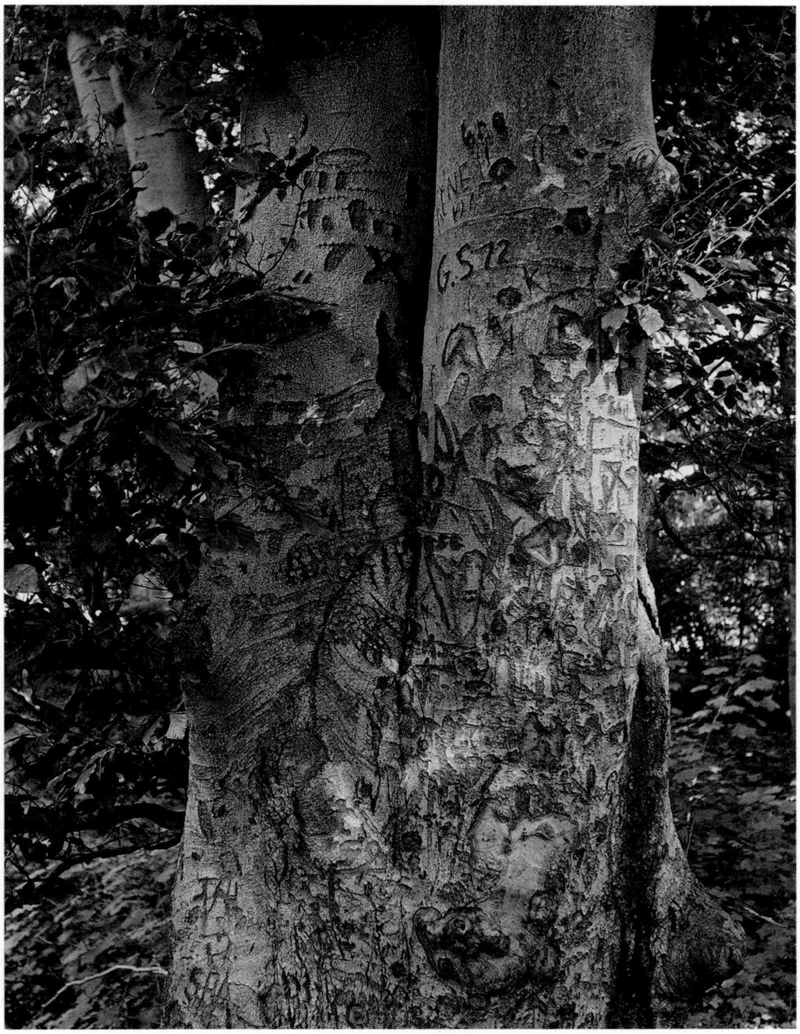
G.S 72

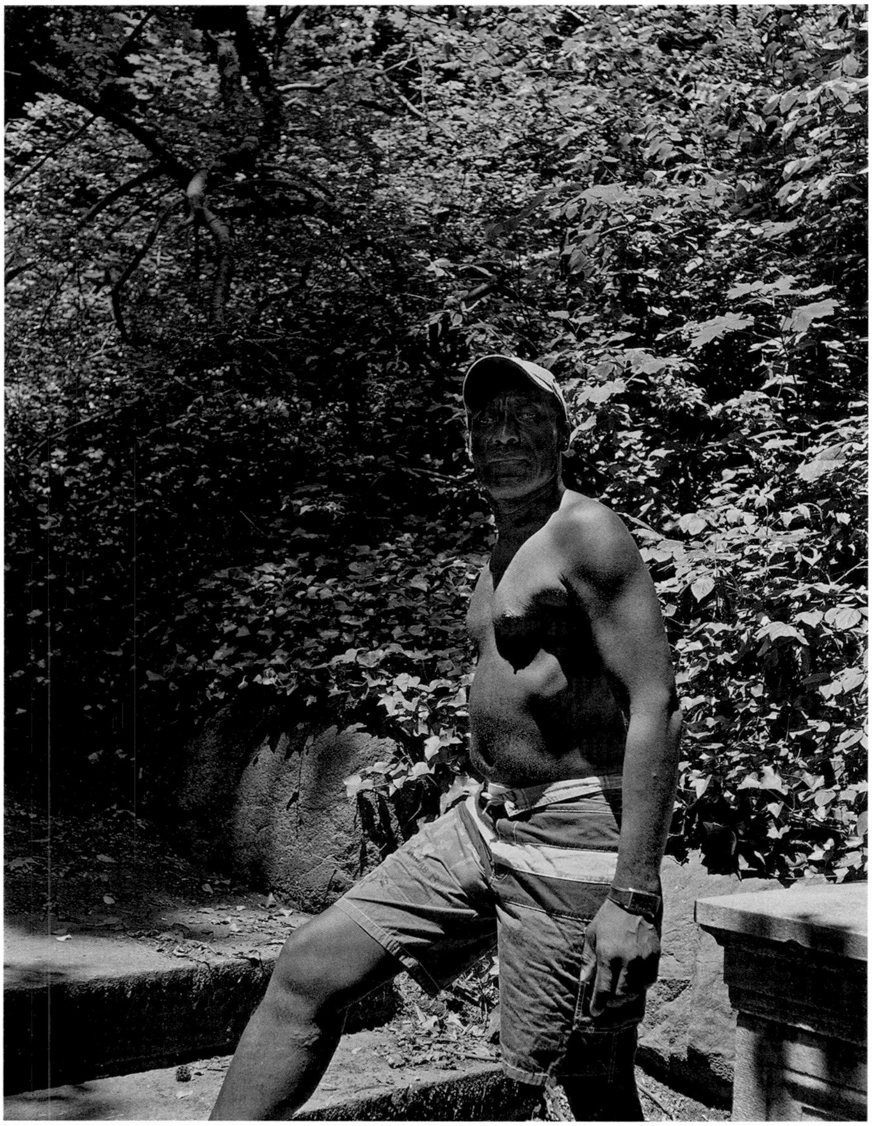

PHOTOGRAPHS BY THOMAS ROMA

IN THE VALE OF

INTRODUCTION BY G. WINSTON JAMES

CASHMERE

POWERHOUSE BOOKS · BROOKLYN, NY

IN MEMORY OF CARL

I will rise now, and go about the city in
the streets, and in the broad ways I will
seek him whom my soul loveth: I
sought him, but I found him not.

The watchmen that go about the city
found me: to whom I said, Saw ye him
whom my soul loveth?

Song of Solomon 3:2,3

> "When I got there, I found the park filled with men in the same horny, hungry state of mind I was in....I can't remember ever seeing so many gorgeous black men in any one place."
>
> — Rory Buchanan

While the Brooklyn Bridge is inarguably Brooklyn's ultimate and most photographed landmark, there are others like Coney Island and the Brooklyn Museum that also enjoy international acclaim. Perhaps lesser known outside of New York City though is Prospect Park, which first opened in 1867. It is to this park, originally designed by the celebrated landscape architects Frederick Law Olmsted and Calvert Vaux, that Thomas Roma has turned his considerable attention with this collection of photographs. However, it was not simply to the 585-acre park's landscape or its neoclassical design and architectural examples that Roma was drawn, but specifically to the setting of one of its arranged spaces: the Vale of Cashmere, and by extension the adjoining Rose Garden and surrounding paths. This book is not a review of architectural history and park design, but rather a photographic examination of this particular urban landscape and its function vis-à-vis gay (sub)culture and social and sexual desire. That is to say, this is not so much a book about a place in Brooklyn's Prospect Park, as it is about the Black, Latino, and other gay and bisexual men who frequent it at odd hours as a place of communion, often in hopes of satisfying both their social and sexual desires.

At first I was apprehensive about writing the introduction to *In the Vale of Cashmere* because somehow over the years I'd convinced myself that the Vale after dusk and the clandestine things that went on there were known only to those who partook of those activities, and as such were only to be discussed in closed company. Although still largely unknown to most, including the majority of Brooklyn residents, it took only a little research to disabuse me of the notion that the files on cruising in Prospect Park were in any real way classified. Despite my misgivings, it was quickly clear that the furtive activities that transpire in the Vale of Cashmere had long been knowledge publicly available to anyone who chose to seek it out. A quick Internet search revealed a selection of short fiction and numerous blog posts that make specific reference to gay cruising in that area of Prospect Park. Among a variety of newspaper articles, a July 12, 2000 *New York Times* headline—"Police Hunt Masked Slasher of Four Men in Prospect Park"—hammers home the extent to which the men pictured in *In the Vale of Cashmere* (and the photographer himself) literally risked their lives each time they plied the Prospect Park paths after dark.

Morgan Shaw, in his essay "Privacy Could Only Be Had In Public: Exploring the Queer Use of Public Parks," states that, "Traditionally, the very definition of 'public space' excludes the possibility of its use for sex. Sex is supposed to take place in the privacy of the home, far from the prying eyes of the public. But for those gays who, especially in the late nineteenth and early twentieth centuries, were married or lived with parents who would not accept their homosexuality, their private desire for homosexual sex could not be expressed within their homes for fear of discovery. They were forced to bring this type of sexual activity into the public realm," thereby transforming heteronormative public space into "queer space." Morgan further asserts that, "The most defining characteristic of queer space is its temporality. Queer space is not a permanent fixture of the urban landscape, but a sudden transformation that briefly renders traditional public spaces as something more dynamic. It may be created at different times of the day or night, on a regular schedule or haphazardly." It is precisely this process of transformation (witnessed by a relative few), this dynamism, this history, that Thomas Roma has photographed here in *In the Vale of Cashmere*.

While I (to my knowledge) do not actually appear among the images Thomas Roma made over the three and a half years he spent photographing in the Vale, I could easily have been, and am metaphorically represented by virtue of my own experiences as an Afro-Caribbean gay man who sought sex in the Vale of Cashmere, and by my very nature as one who has been given to erotic chase in public spaces. Roma's photographs exemplify a socio-sexual milieu and paradigm that has drawn multitudes of men and persisted for decades despite violence, murder, and assorted official attempts by city and borough governments (and even gay organizations) to tamp down on cruising behaviors that are seen by many as socially unacceptable, perilous in terms of risk of bodily harm and potential exposure to sexually transmitted diseases, and deviant, irresponsible, and illegal. I believe that Roma makes a conscious choice here to focus his lens on, and ask permission of, Black men in particular, but this choice is not meant to mislead readers into believing that only such men like me make (and have made) carnal use of this space, or that cruising by Black men in Prospect Park is limited to the Vale of Cashmere. While African American and Caribbean men currently predominate as a result of patterns of immigration and other factors, those who frequent the Vale of Cashmere in search of community and sexual gratification have been as diverse and demographically mutable as the communities (far and near) that surround Prospect Park.

The images that Thomas Roma presents carry with them the economic, racial, sociocultural history of New York and Brooklyn as well as the struggles (personal and political) related to the development and defense of sexual identity and community that continue to play out locally, nationally, and internationally. George Chauncey points out in *Gay New York: Gender, Urban Culture, and the Making of the Gay Male World, 1880–1940* that in the 1920s and 30s "cruising parks and streets provided many young men and newcomers to the city with a point of entry into the rest of the gay world.... The parks and streets were perhaps the most common place for newcomers to meet men more familiar with that world, and these men became their guides to it." While some of that paradigm still exists, I believe that the late twentieth and early twenty-first centuries have seen Prospect Park and the Vale of Cashmere evolve into a final destination for a segment of the population rather than merely a way station to the greater gay world. Rory Buchanan's short story "Summer Chills," from *Brother to Brother: New Writings by Black Gay Men*, evidences this, as he wrote of Prospect Park in the late 80s, "I can't remember ever seeing so many gorgeous black men in any one place." He wrote this despite the fact that Mr. Buchanan, with whom I was acquainted, was a member of the social organization Gay Men of African Descent, which had been formed in 1986. Like me, Buchanan was thereby already privy to the existence of several established Black gay bars, clubs, and social organizations that were present during the period in which this short story was set. The story's protagonist goes on to say that, "Passing through the trees and bushes transported me through time. I found myself in a lush tropical jungle. I could feel the humidity wrap itself around my body. I could smell the vegetation smoldering and seething with a life all its own. I looked at the brothers near me and felt I was in an uninhibited village in Africa." The sensations Buchanan describes are in fact a list of some of the reasons men consciously choose to venture into the Vale of Cashmere, knowing that no bar or nightclub can offer them an equivalent experience.

Clearly, rather than simply being driven into concealment by a heteronormative and homophobic society, many men (myself included) entered the Vale of Cashmere after dark because we enjoyed it (even drew a sense of power and resistance to societal norms from it), not because we had few or no other options through which to engage with other men. Journalist Kai Wright writes in his book *Drifting Toward Love: Black, Brown, Gay, and Coming of Age on the Streets of New York*, that, "New York is a place where scarce space is jealously defined by whomever has most recently laid claim to it.... New Yorkers stake out their space and draw power and belonging from it... and so, central Brooklyn's young Black and Latino gay men mark Vaux and Olmsted's rambling woods as theirs...." Gathering at the fountains and along the benches in the Rose Garden above the Vale of Cashmere during the day is as much (or more) an act of fellowshipping and strengthening of community ties as it is one of cruising for sex.

After the sun has set, however, this equation tilts strongly towards the carnal. Cruising at night, in my experience, heavily weights the values of anonymity and transitory sexual contact as an alternative to the "more structured" status quo gay world. For some, danger (from law enforcement more so than violence) is an added lure that no longer exists in the world of bars, nightclubs, and licensed sexual establishments as it did before and during the era of Stonewall.

Thomas Roma, to his great credit, manages to chronicle through his photographs both the carnal and communal elements of the Vale of Cashmere—including multiple photographs in which the subjects are clearly known to one another and share an affection that goes beyond the sensuous—with a continuous emphasis on the natural setting in which these relationships manifest. Roma succeeds at imaging this world despite the limitations of still photography and the art form's inability to capture the sounds of the wind through the trees, of insects making their way through detritus, of bats, footfalls, and moments of utter silence.

The cover of *In the Vale of Cashmere* depicts a late fall or winter scene in which a young Black man makes his way, seemingly aimlessly, along a heavily beaten path among denuded trees. This is a perfect image with which to begin the collection and to convey the sense of wandering, of having an idea of what one desires, but being uncertain in which guise or direction one will find the object of one's pursuit. This entrée into the collection recalls for me the uncontrollable trembling I sometimes felt as I entered the park awash in a mixture of anticipation and angst. The thudding of my heart that I experienced at moments, knowing that I was by myself under the night sky, but not at all alone. Roma does a masterful job with photographs such as this—and the second image of a much carved into tree that likely began its life as two separate trees that over time fused together—which speak volumes about purpose, and the persistence and complications of desire, by either absenting individual men from the images or presenting them as nearly insignificant in contrast to the landscape, suggestive forgotten items (such as a towel, strewn condoms, a lone glove, a newspaper, or torn photos), refuse, and other elements of the environment.

Many of the other photographs, however, present portraits of the park's denizens for which Roma received permission and cooperation. These images represent both a coup for Roma and a constraint in that their formal quality speaks to the rapport and trust he developed with these men (in a milieu in which namelessness and facelessness are often considered priceless), but cannot convey the raw nature of what it is to hunt or to offer oneself to other men in failing light or utter darkness knowing that the ever-present risks will endure far longer than the fleeting instant of orgasm as reward. Brilliantly, Roma also includes images that suggest filmstrips, which serve to reintroduce the notions of movement, spontaneity and, importantly, anonymity which are cornerstones of the public sexual functioning of environments such as this.

It is refreshing that there is no artifice involved in these photographs aside from Roma's ingenuity in constructing his own camera. Journalistic in their artistry, these black and white images do not betray any particular stance regarding the scenes they present—neither glorifying nor denigrating the men or the activities in which they partake. Where men do not appear, Roma paints for us an image of this landscape called Prospect Park, its slender, gnarled and broken trees and shrubs, its slants of light and blankets of shadow, which serve at different times as obstacles, implements, and camouflage. The Vale of Cashmere and its adjoining grounds epitomize the ways in which designed spaces (like men) sometimes return to their natural character at intervals intentionally, but most often through the happenstance of being.

In so producing and assembling these photographs, Roma has created an imagistic work, using the everyday language of humanity and reality to enlarge and continue the conversation regarding controversial sites of public sexuality such as the Vale of Cashmere, which are in a constant struggle against both heterosexual and homosexual agents and organizations that see nothing redemptive or positive in their queer use. It is as Morgan Shaw states that, "rather than looking at cruising grounds and places of public sex as places that foster a gay community, these officials argue that this type of behavior makes public acceptance of queer culture more difficult, supposedly weakening the moral position of those who would prefer assimilation into what is held-up as the shining image of heterosexual middle-class morality."

Thankfully, *In the Vale of Cashmere* is no morality play of images. Roma's project raises, perhaps impartially, the question of whether it is necessary, possible, and valuable to have privacy in public, and whether the queering of a public space on a temporary or covert basis can be beneficial to individuals or even a community without being pernicious to other parties or society at large. At its simplest and most profound, however, Roma's photographs are additional evidence of a locus of gay social and erotic life that has remained largely unchanged despite advances in social acceptance of homosexuality and even technology. The faces, races, and classes of the men pictured here would undoubtedly change if Thomas Roma were to repeat this project over the coming decades, but what would remain true is that the men of the Vale are and always have been some of our friends, family members, colleagues, and our neighbors. — G. Winston James

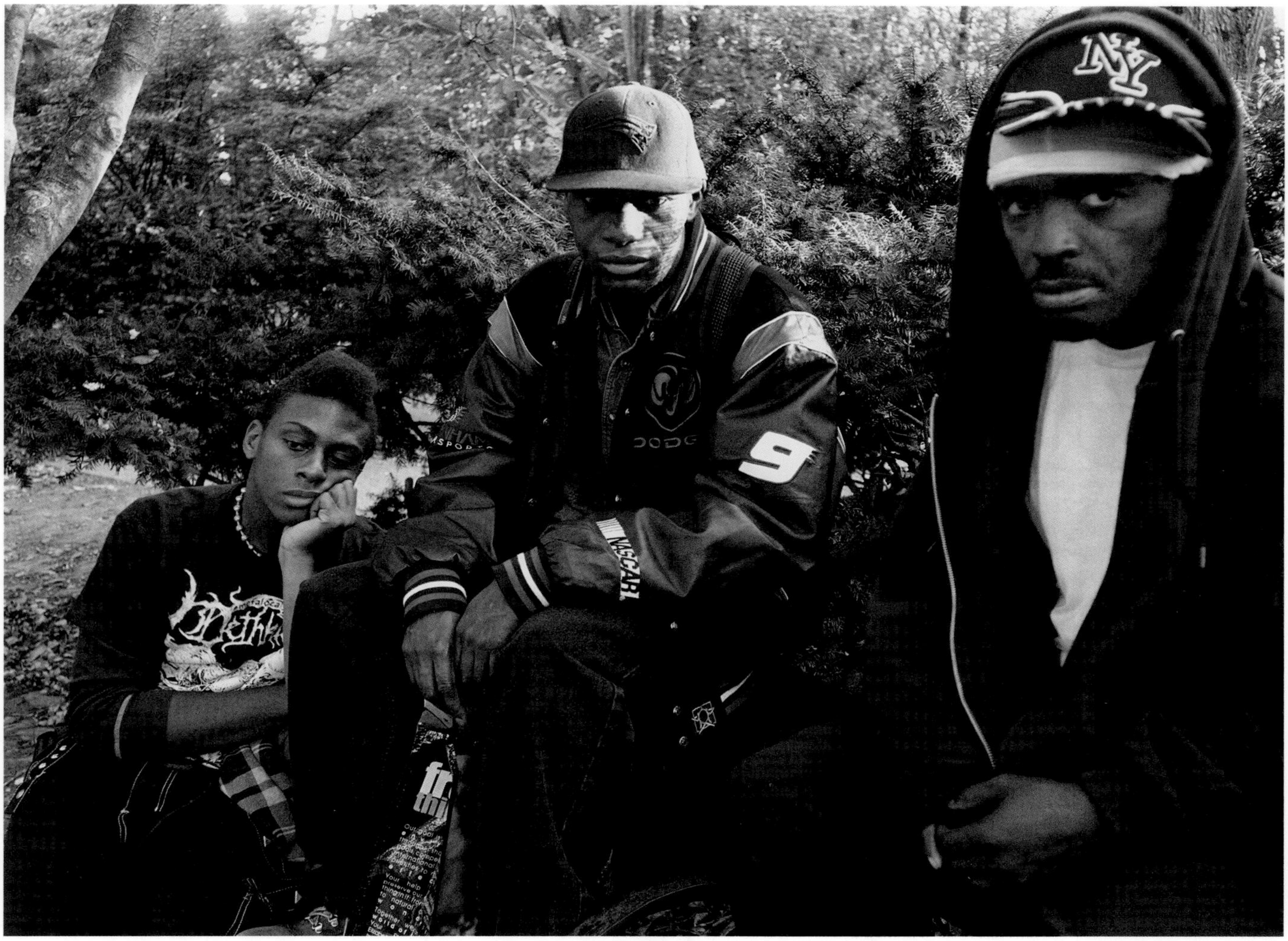
NY
9

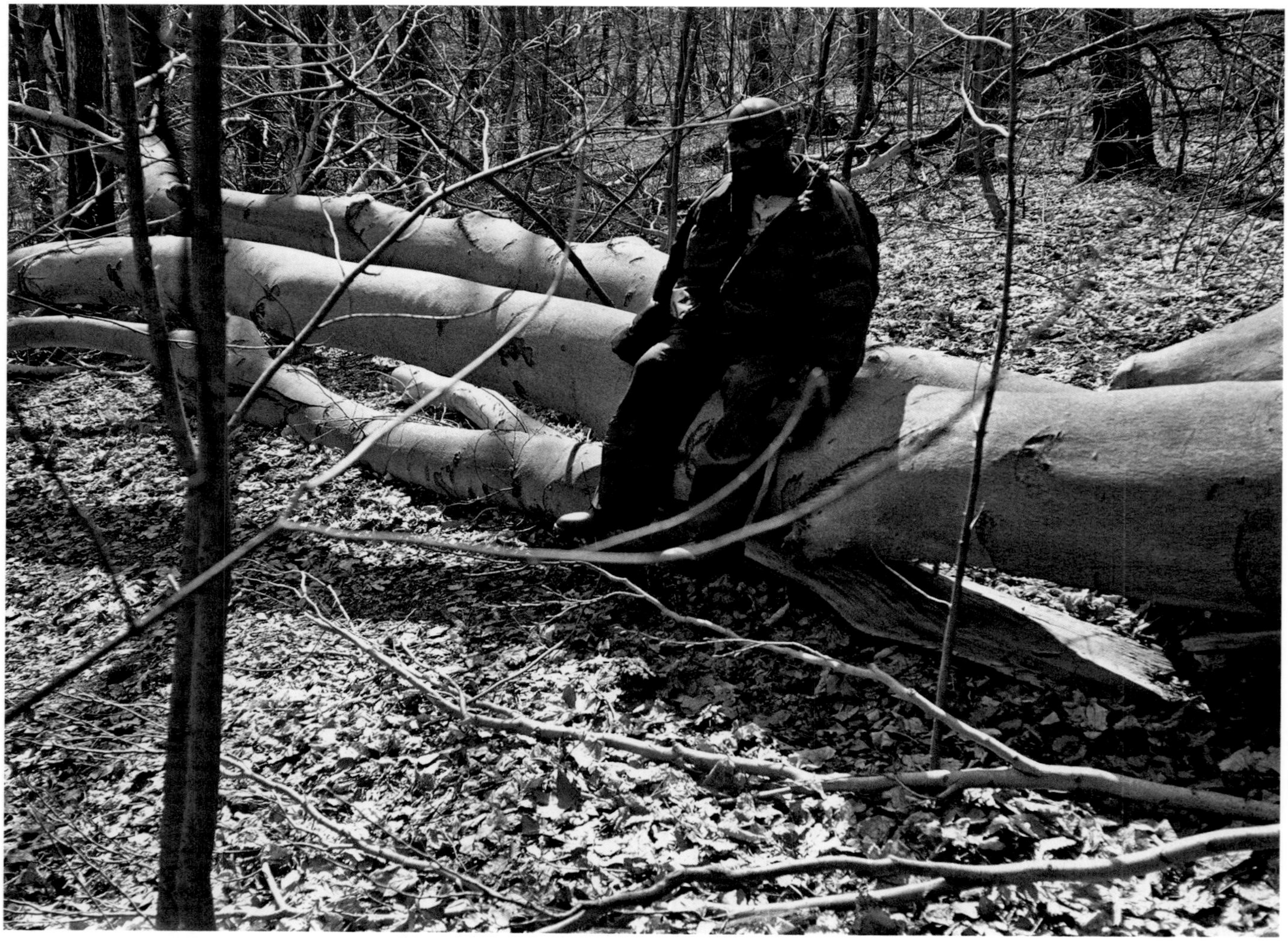

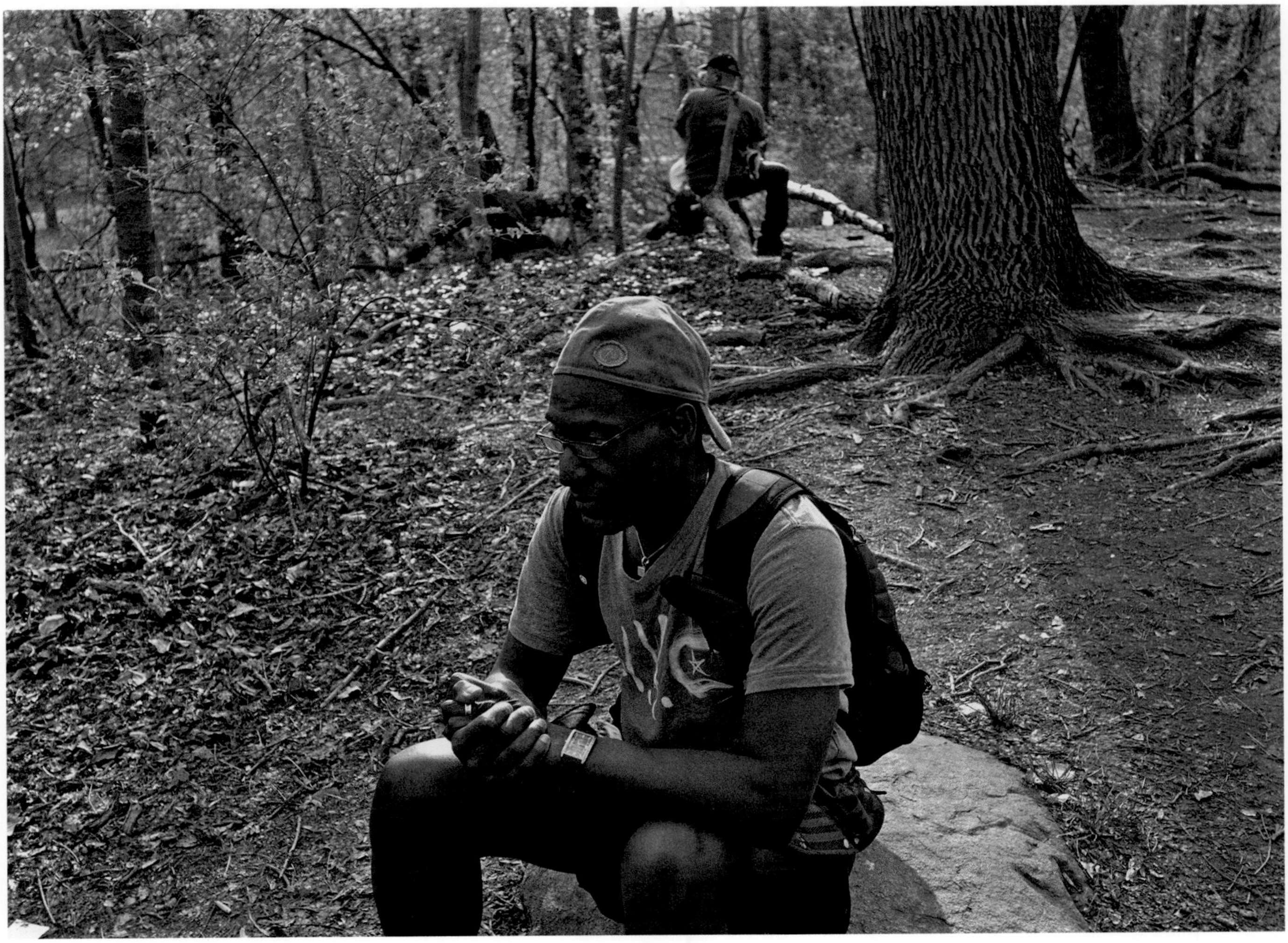

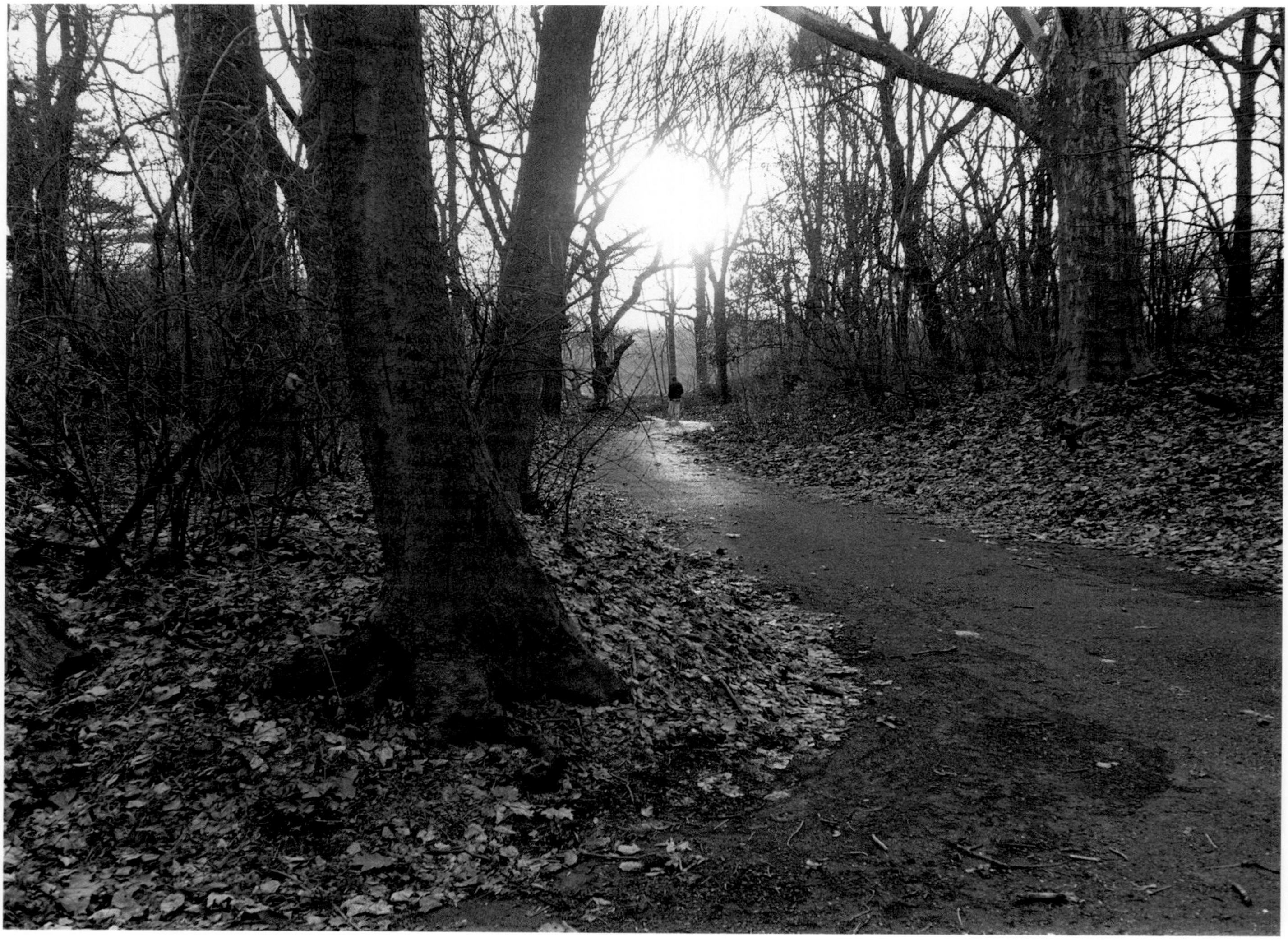

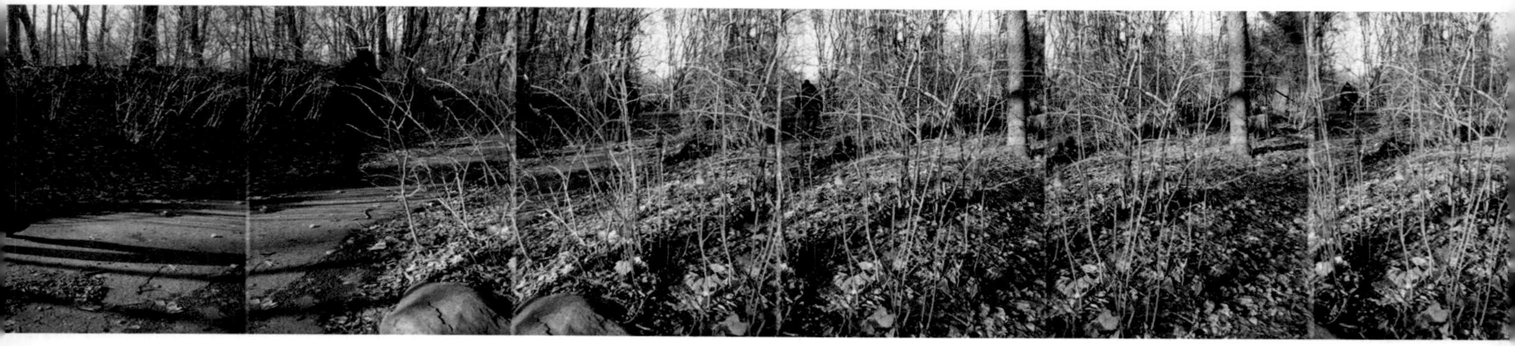

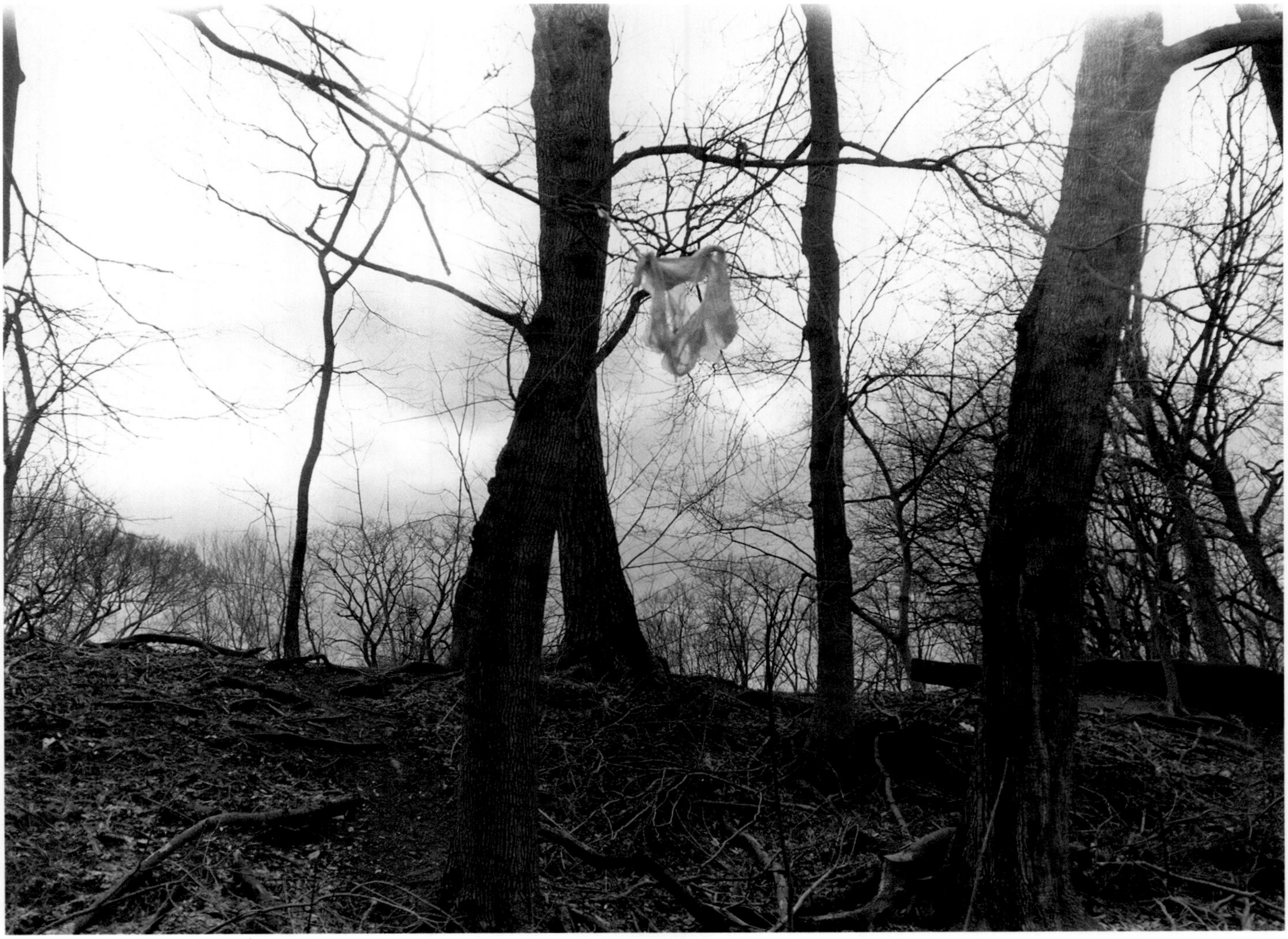

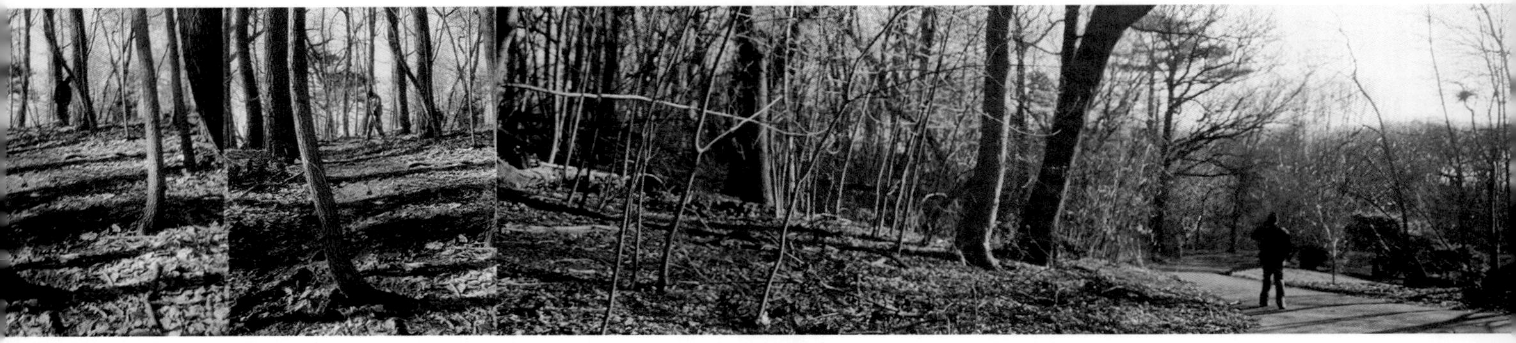

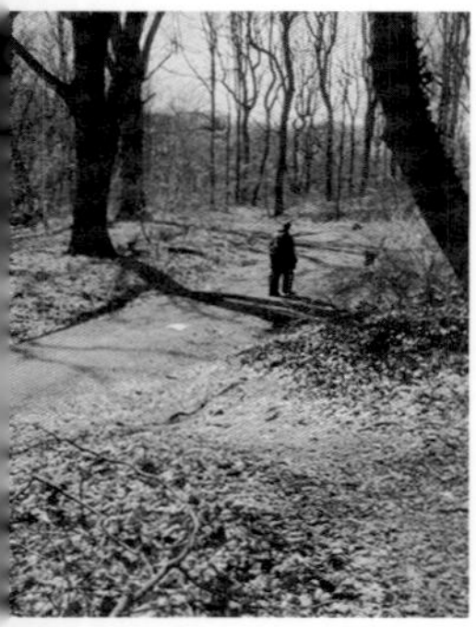

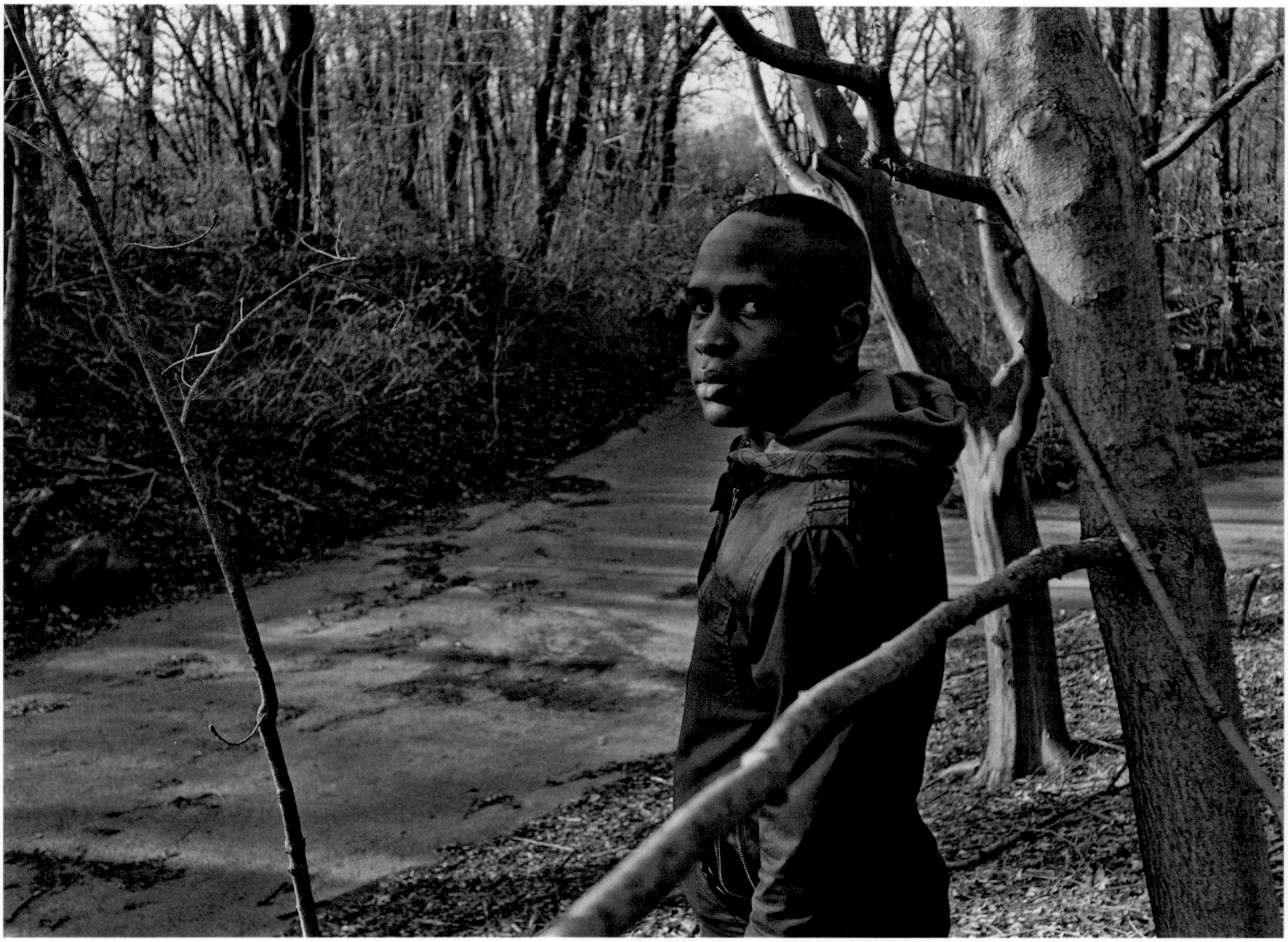

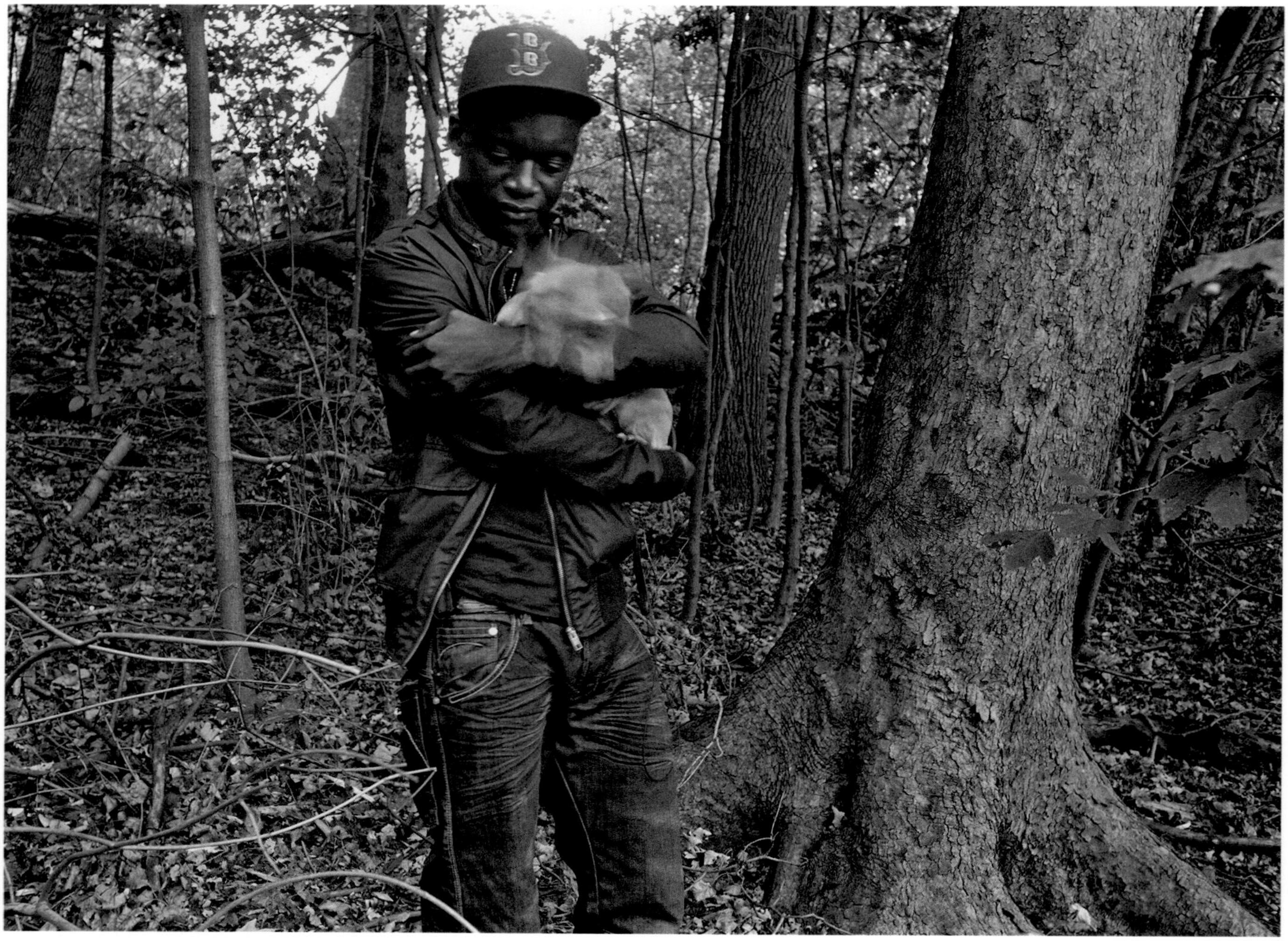

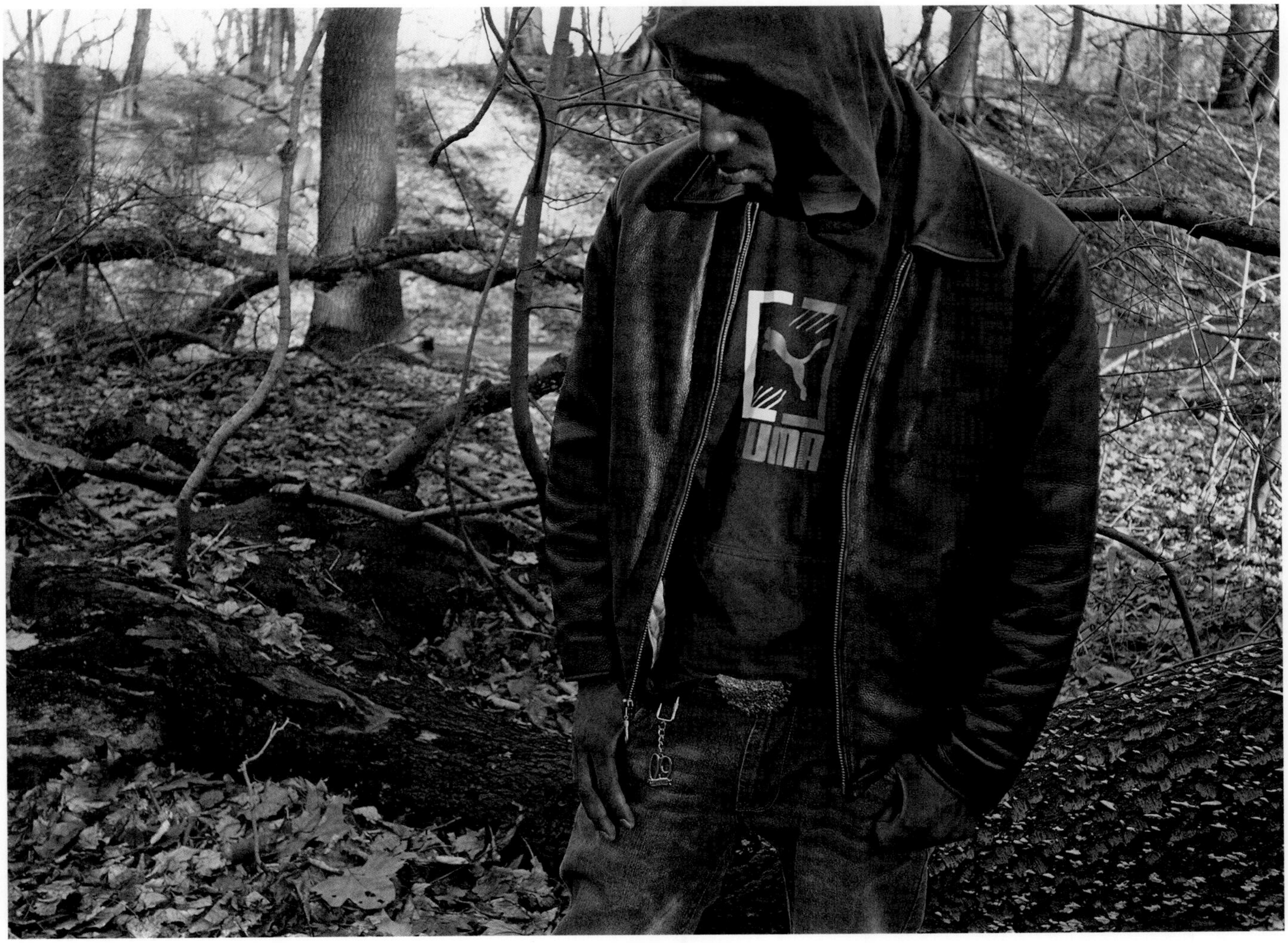
UMA

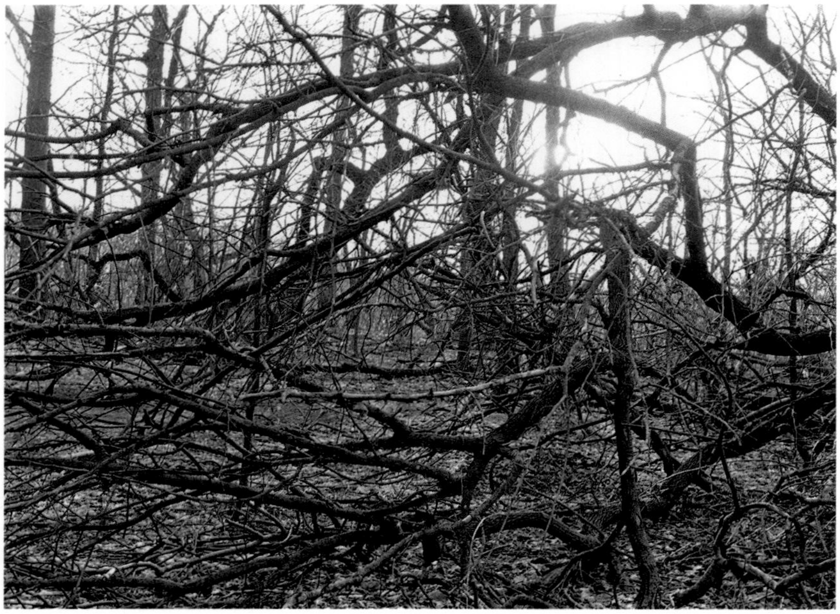

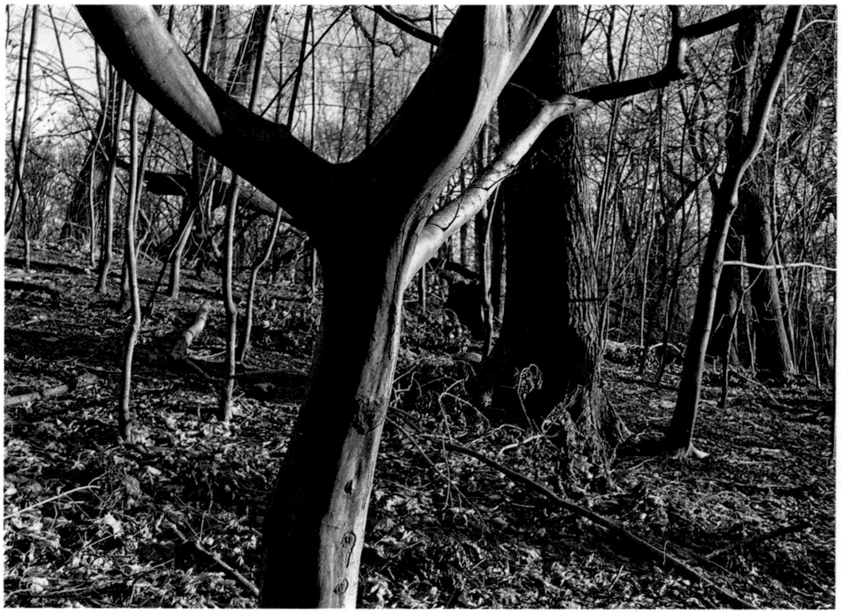

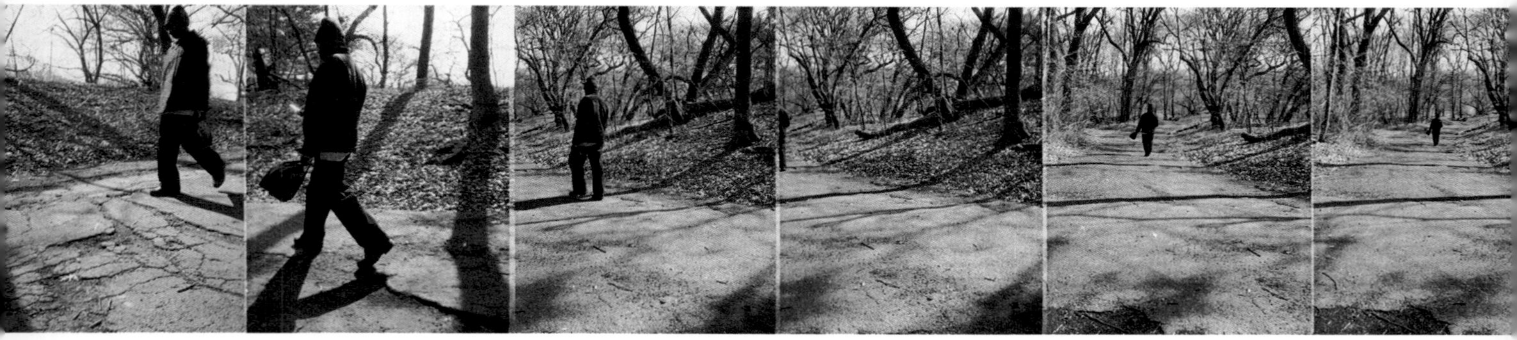

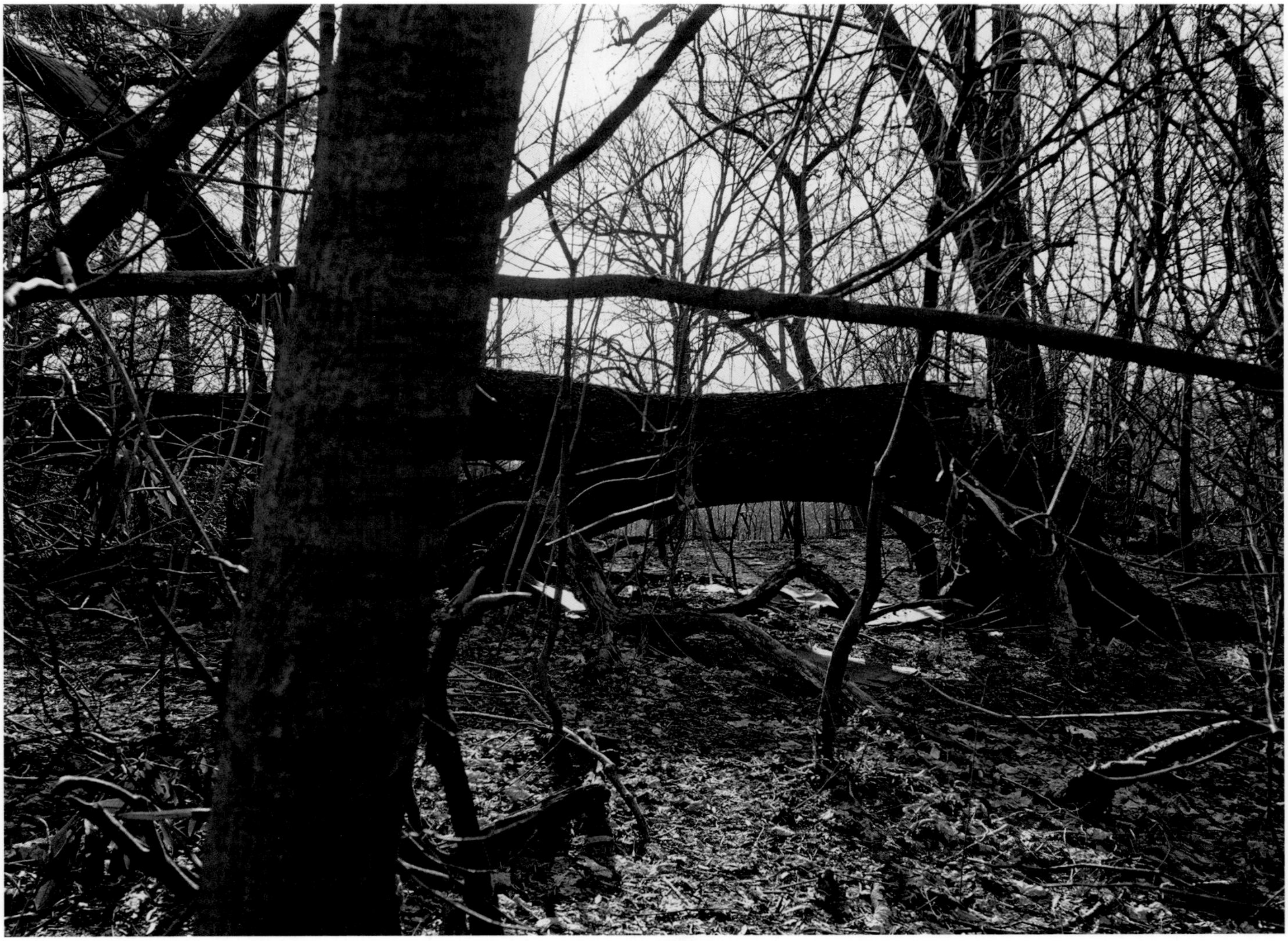

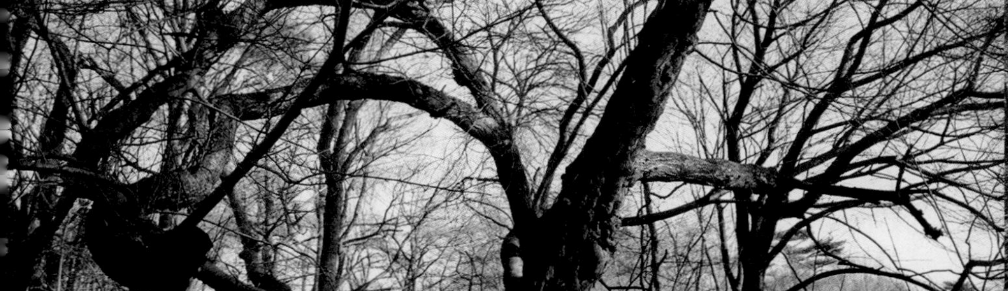

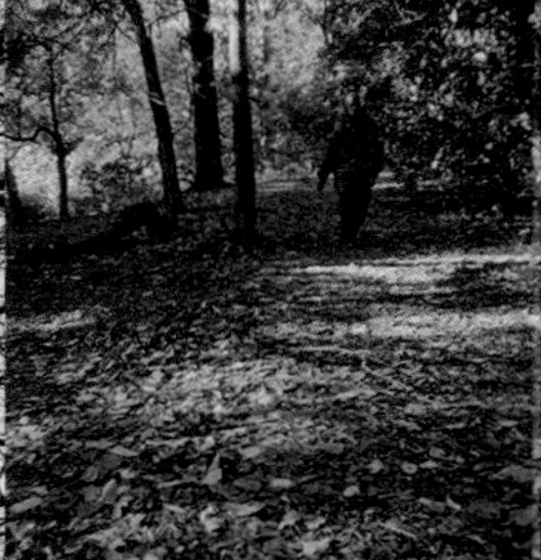

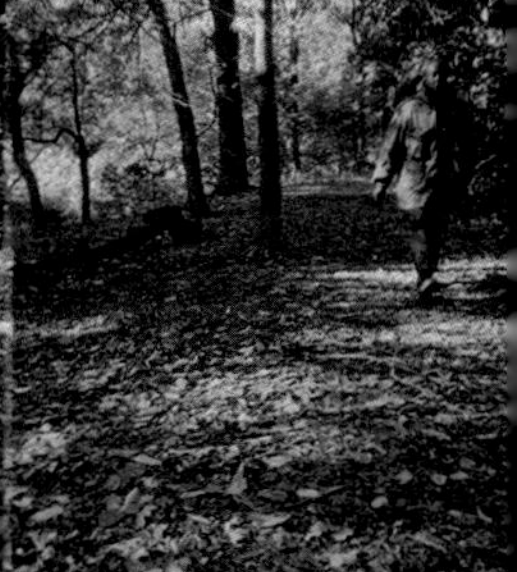

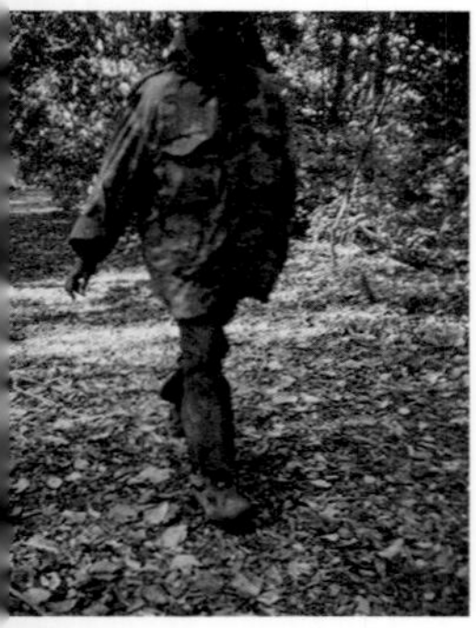

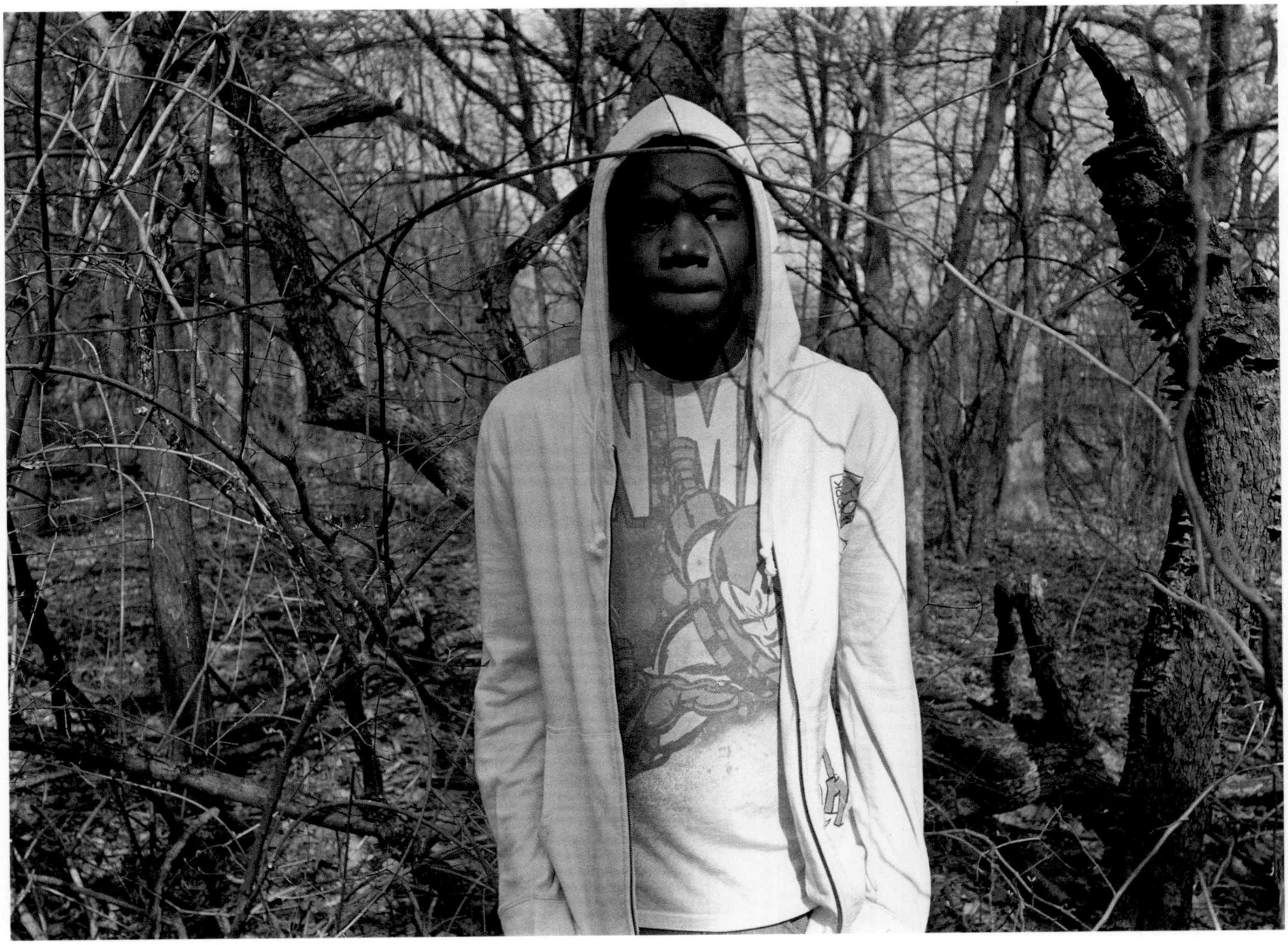

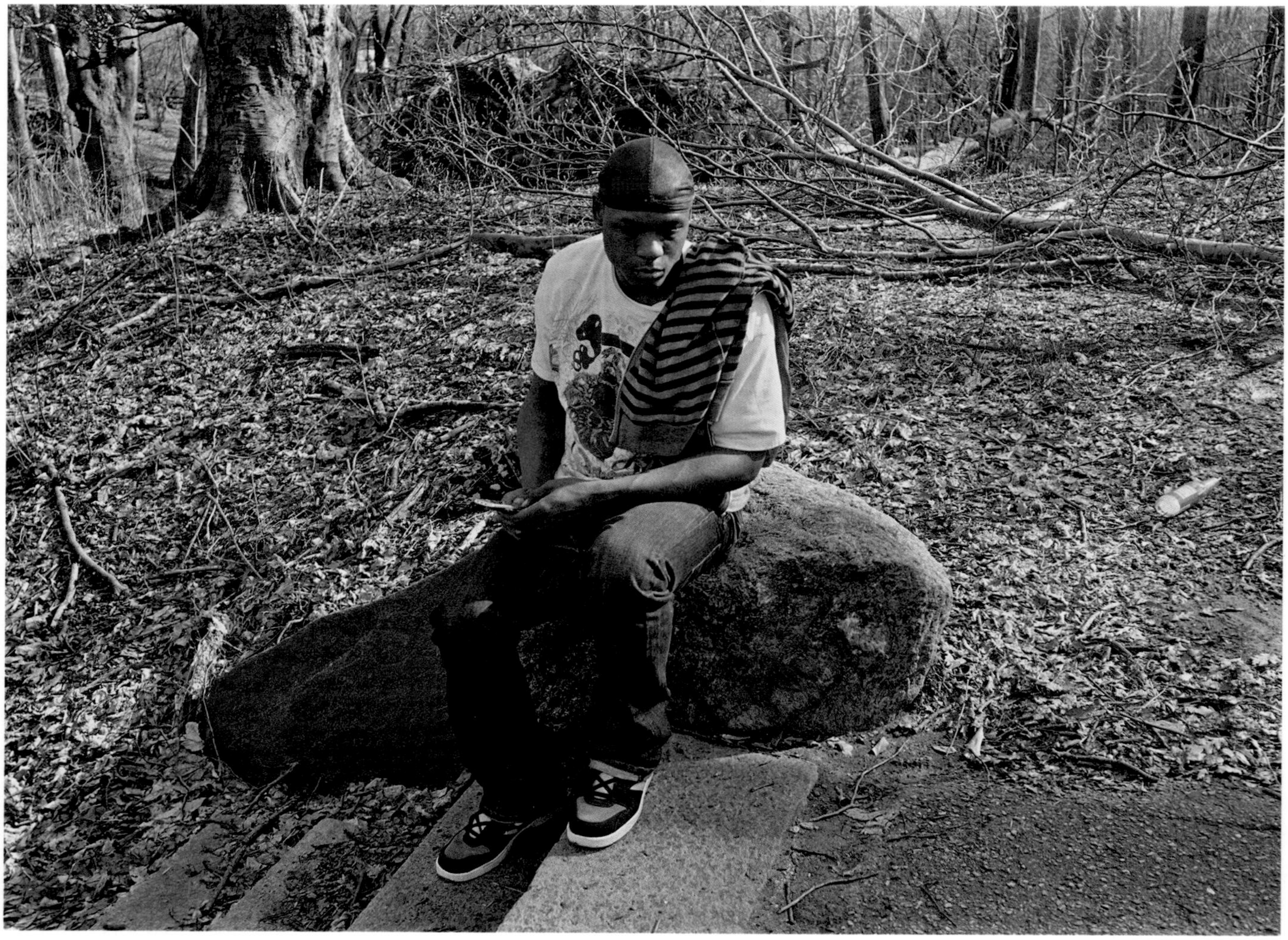

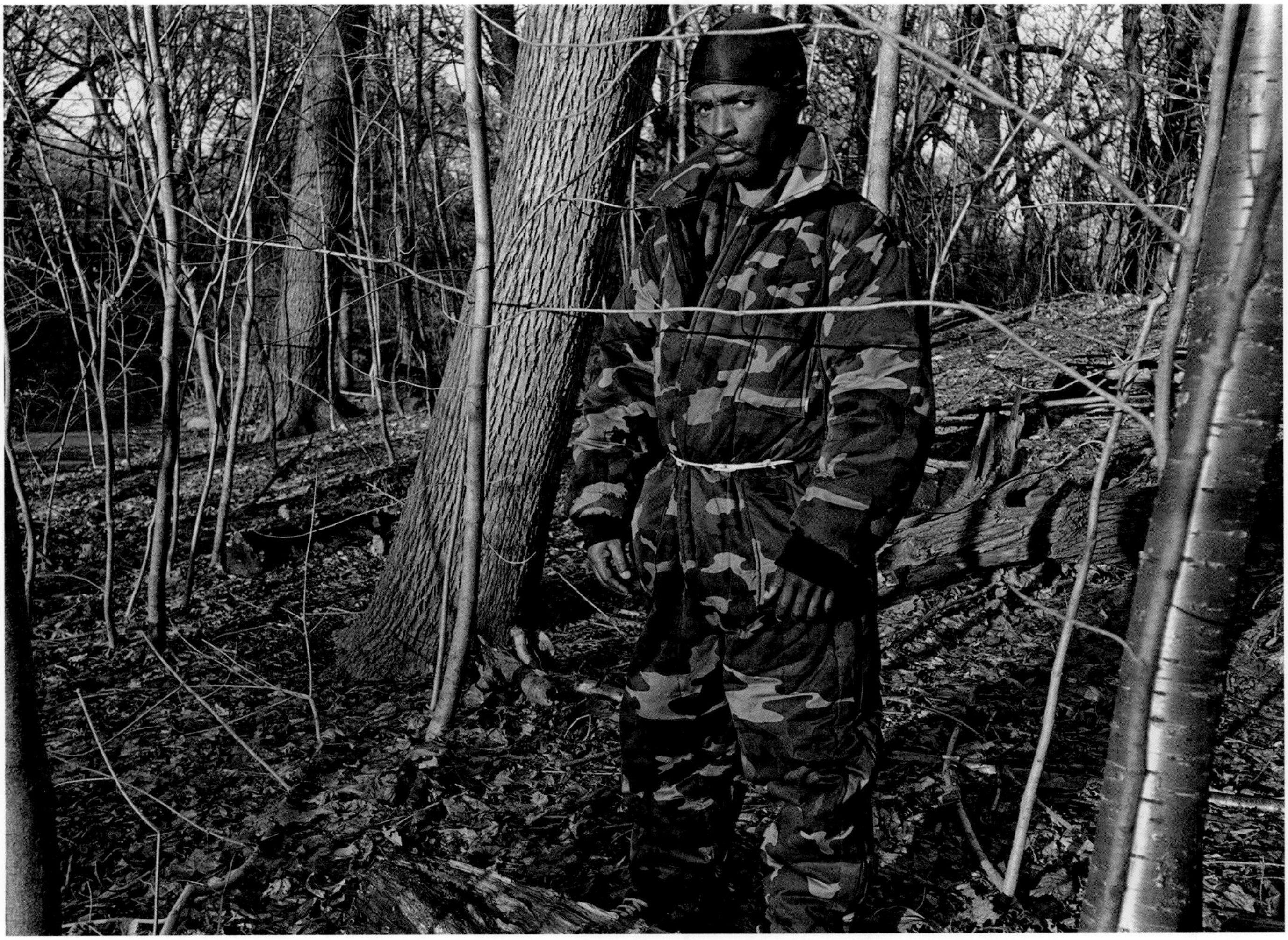

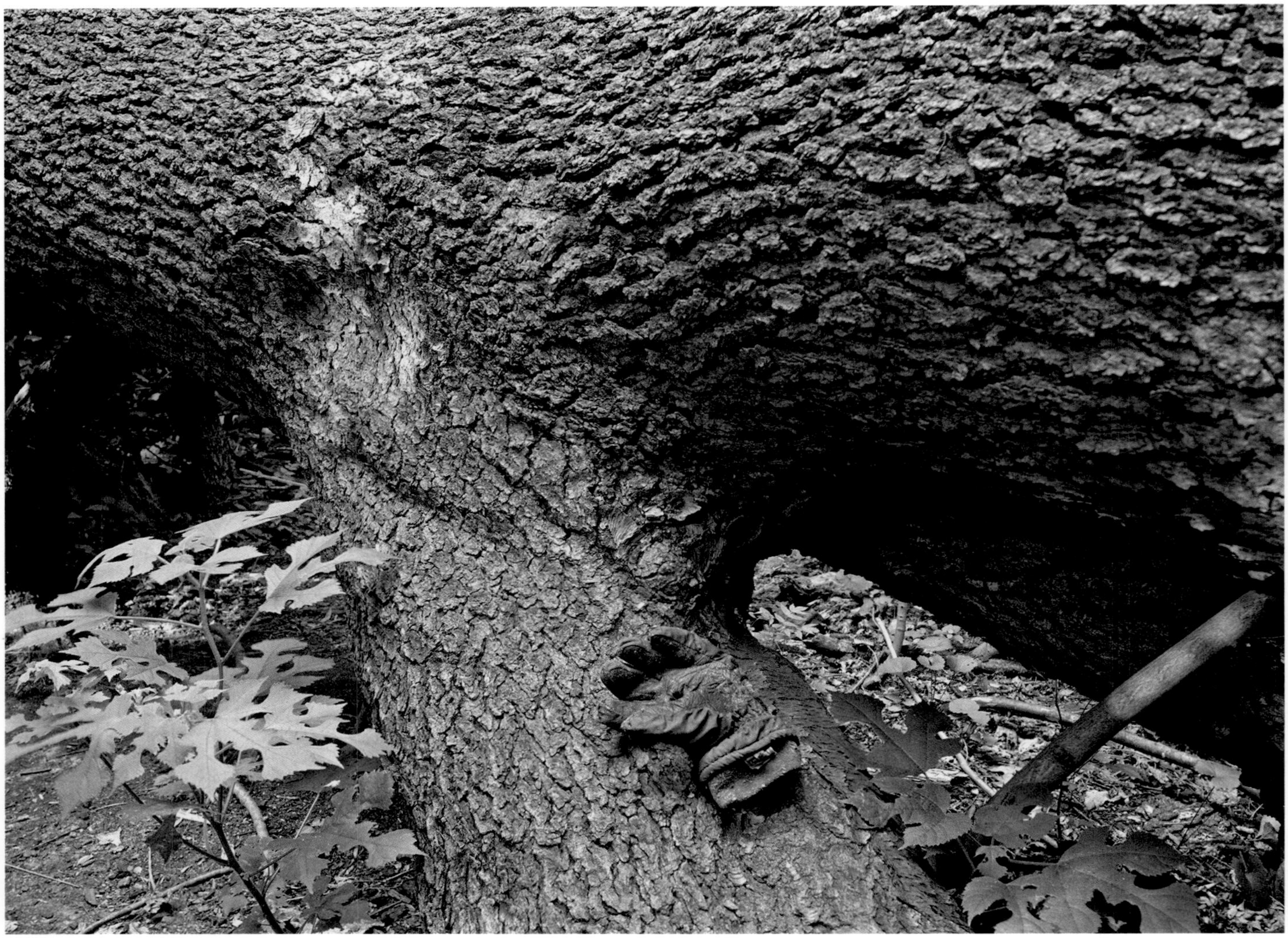

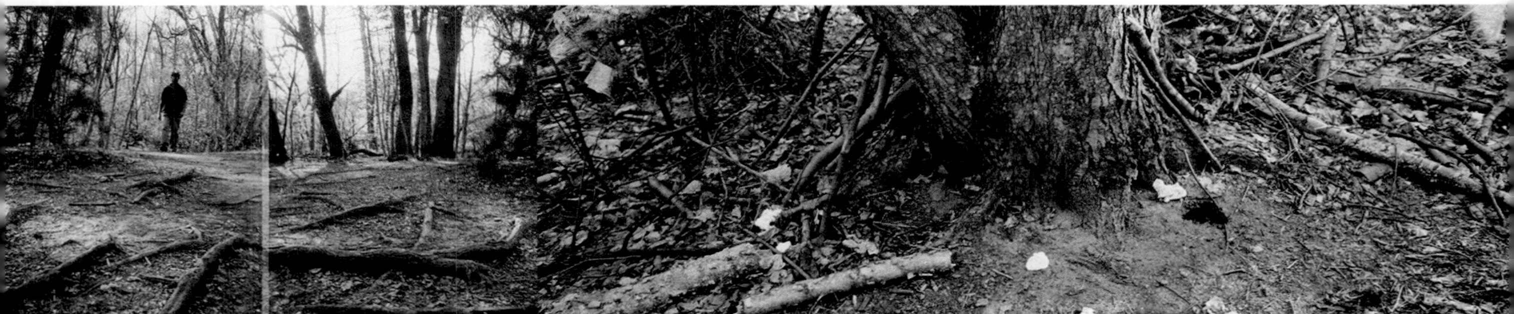

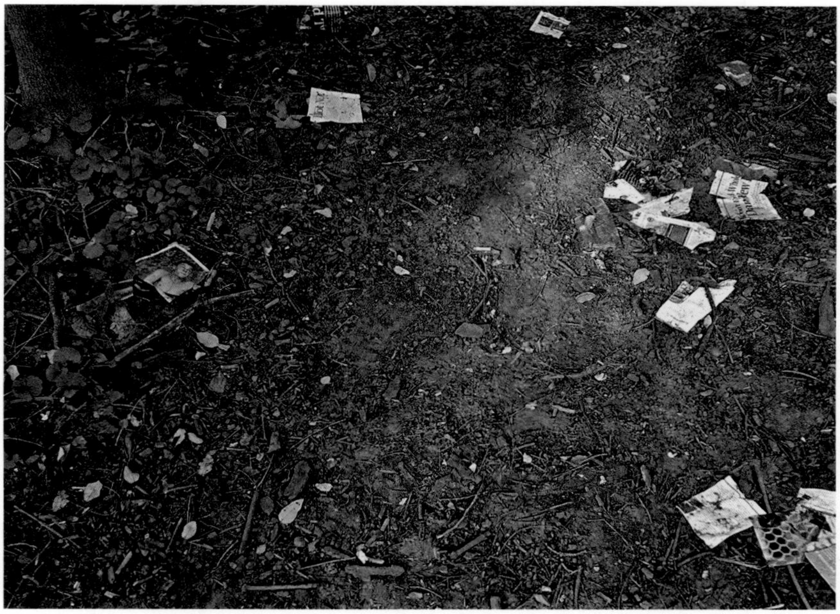

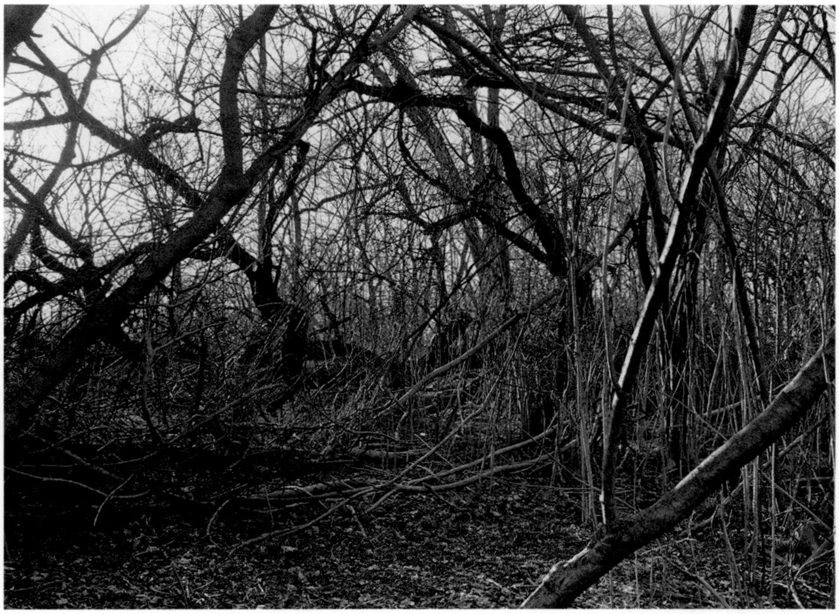

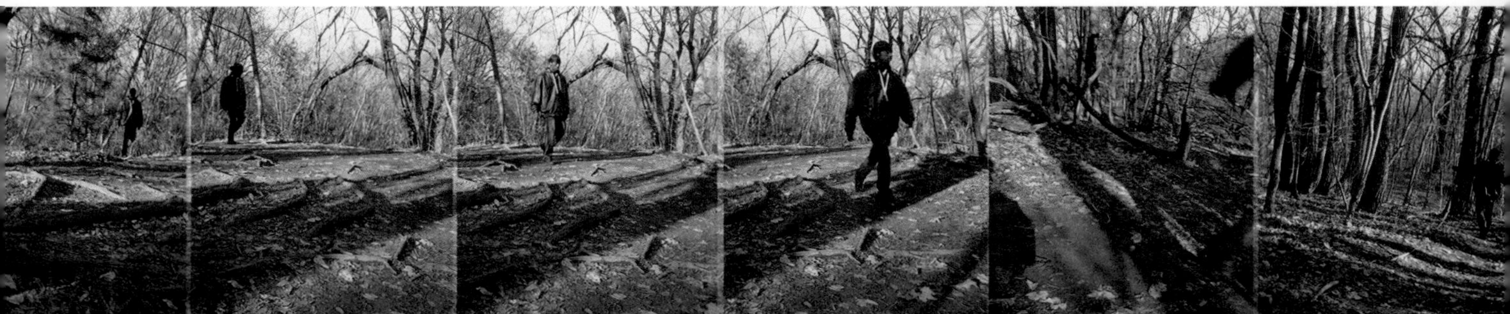

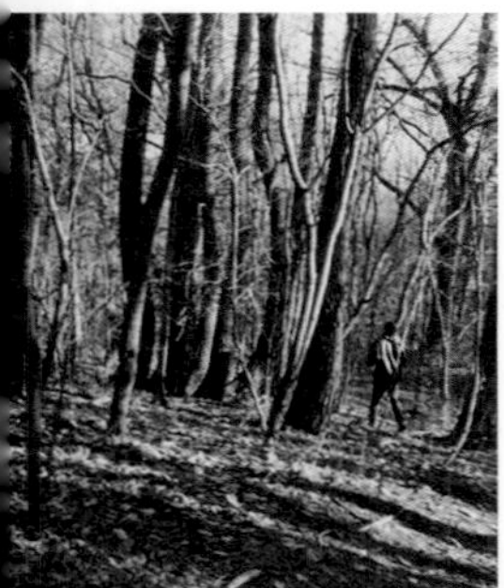

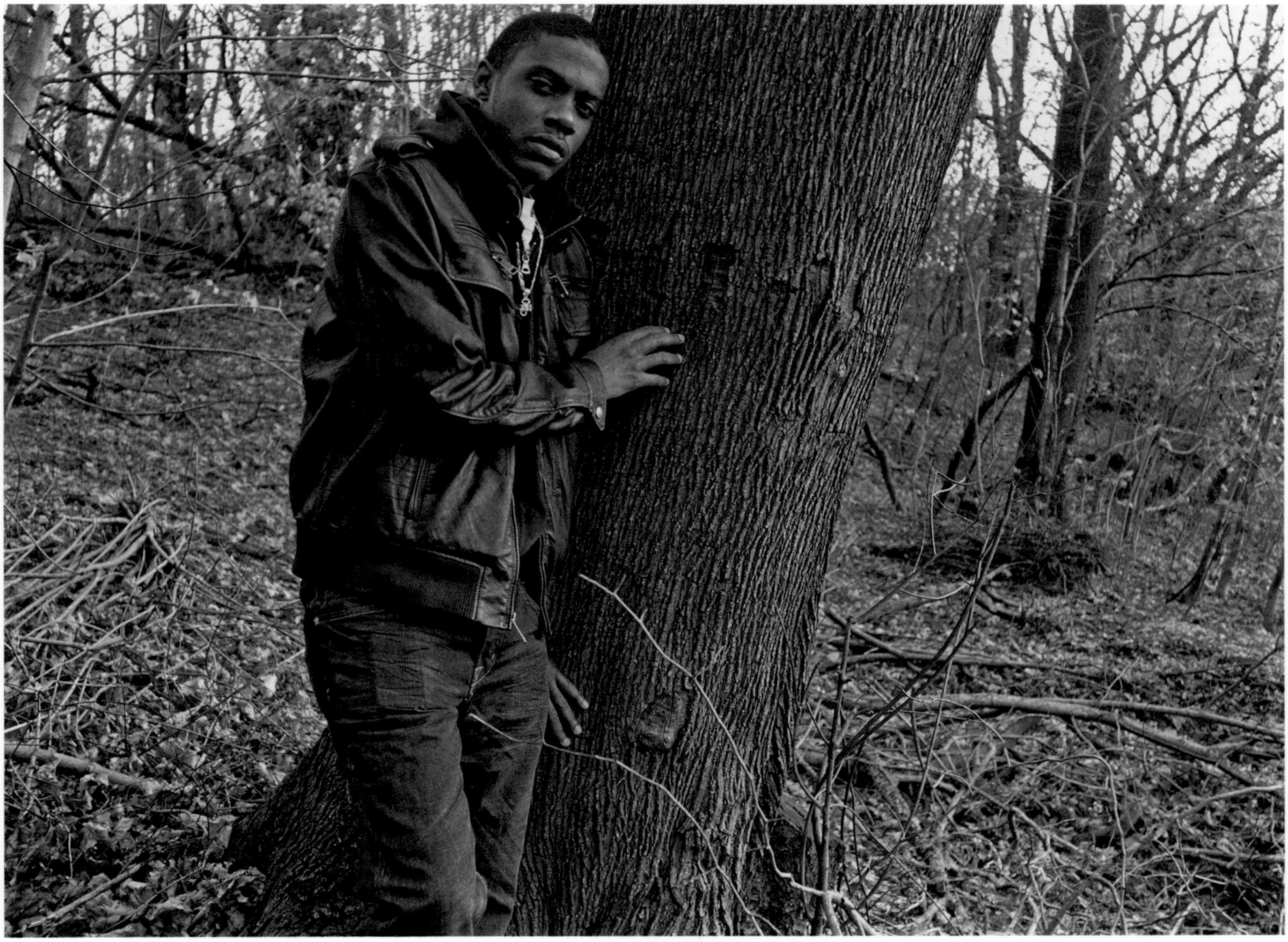

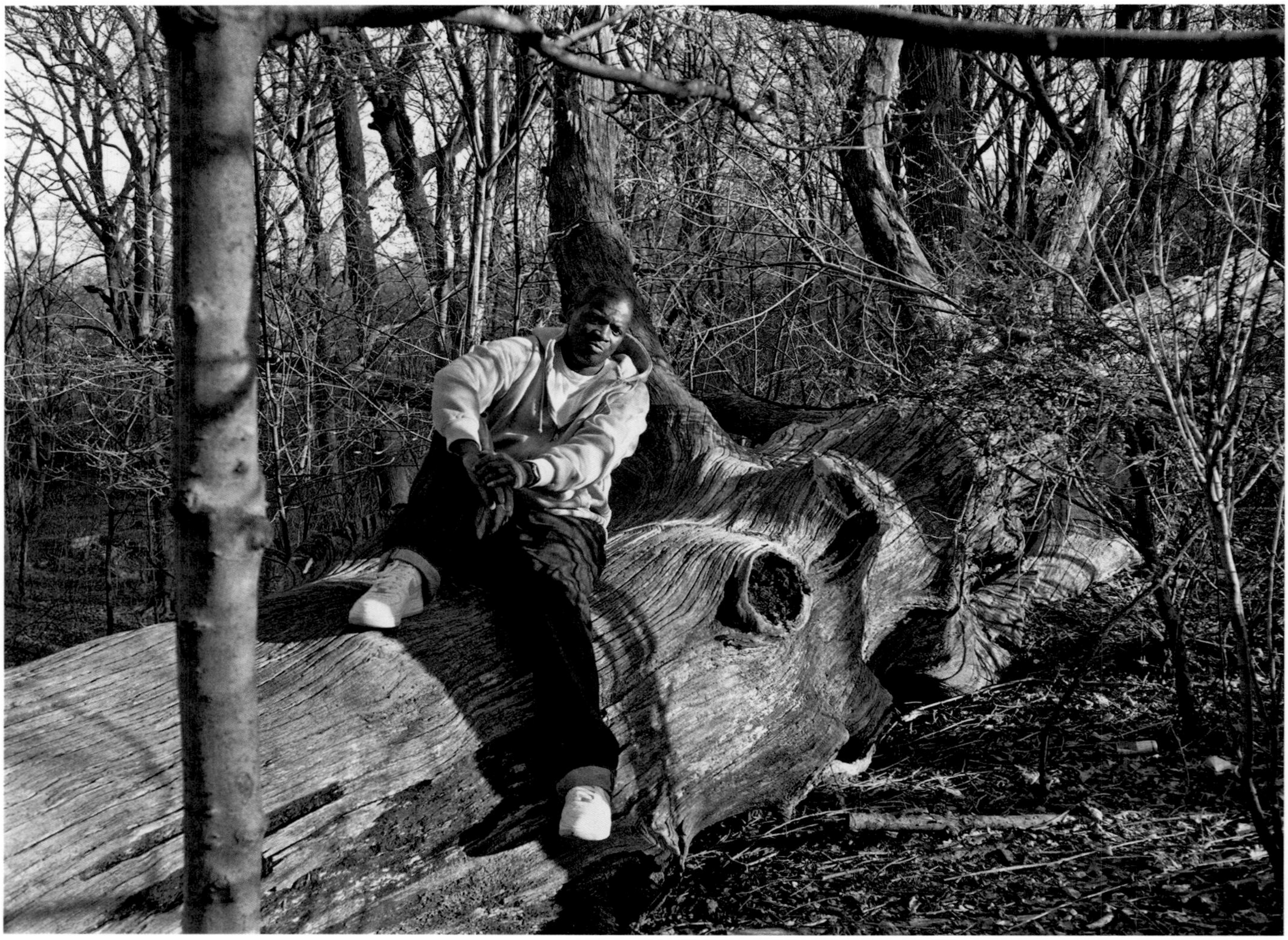

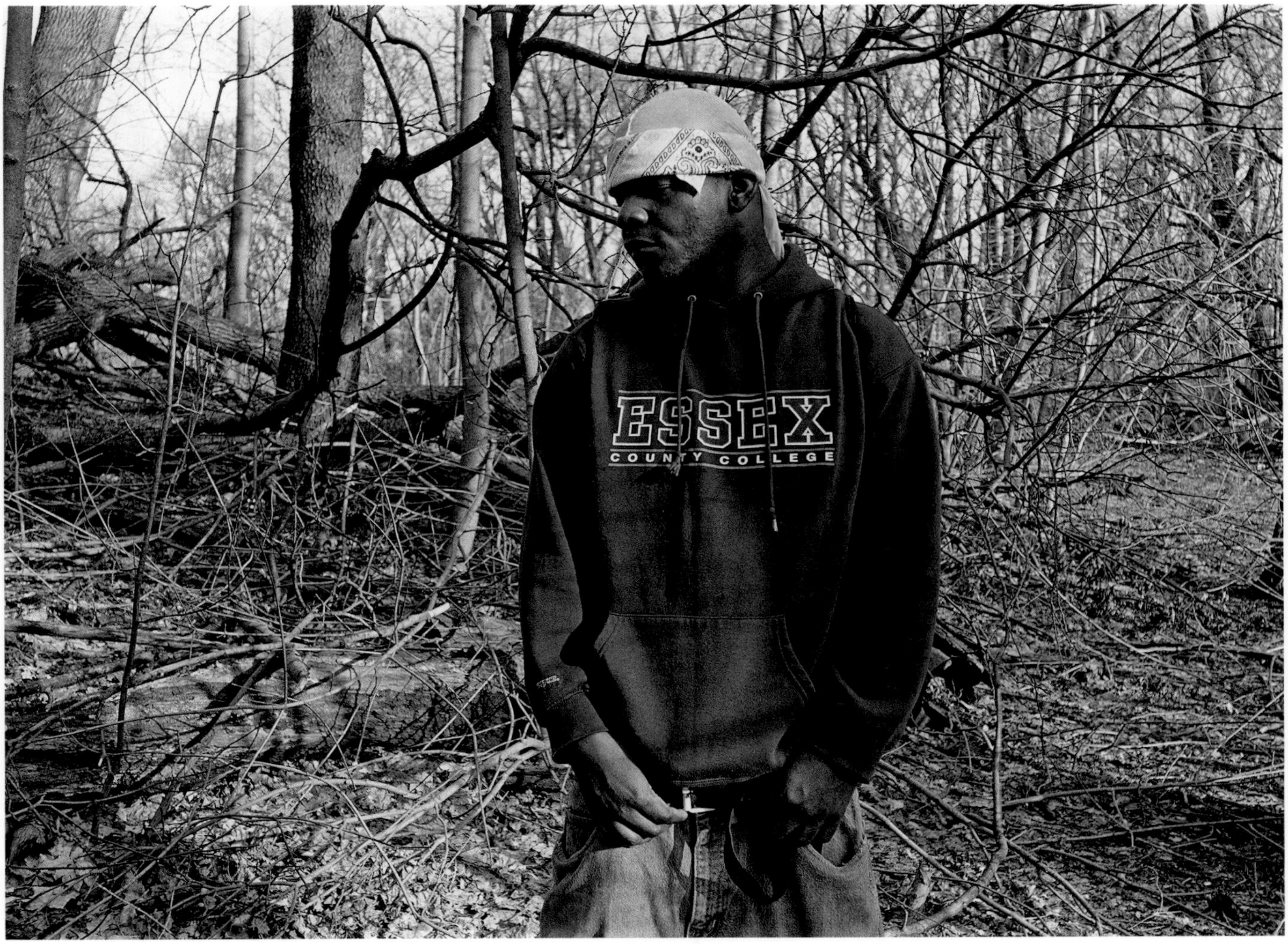
ESSEX
COUNTY COLLEGE

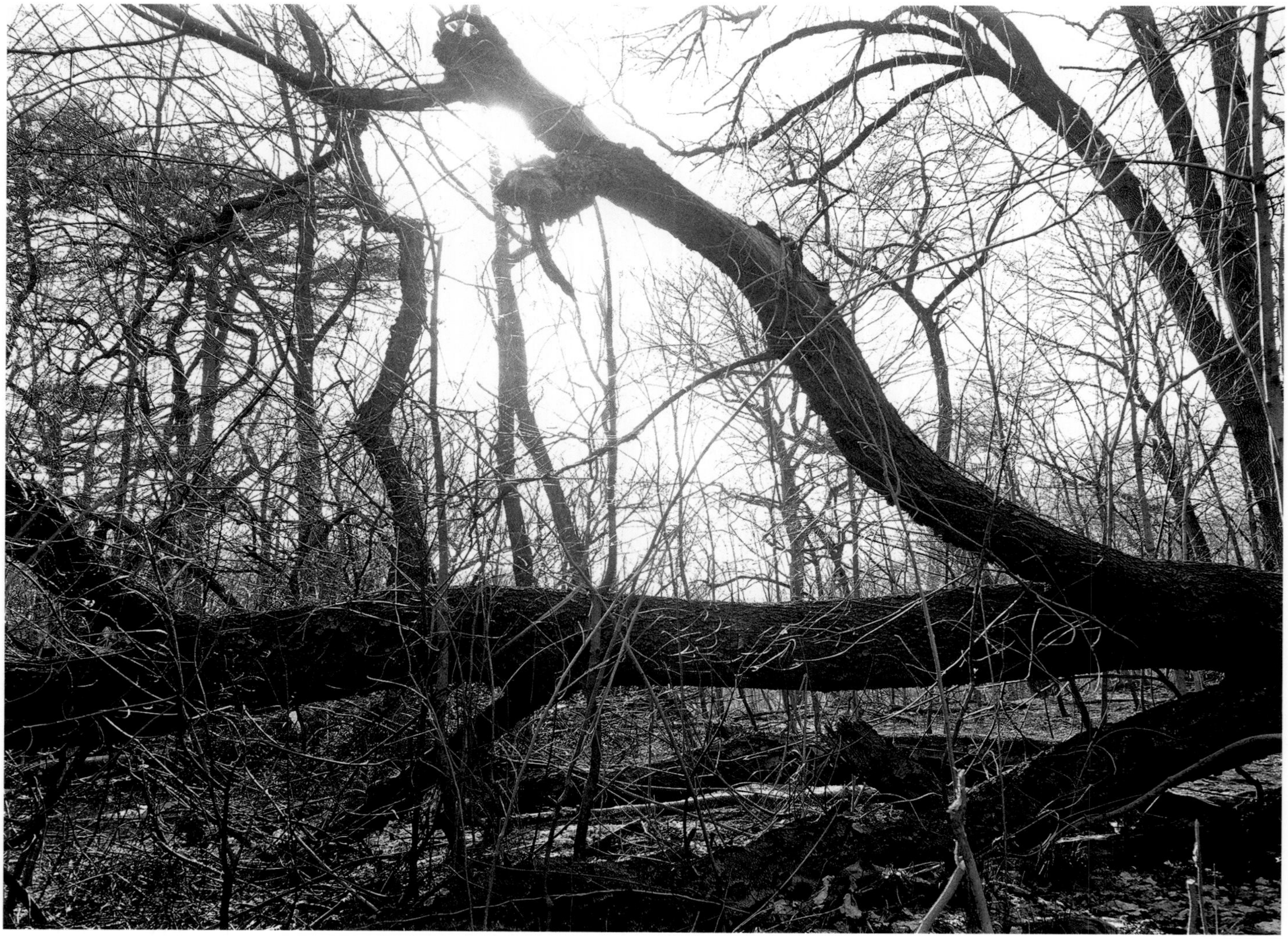

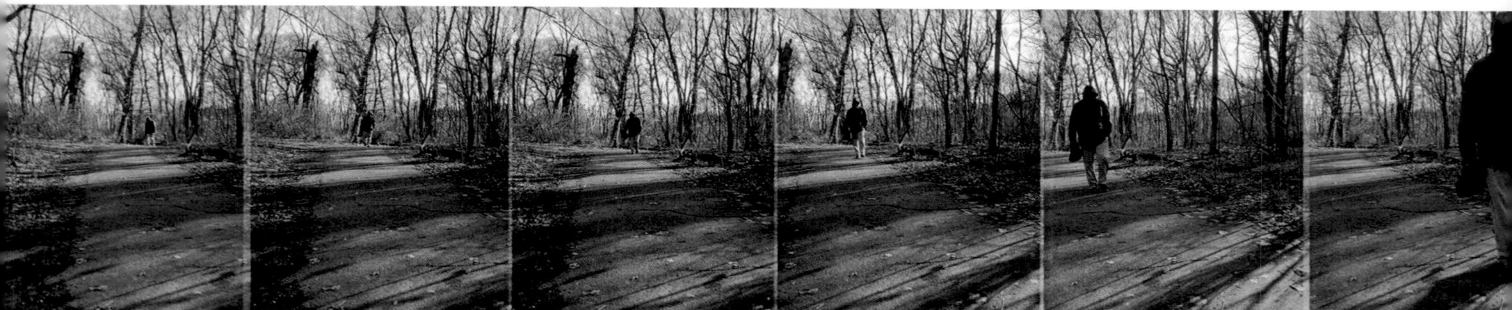

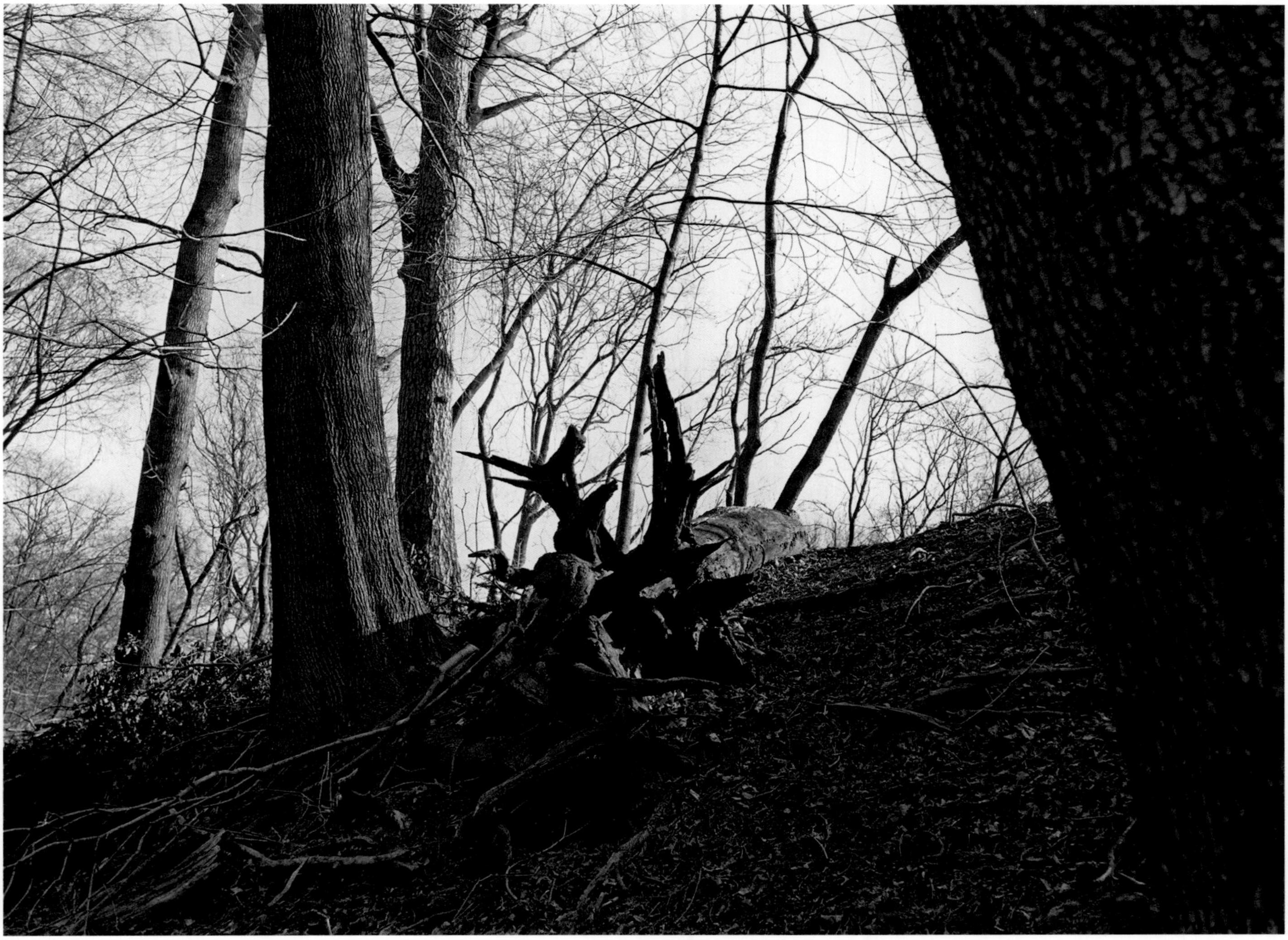

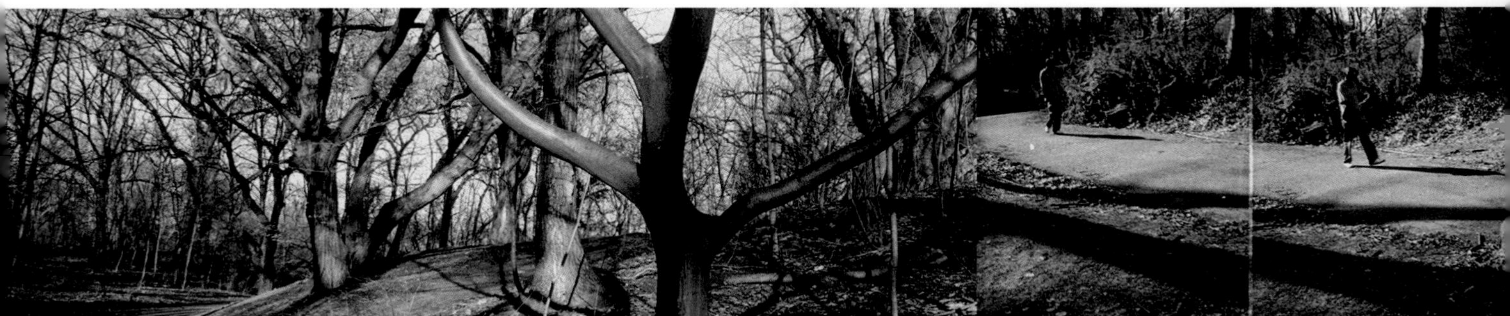

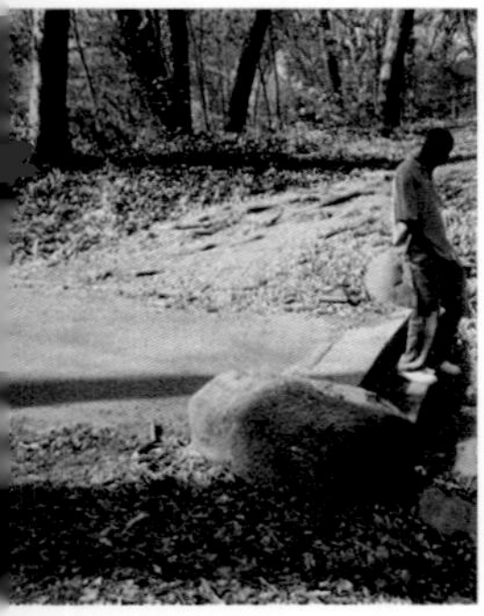

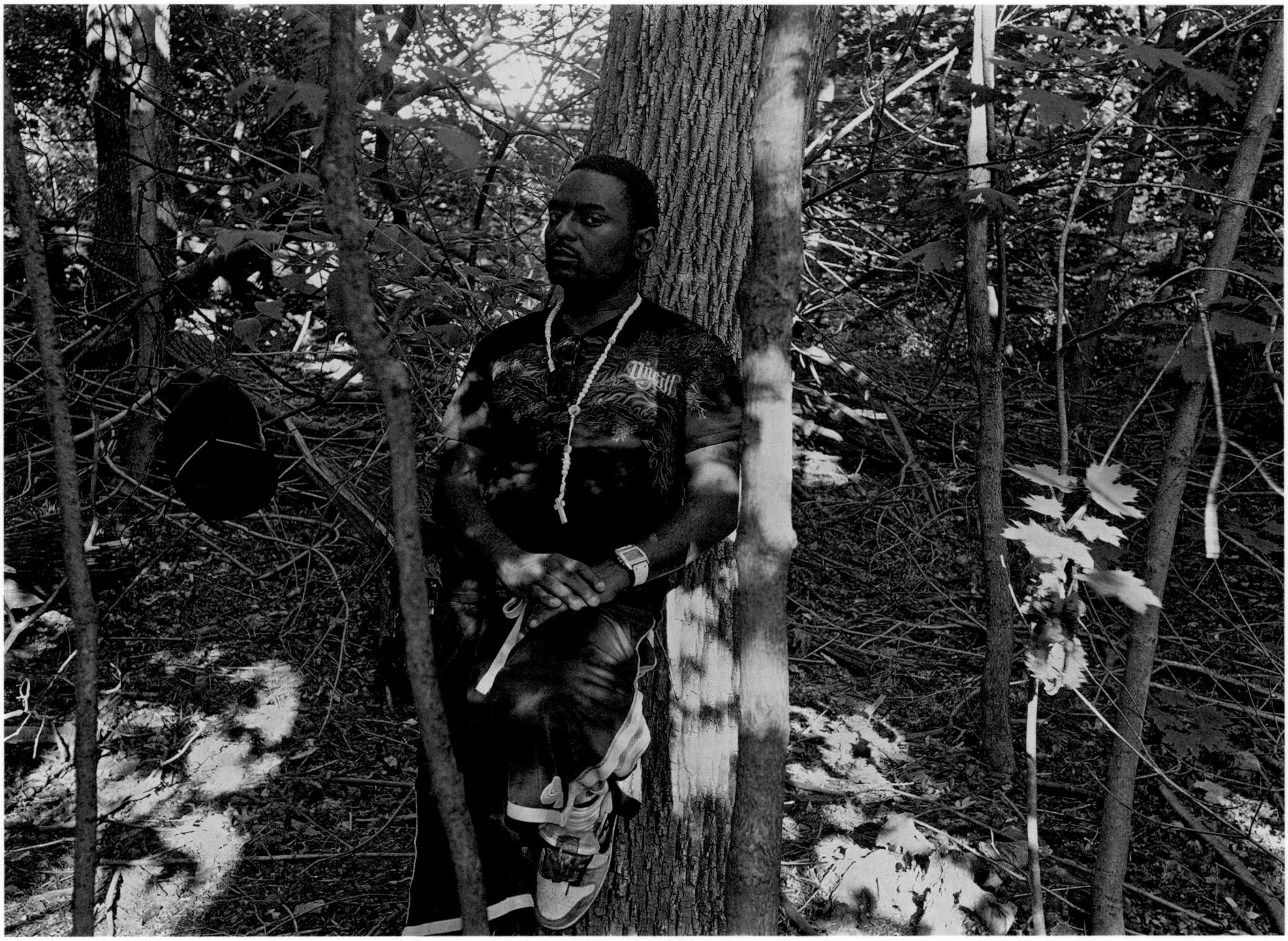

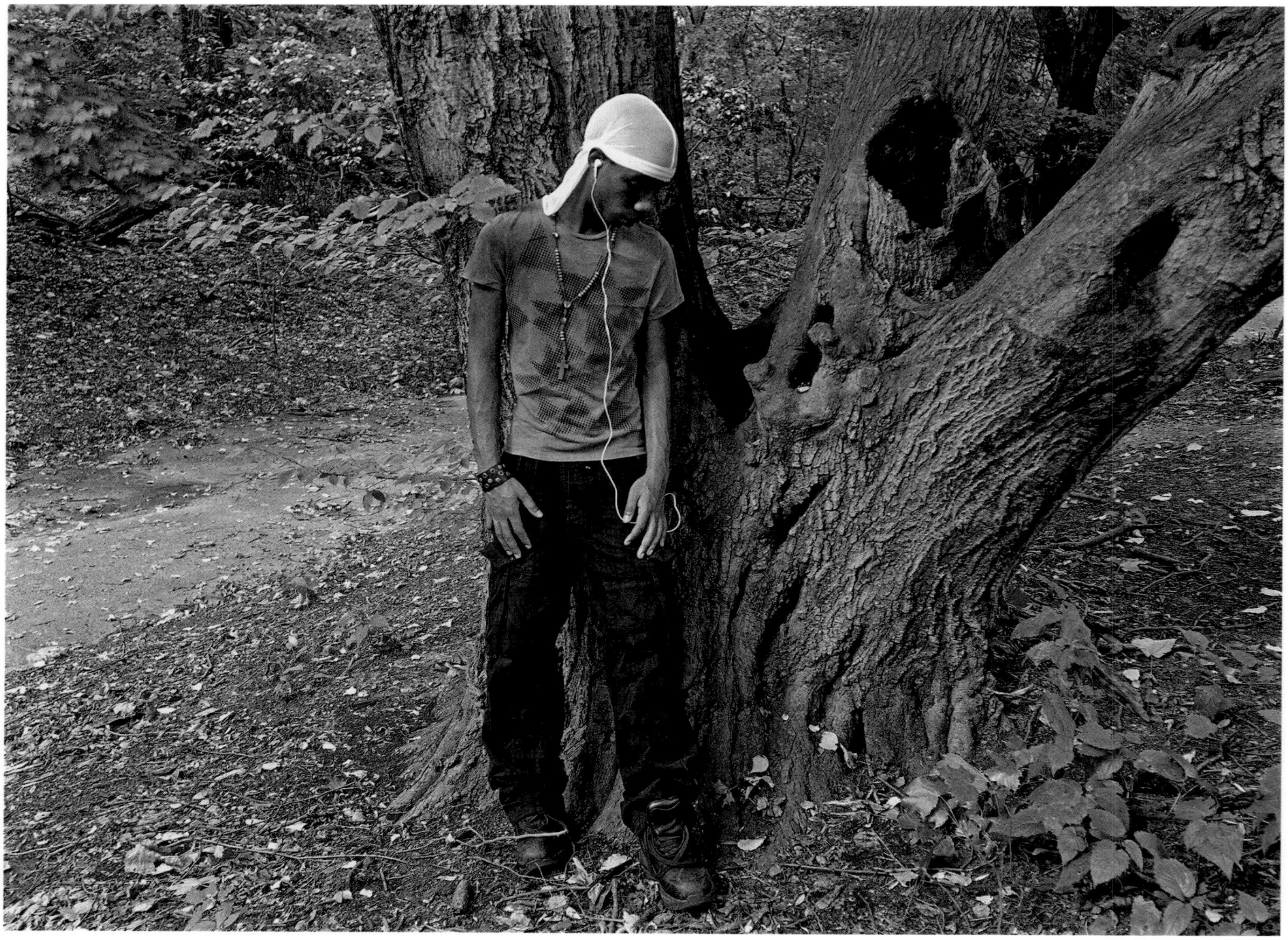

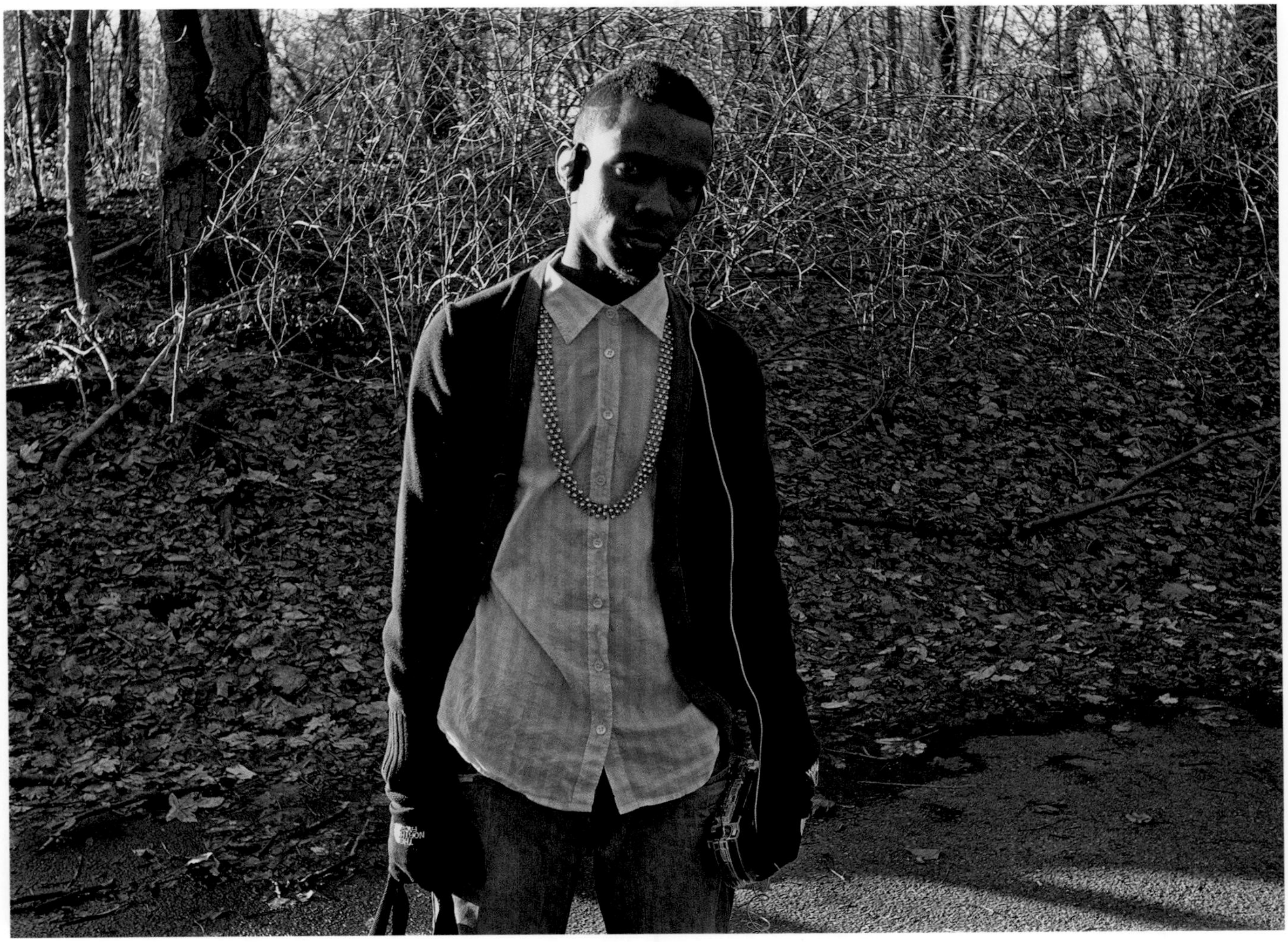

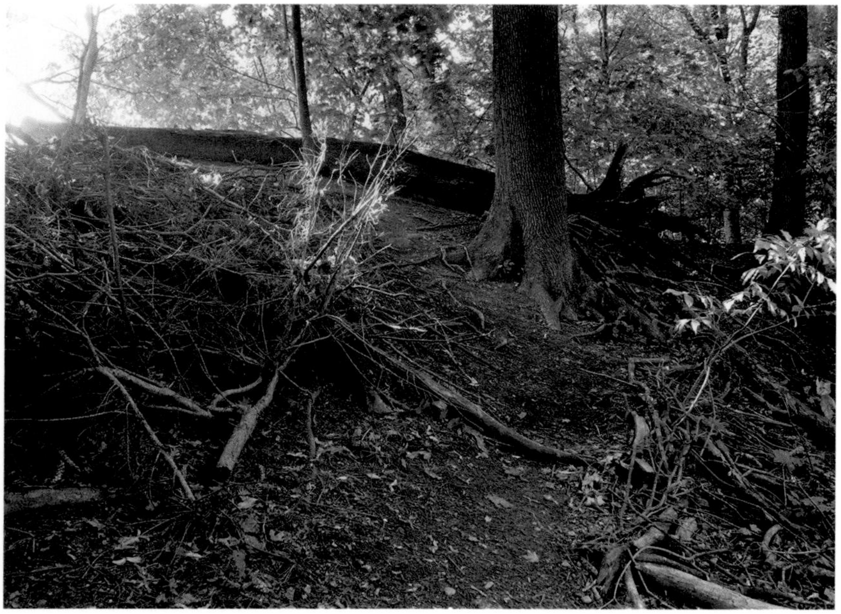

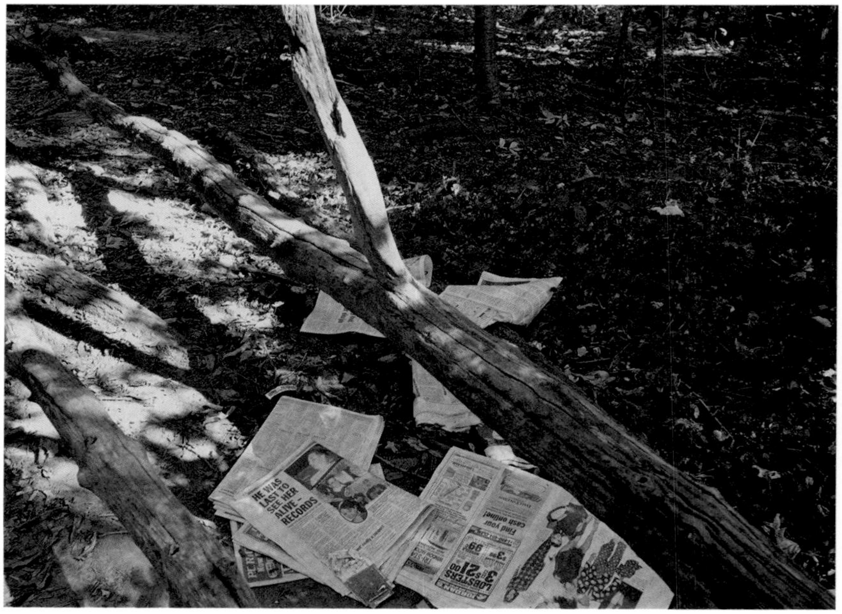
HE WAS LAST TO SEE HER ALIVE - RECORDS
Find your Cash online!
LOBSTERS
3 for $21.00

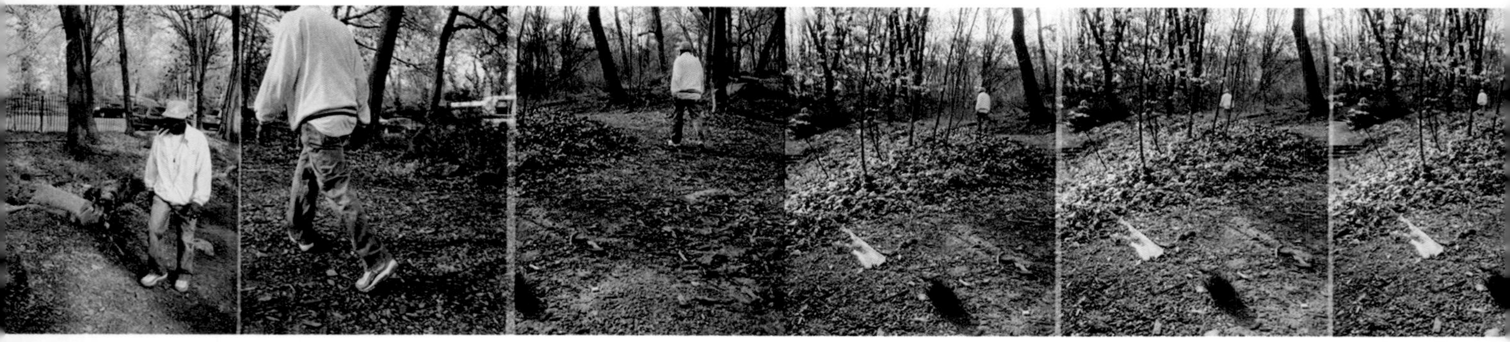

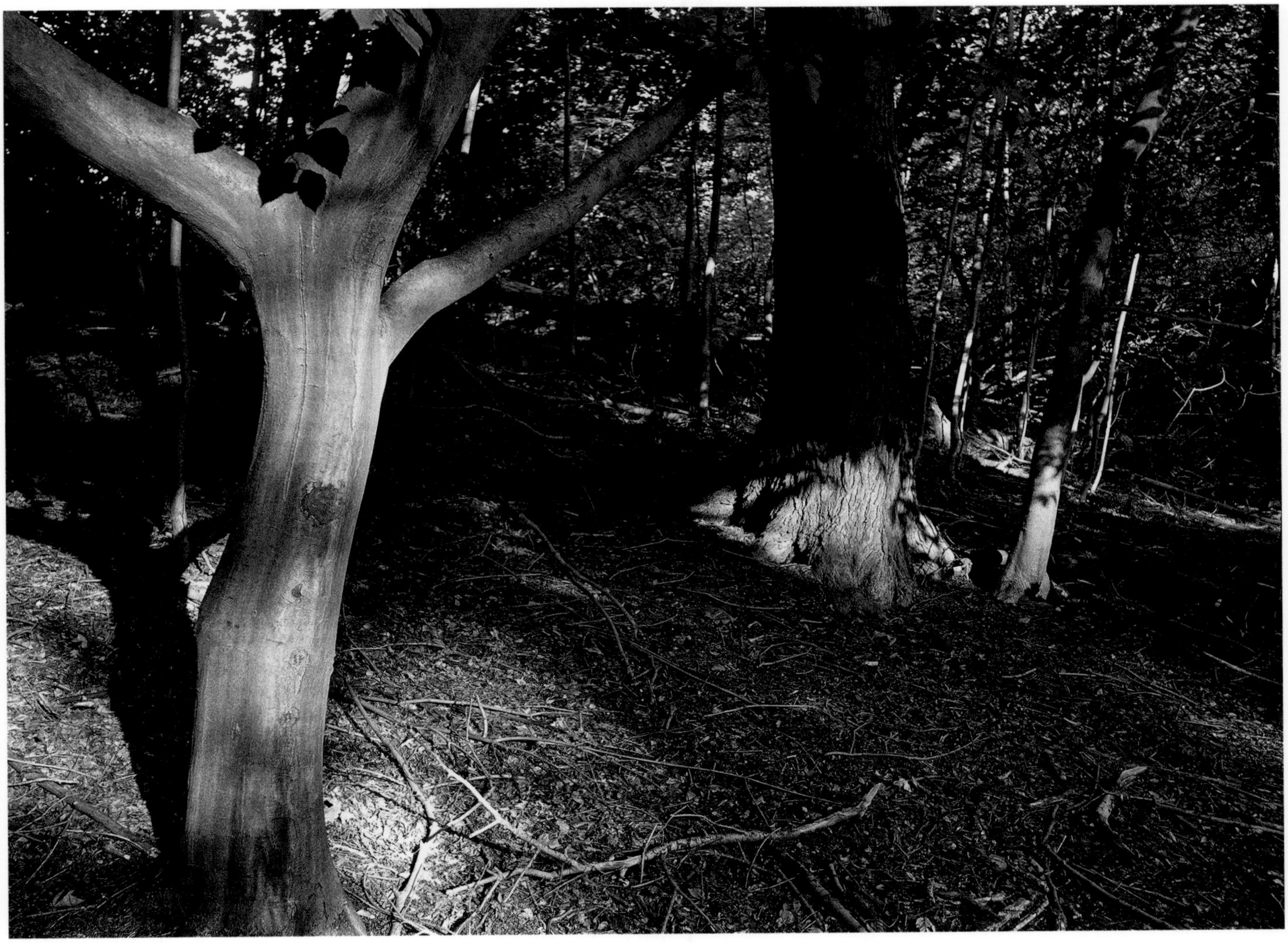

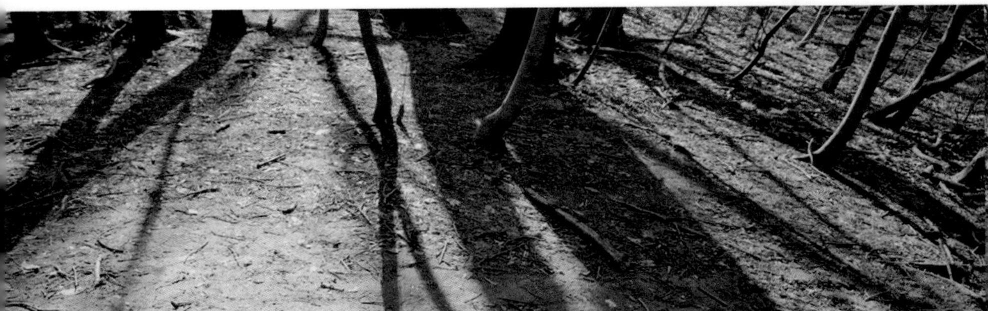

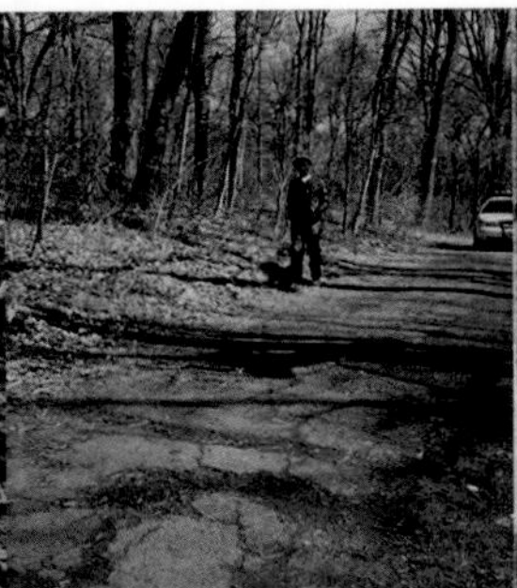

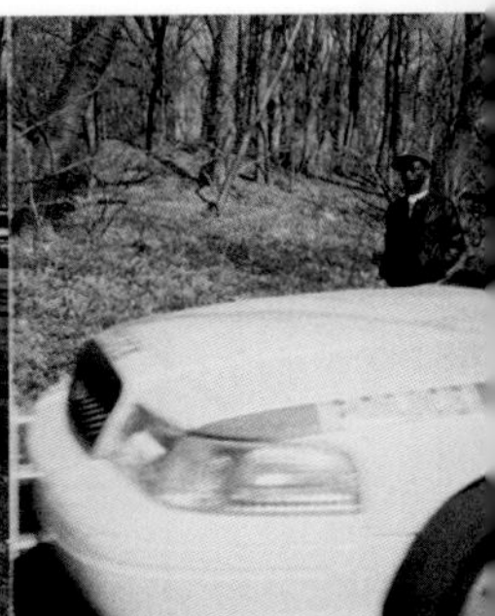

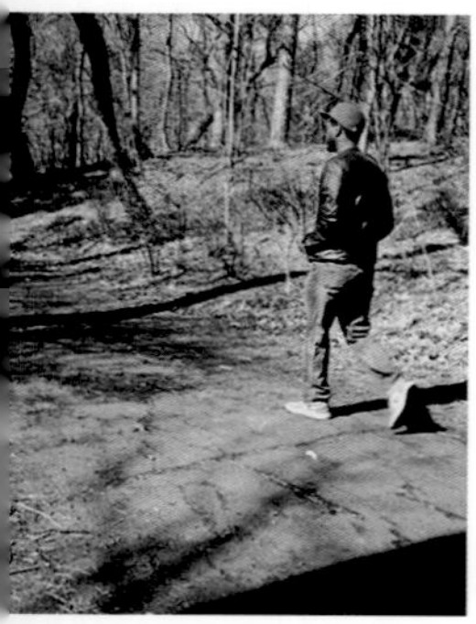

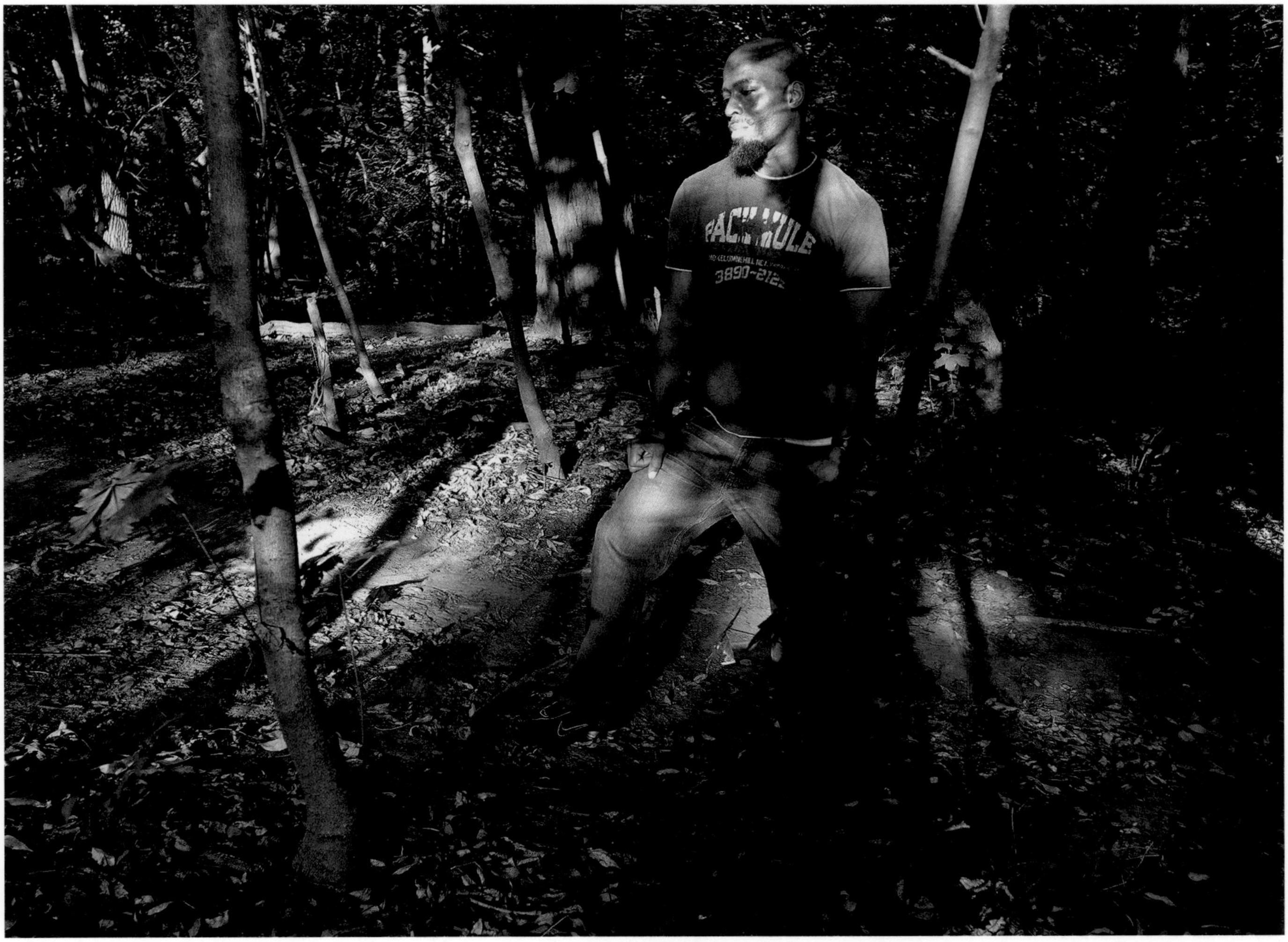

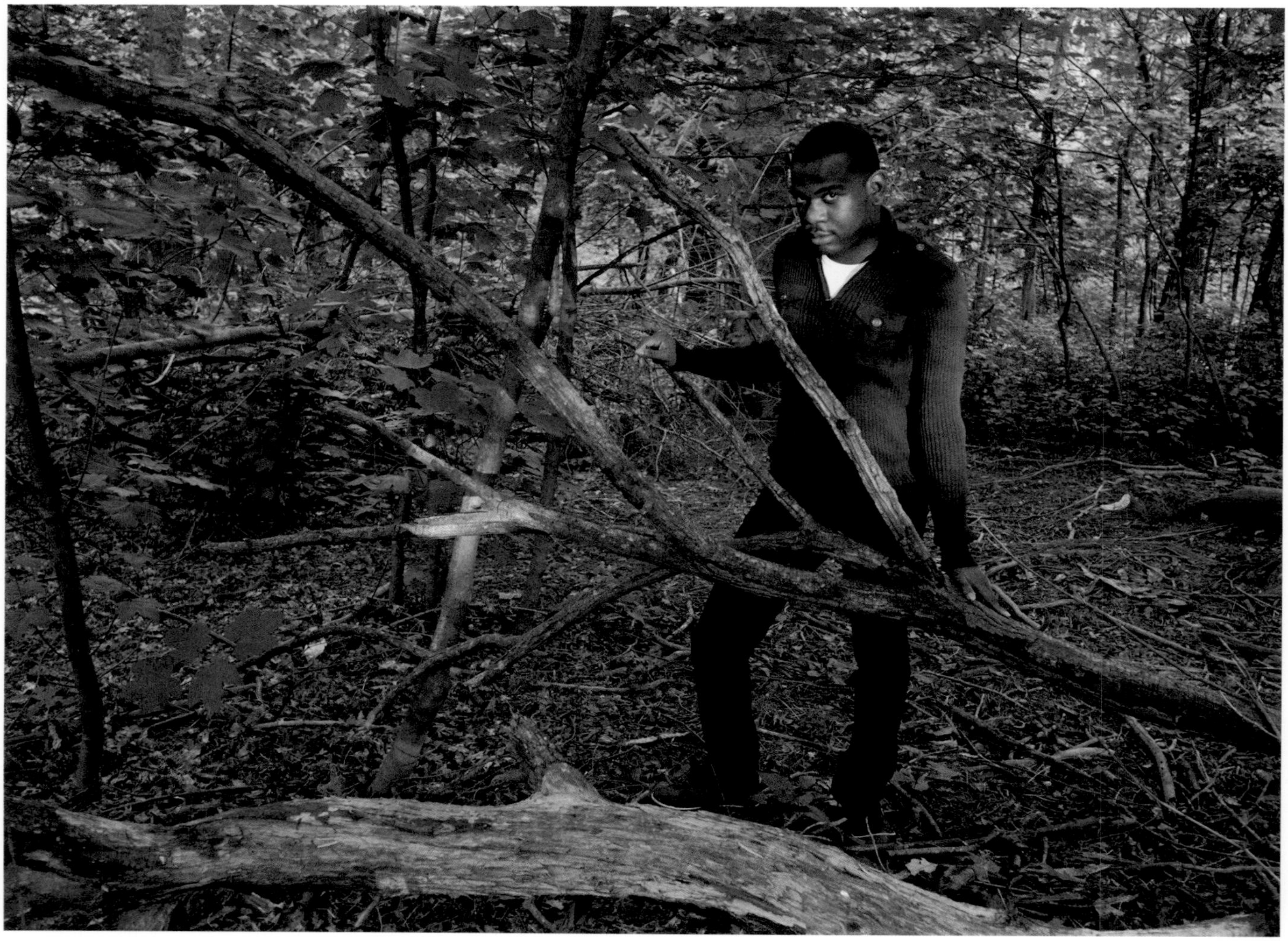

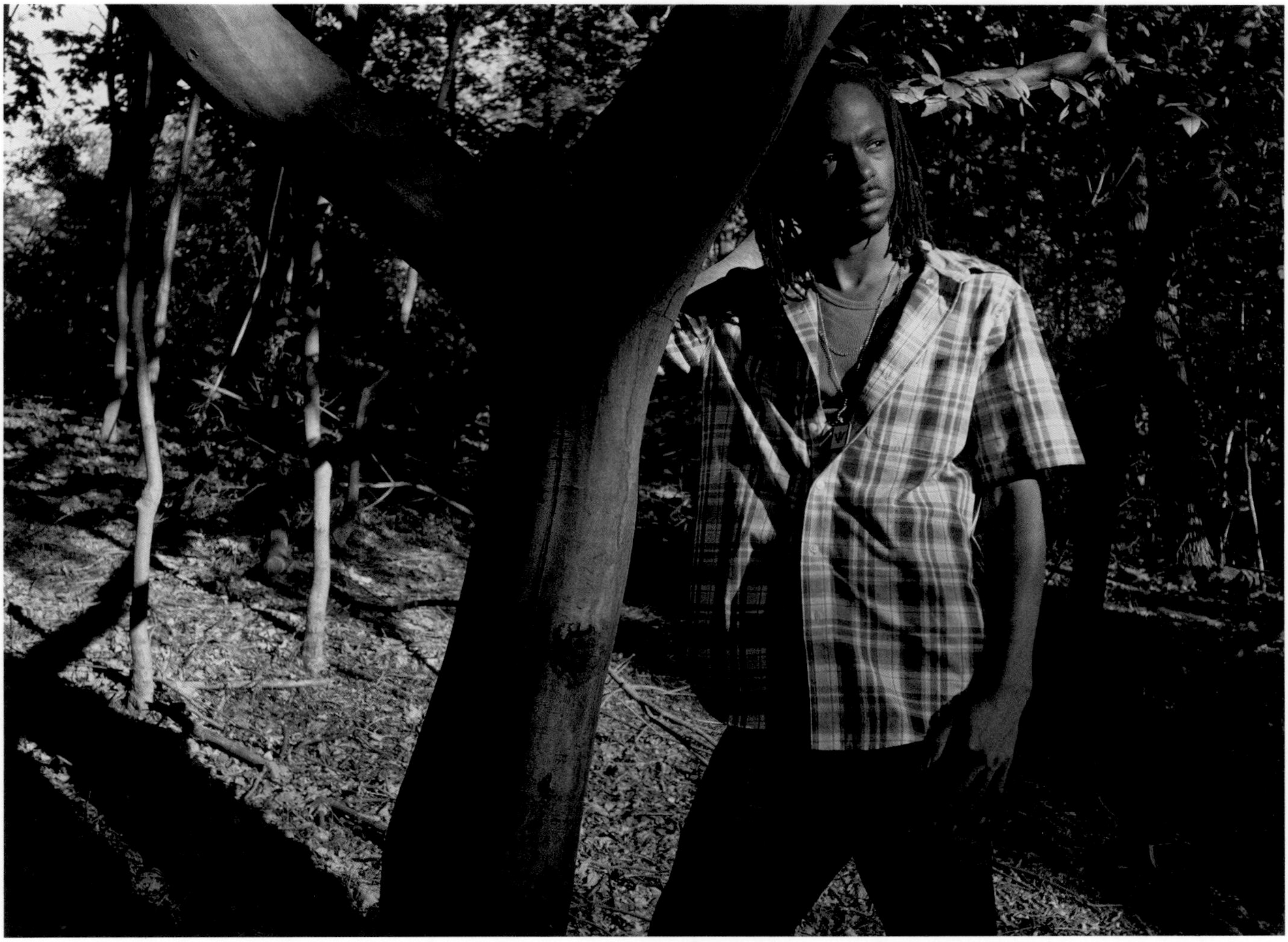

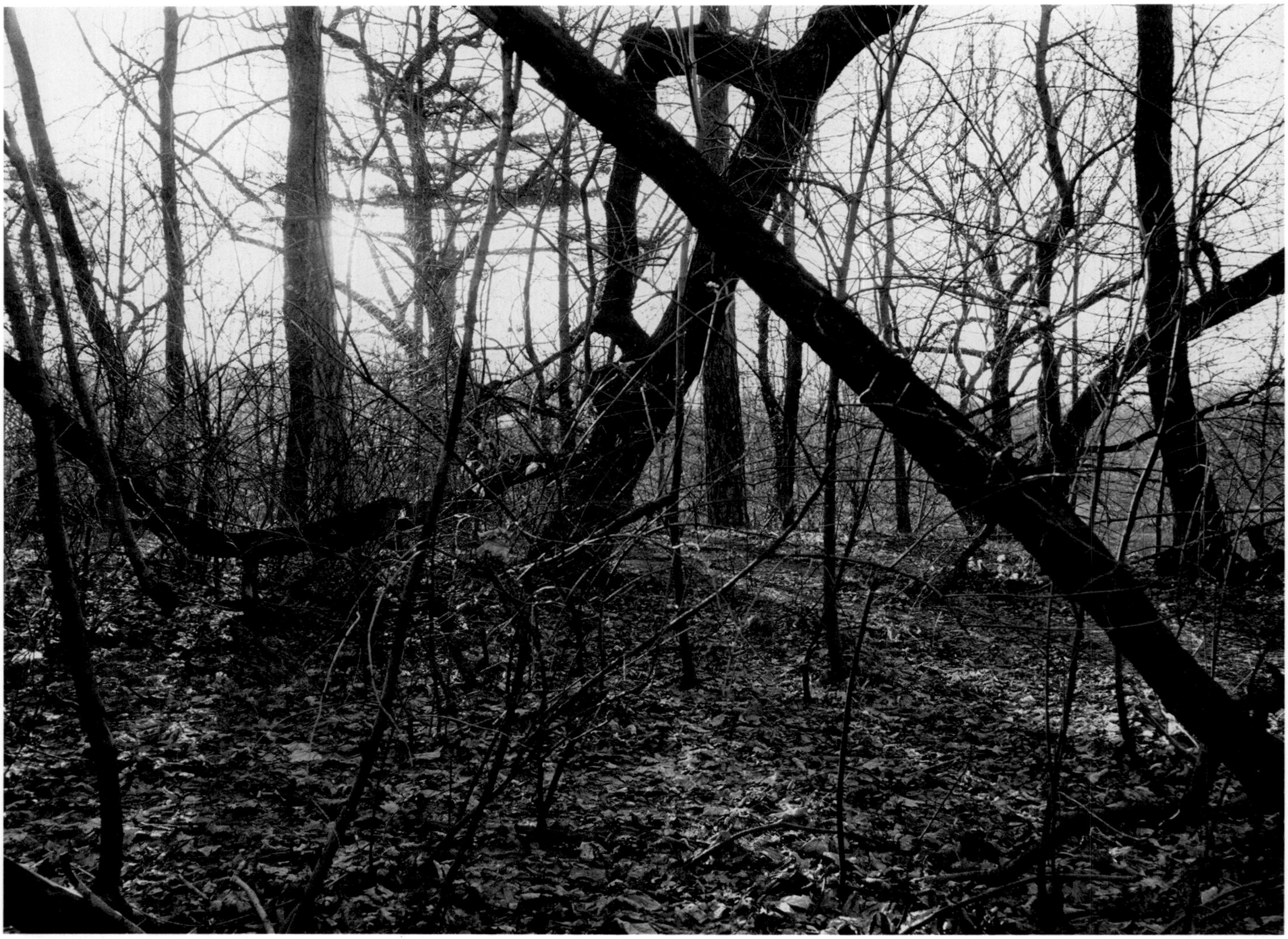

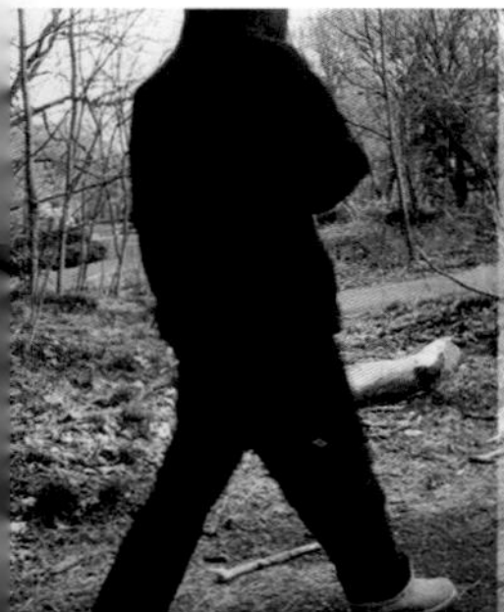

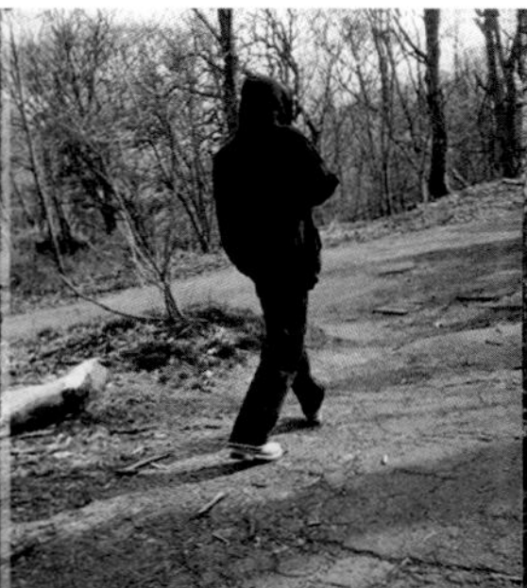

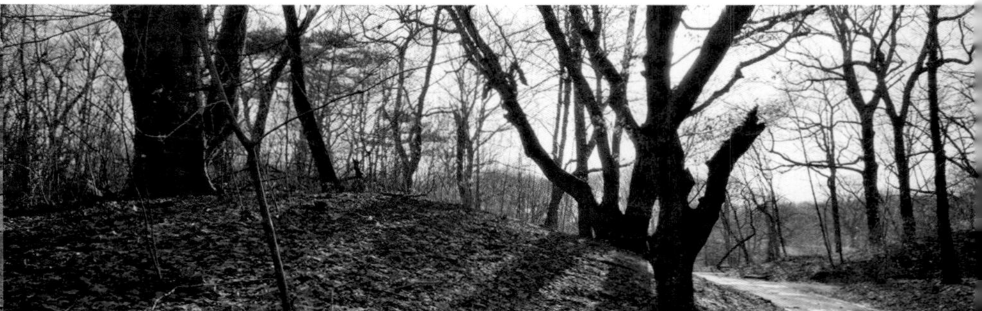

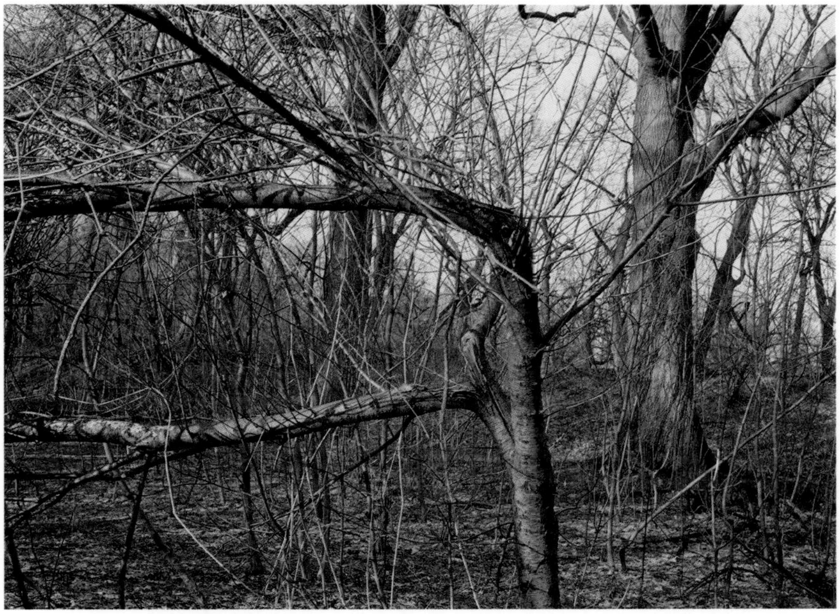

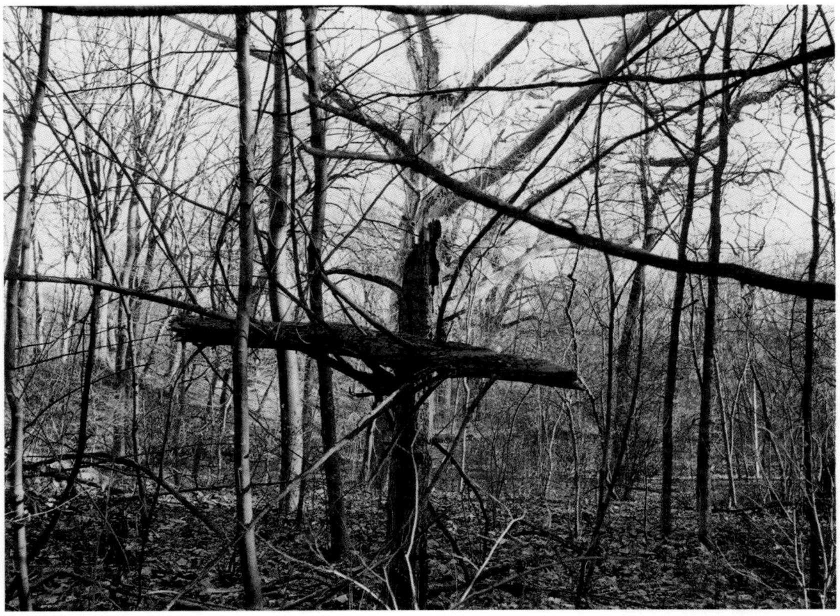

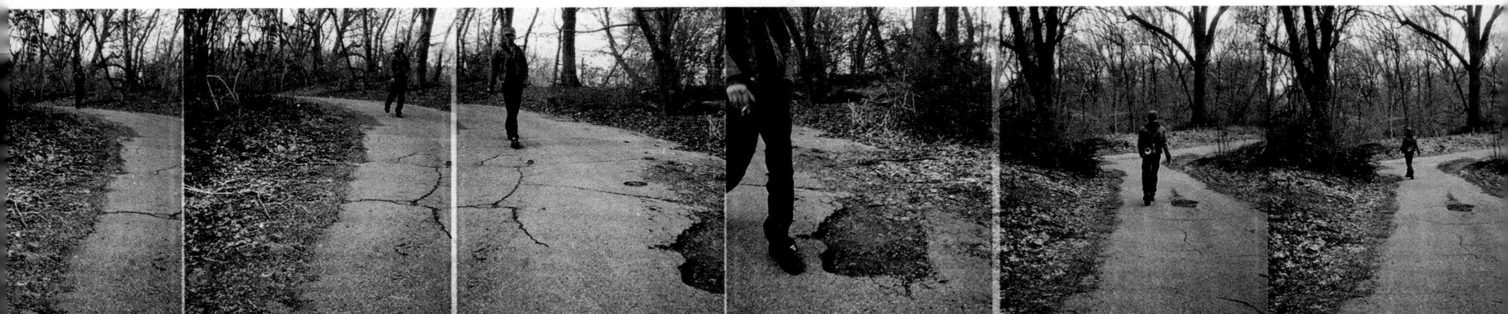

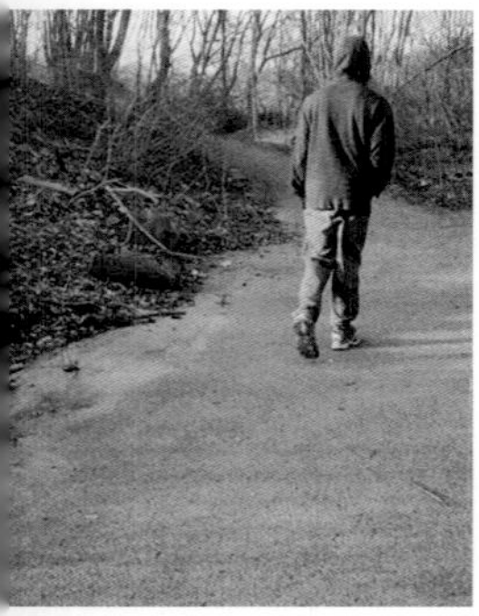

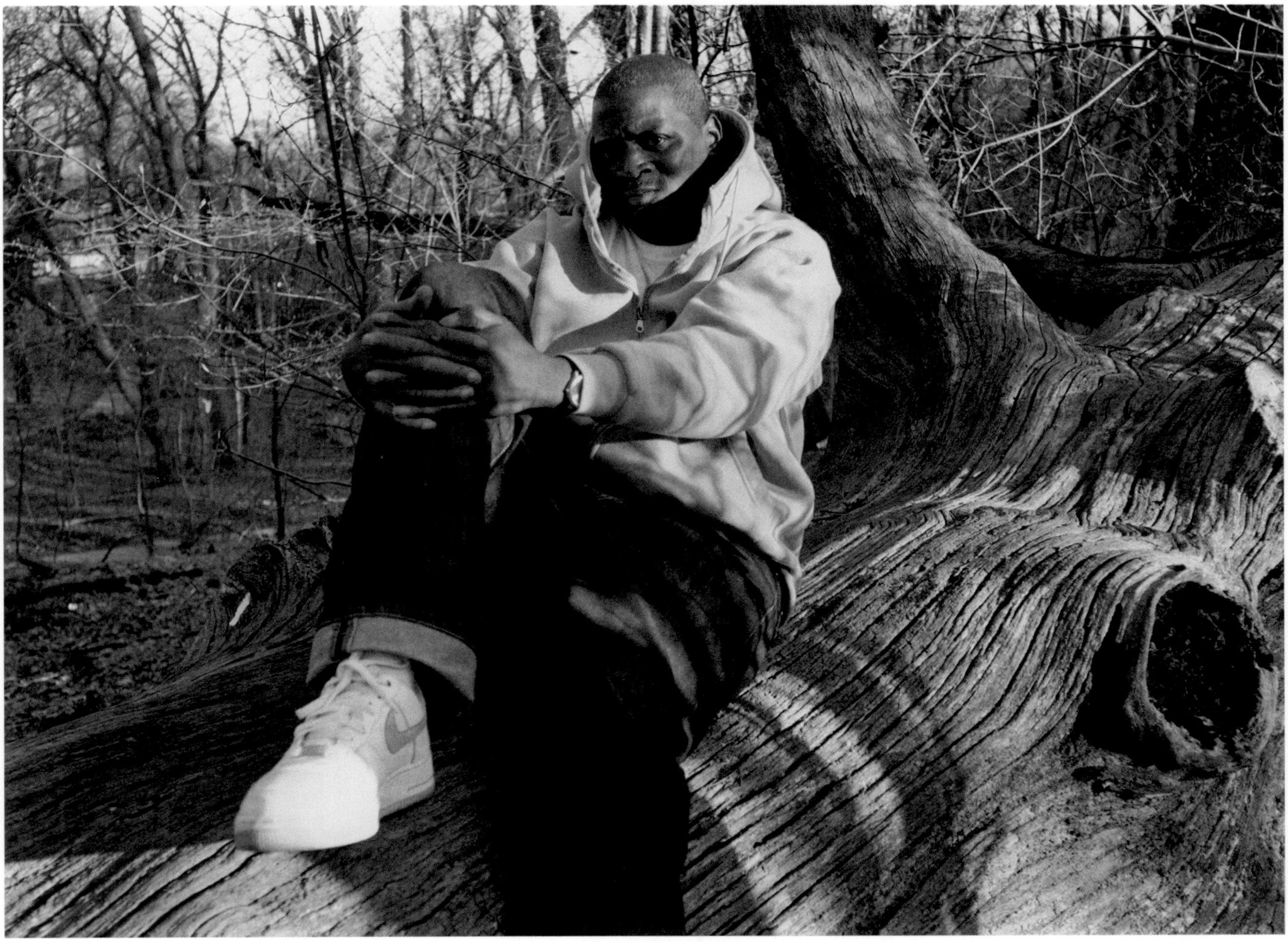

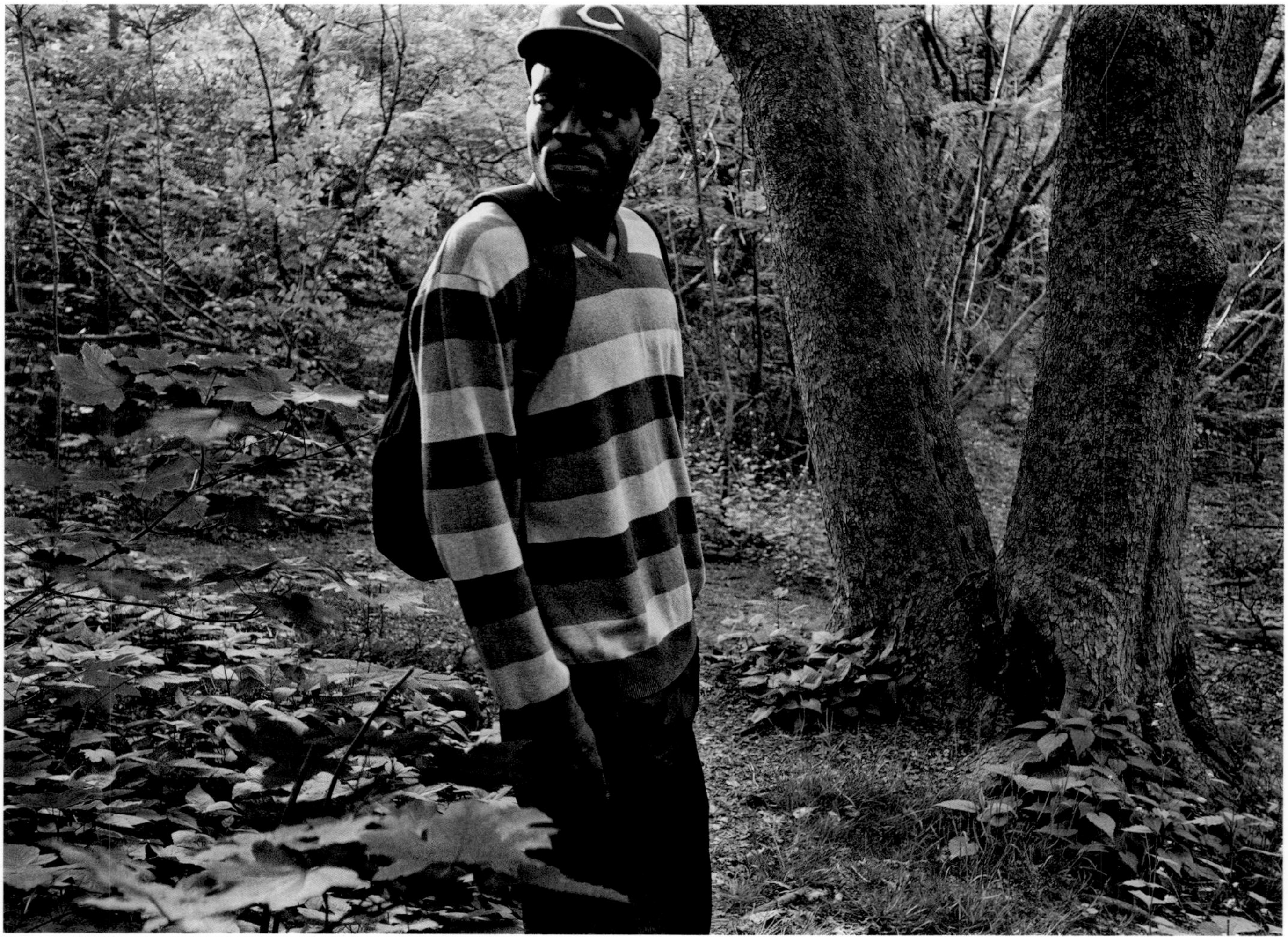

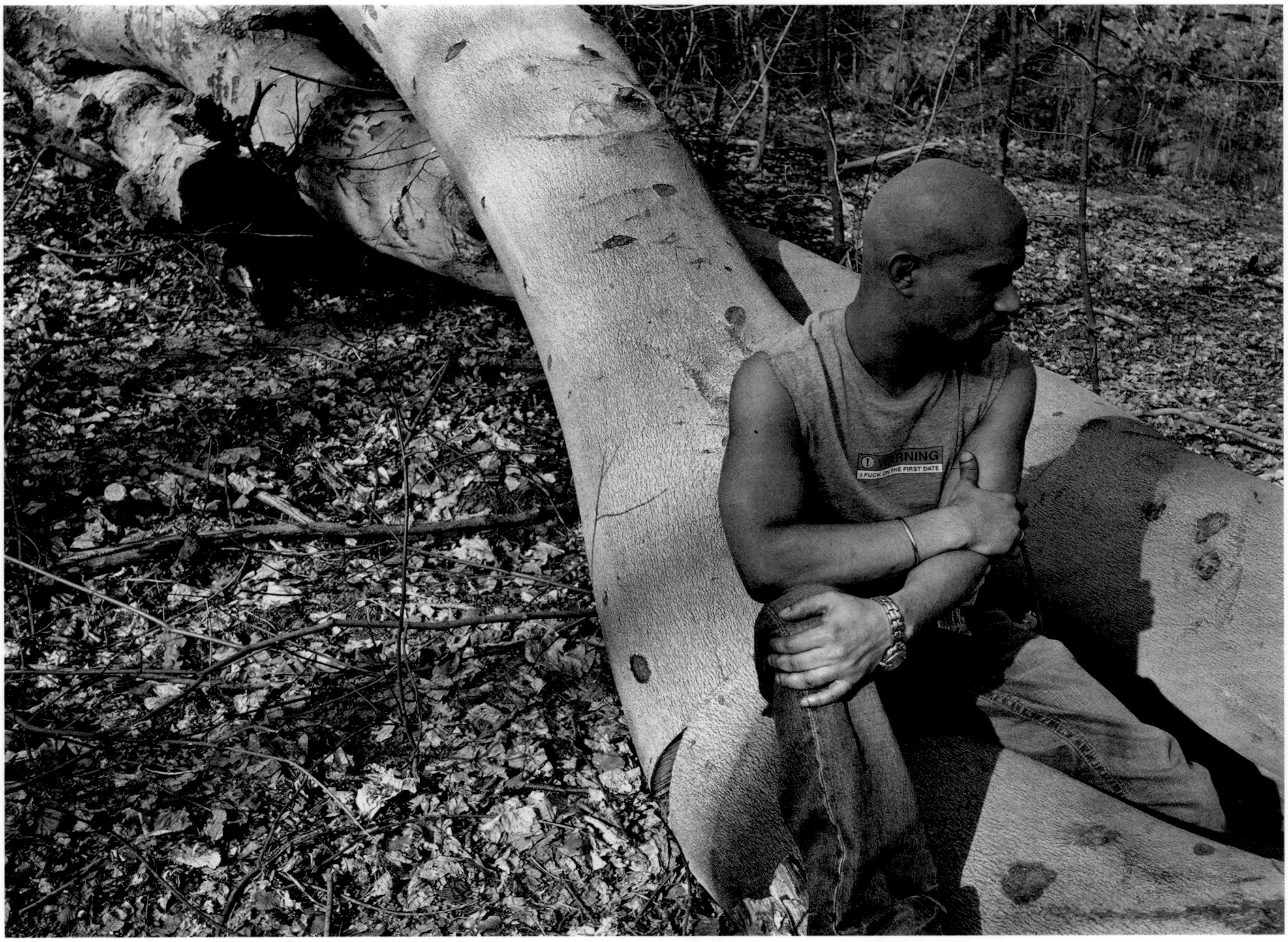
WARNING
I FUCK ON THE FIRST DATE

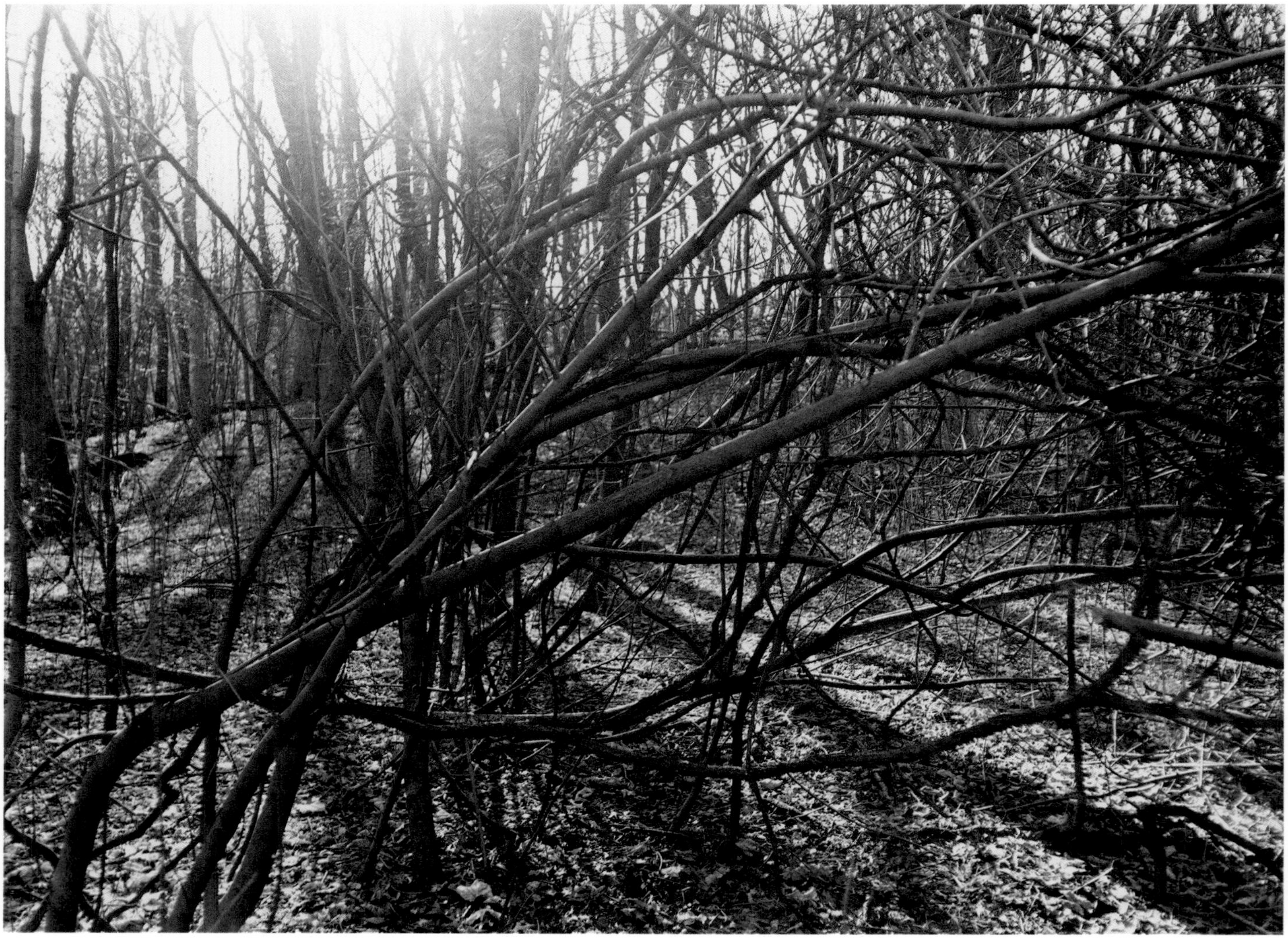

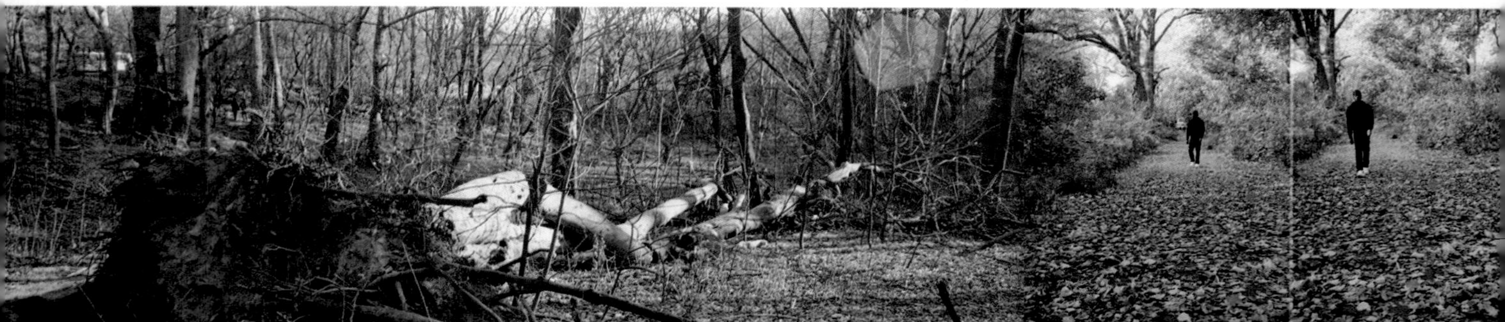

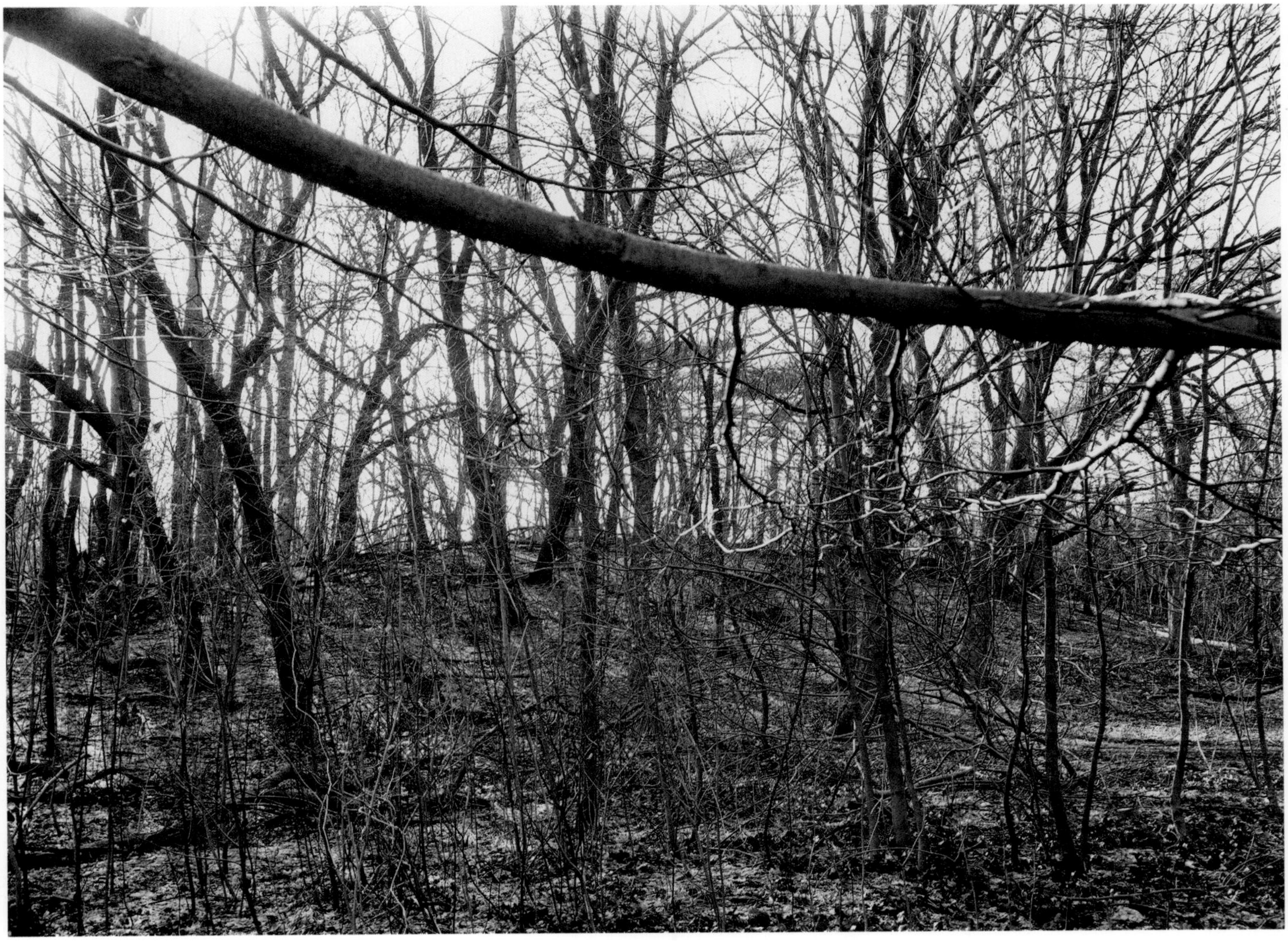

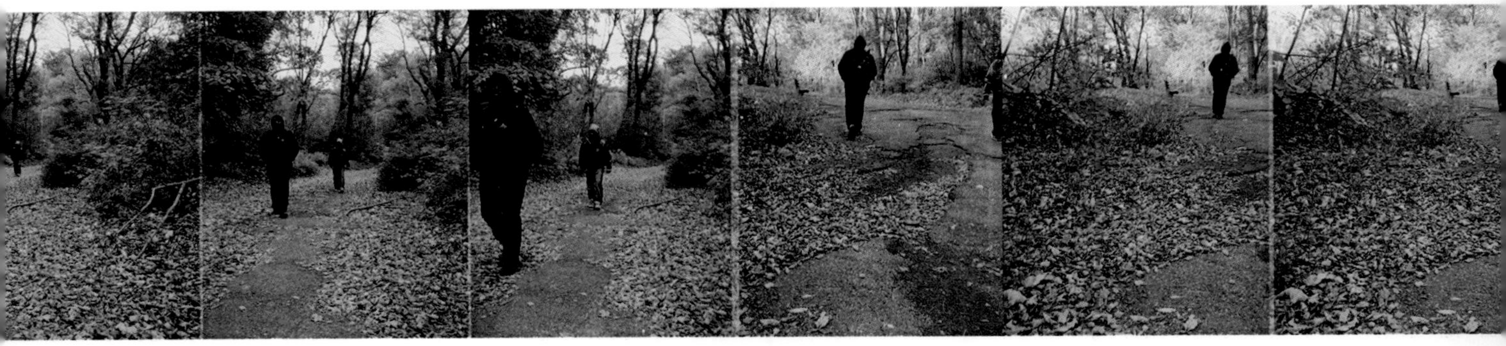

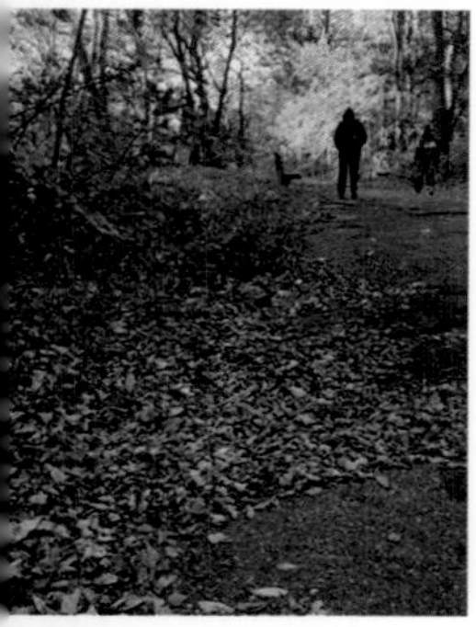

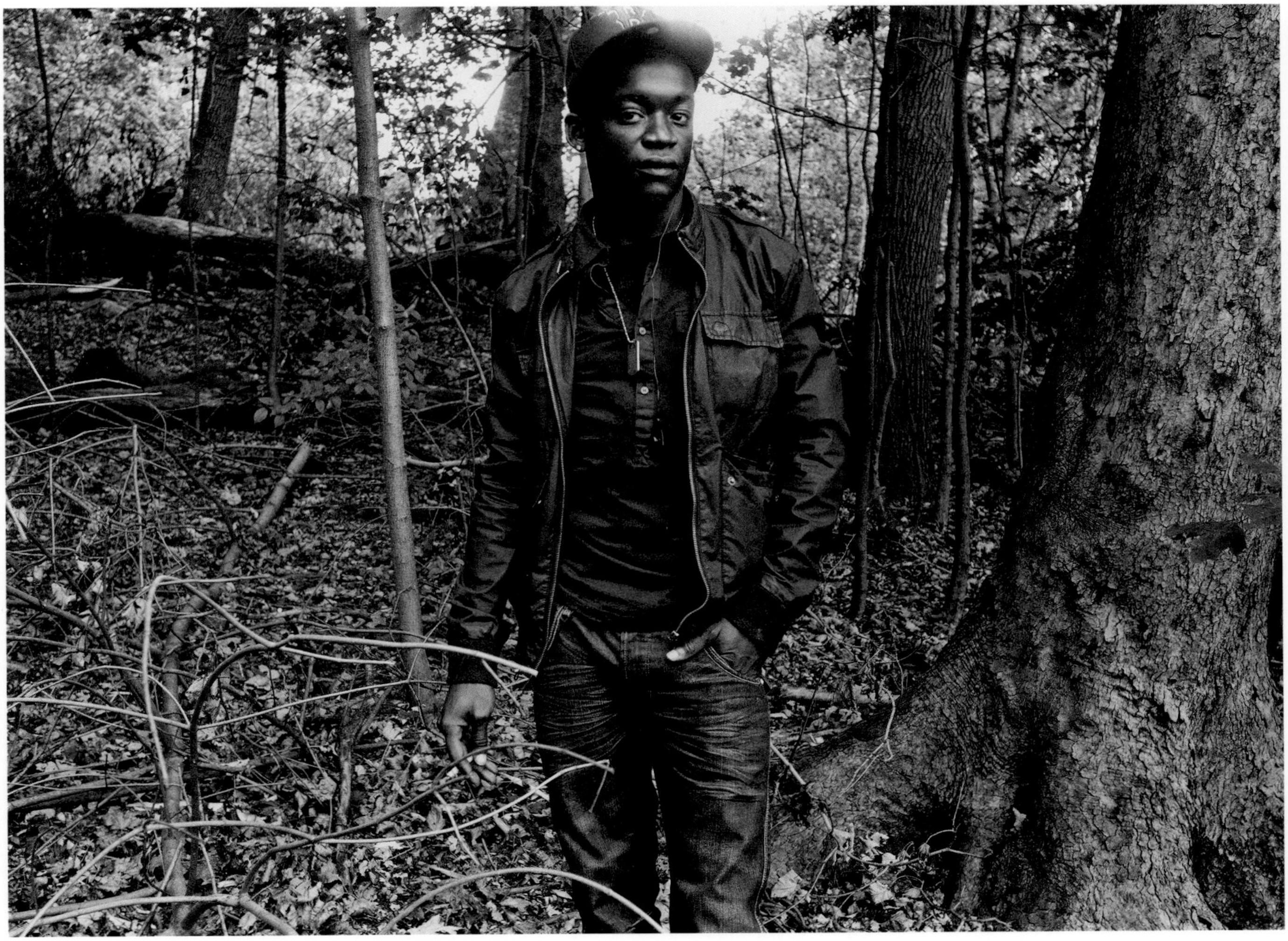

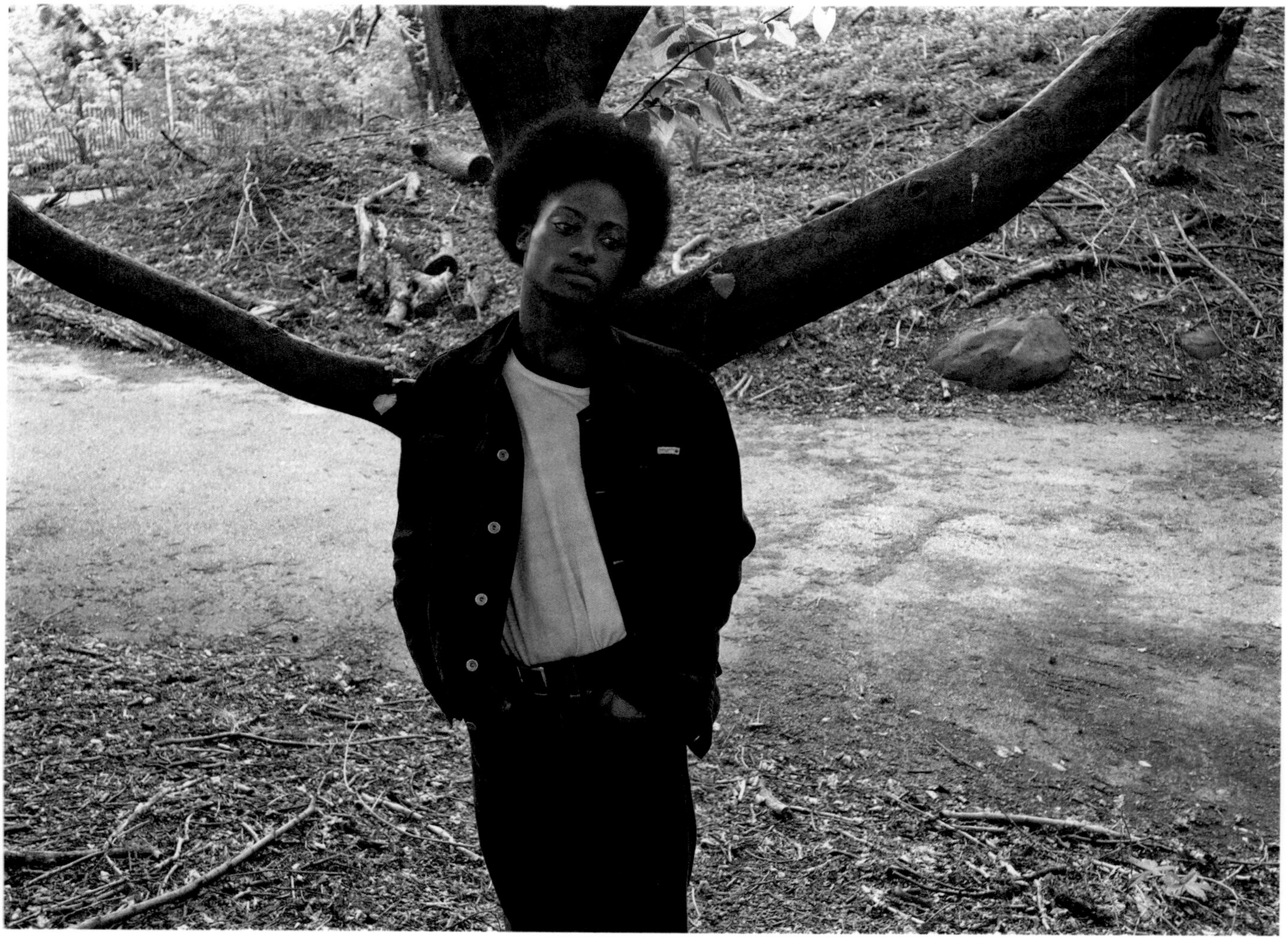

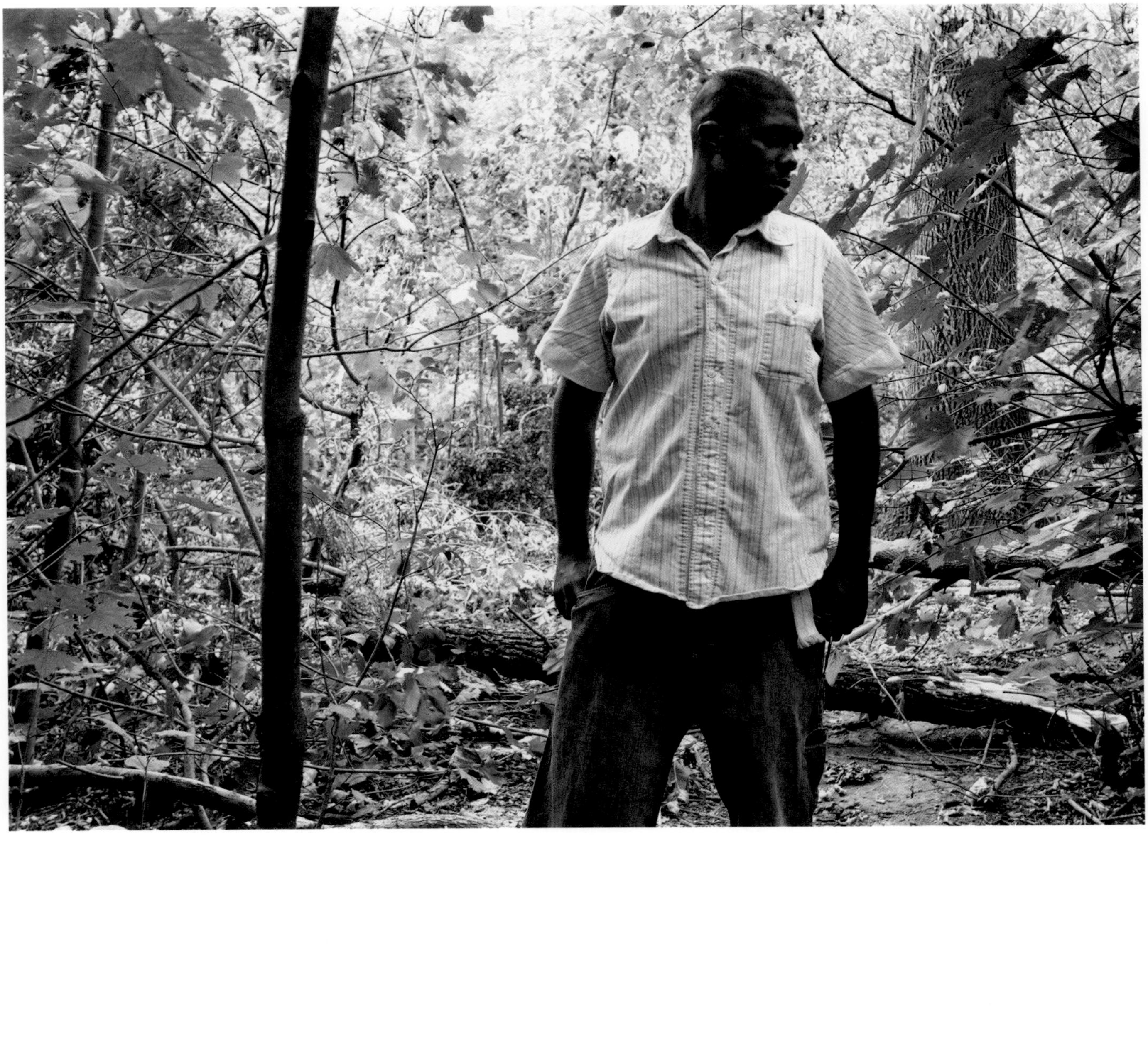

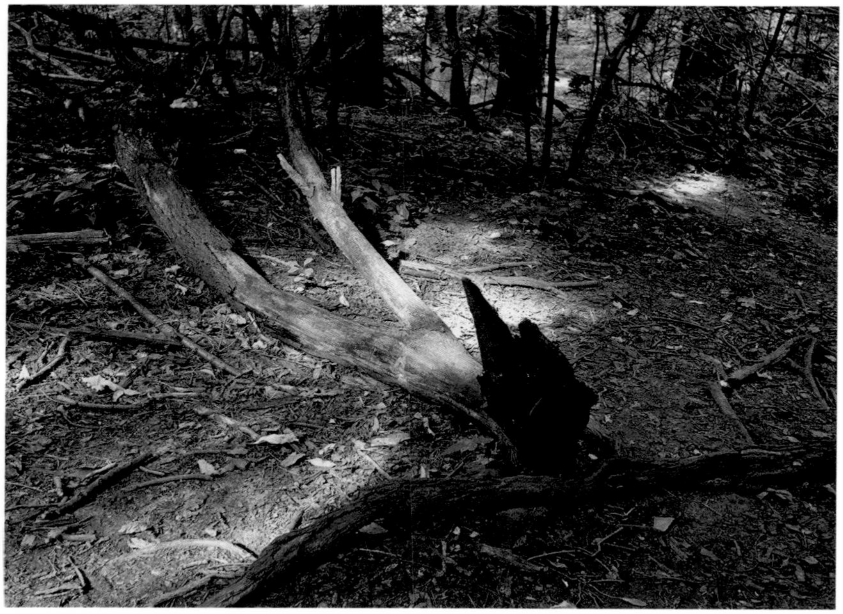

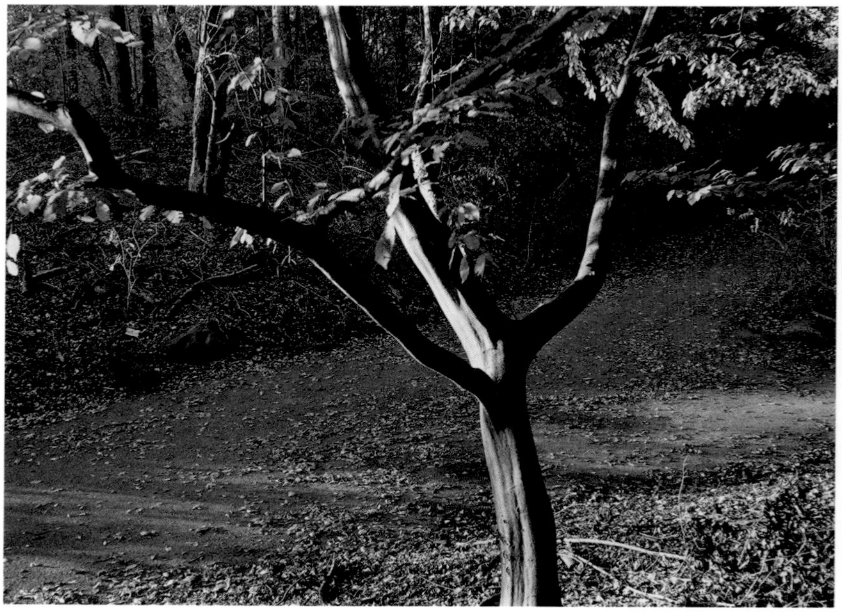

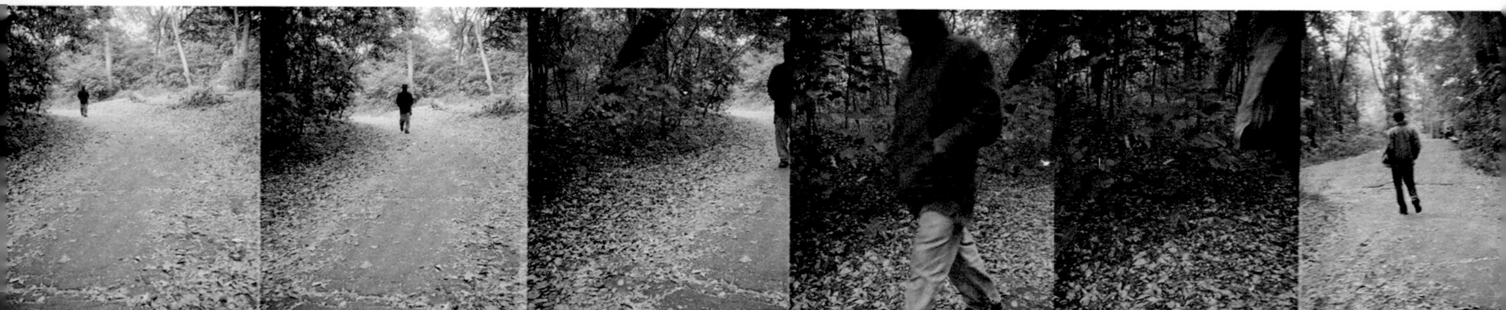

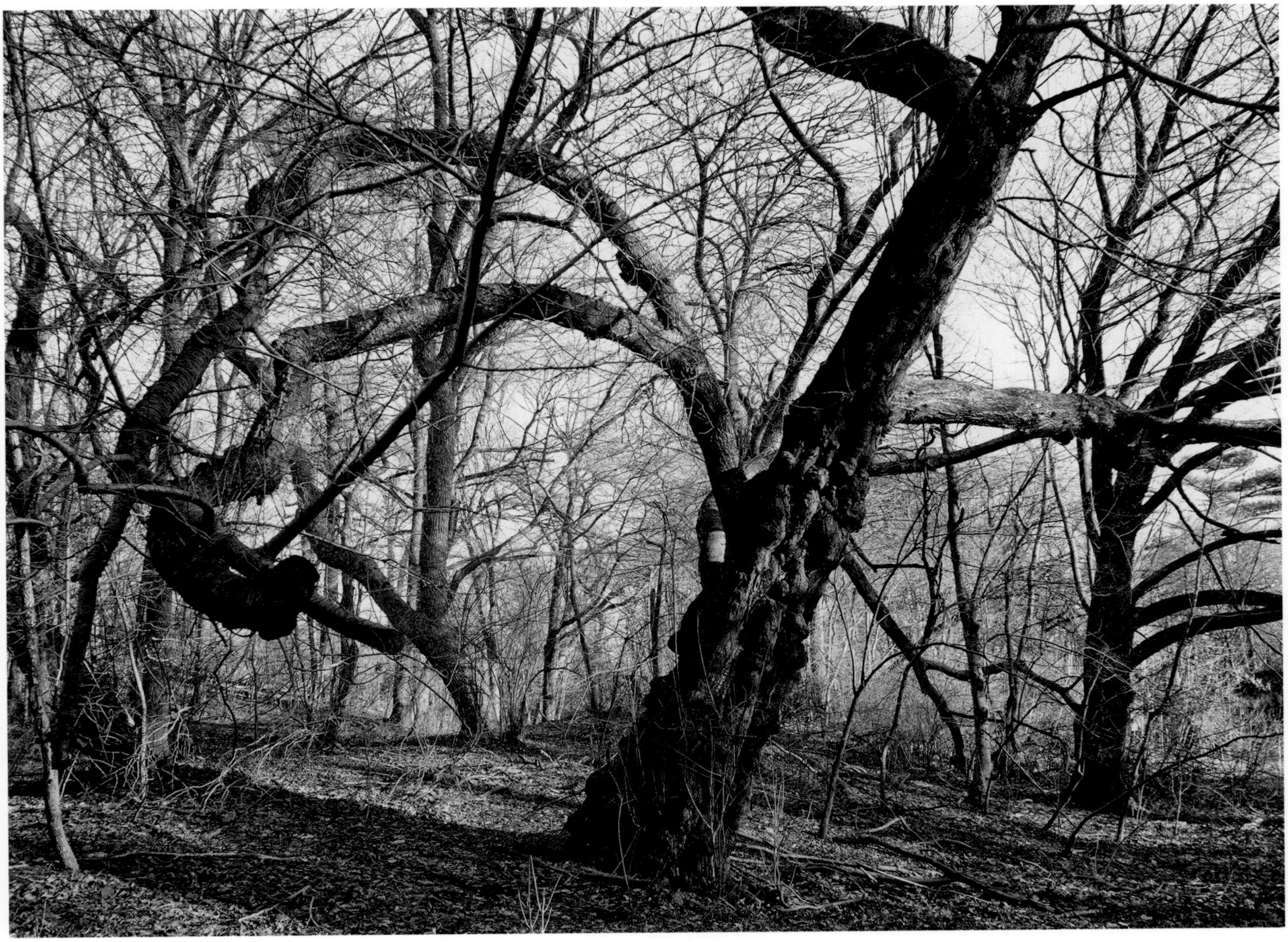

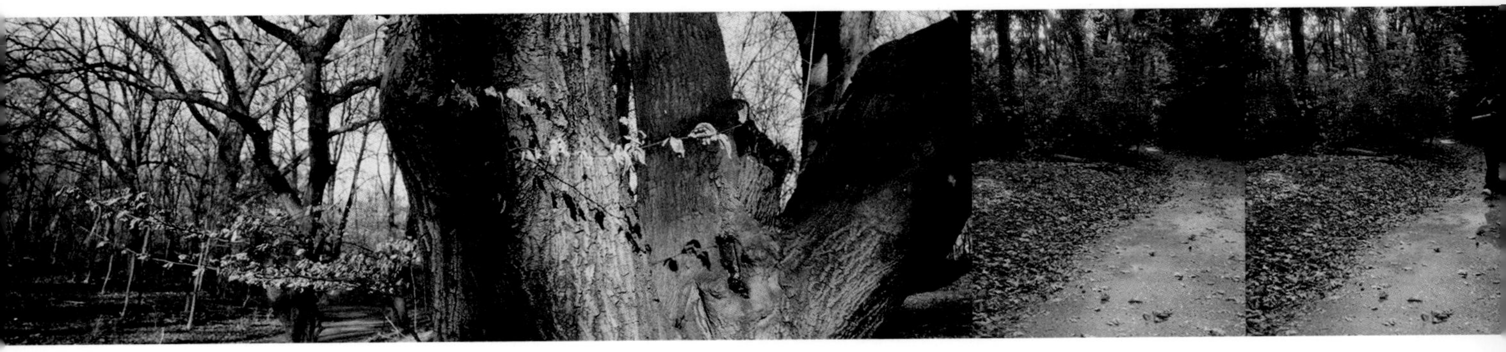

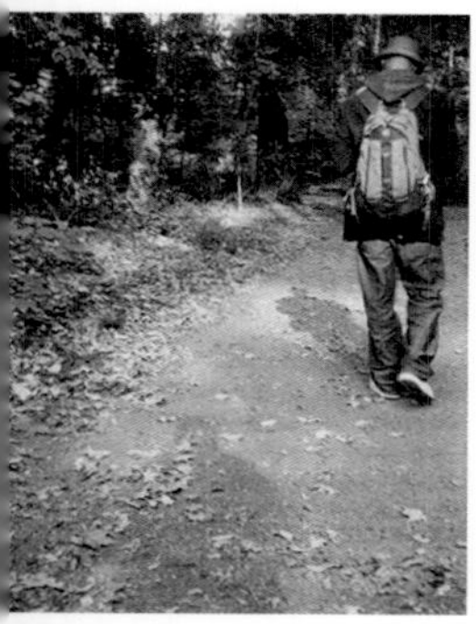

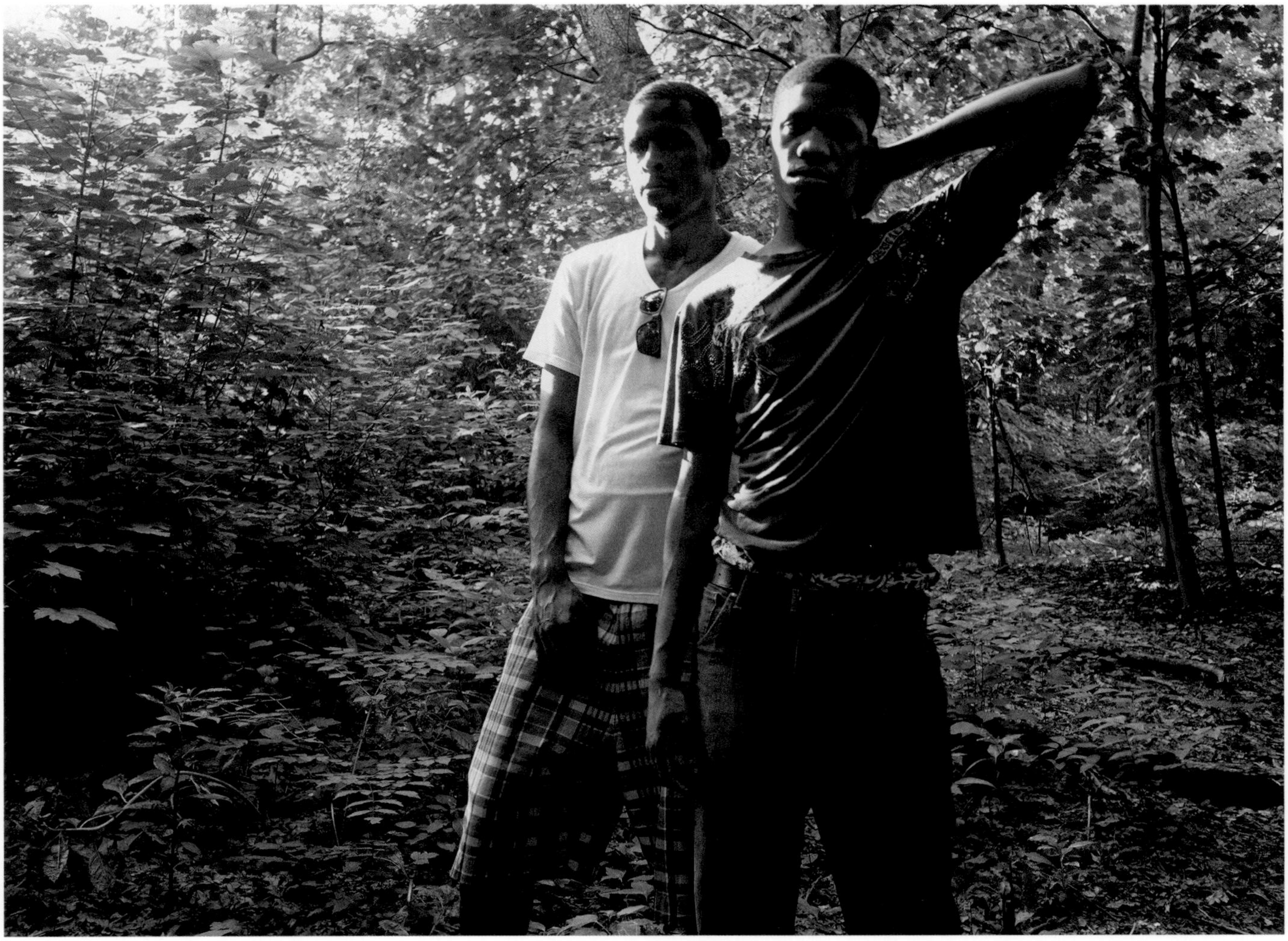

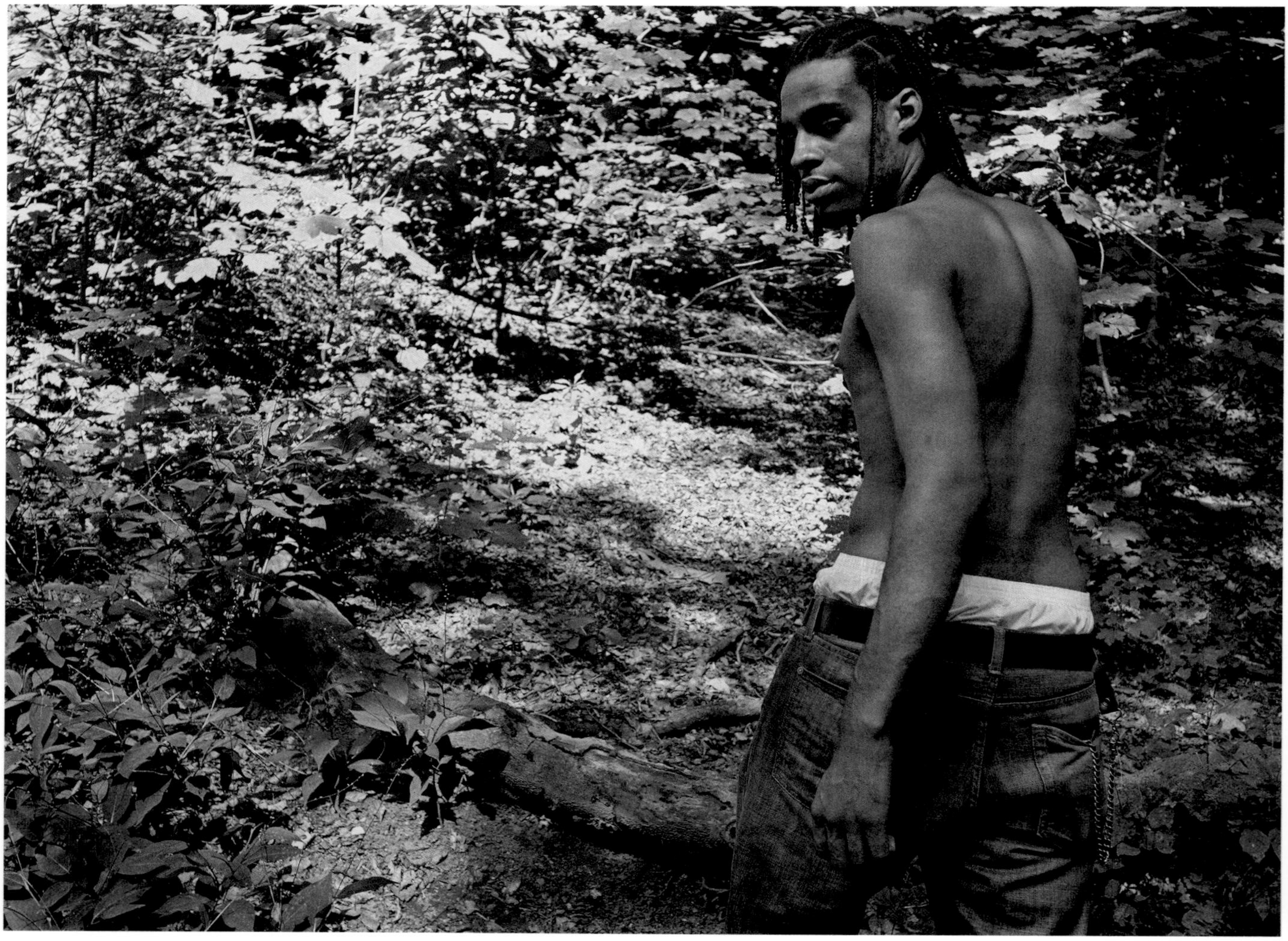

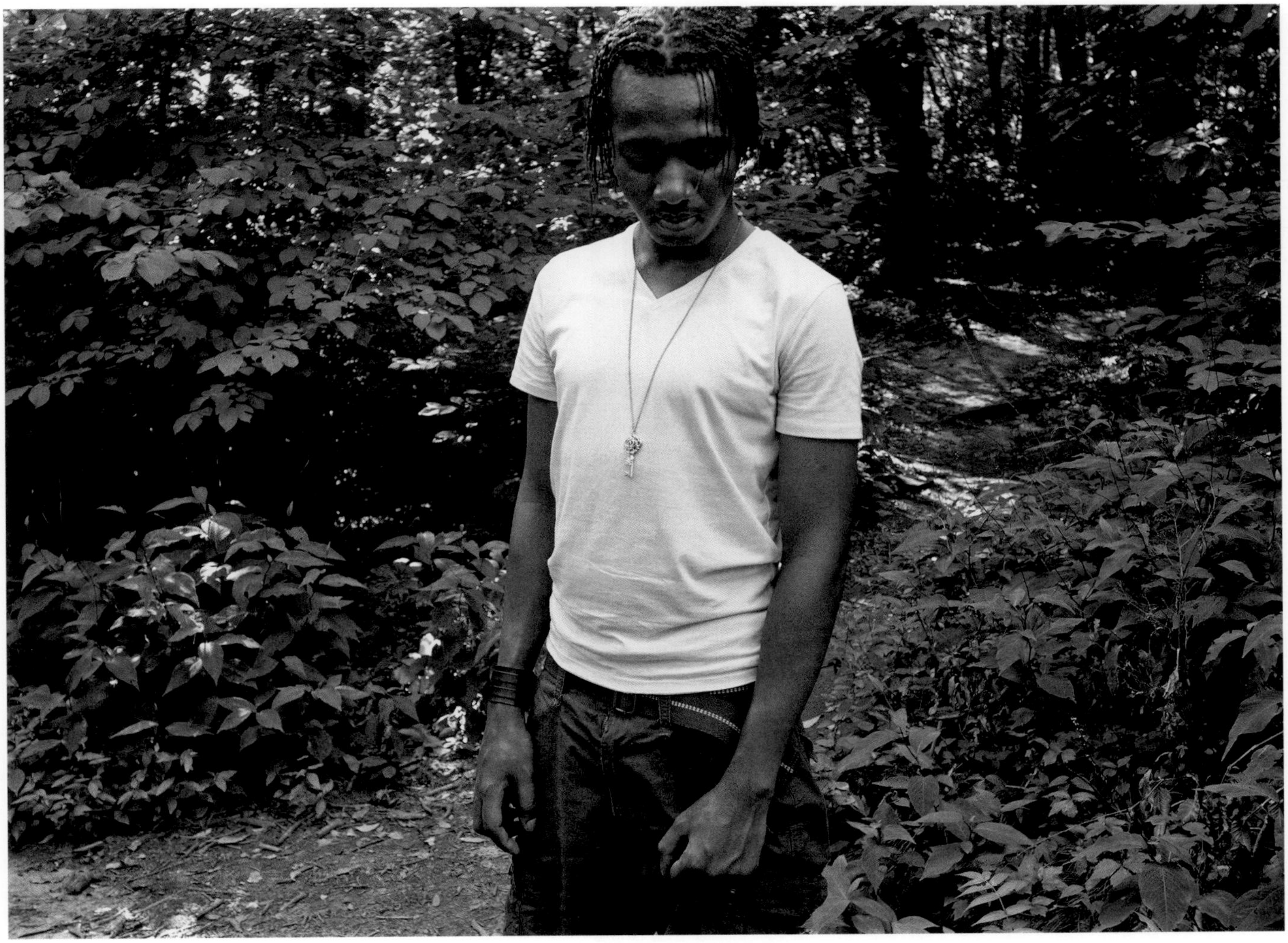

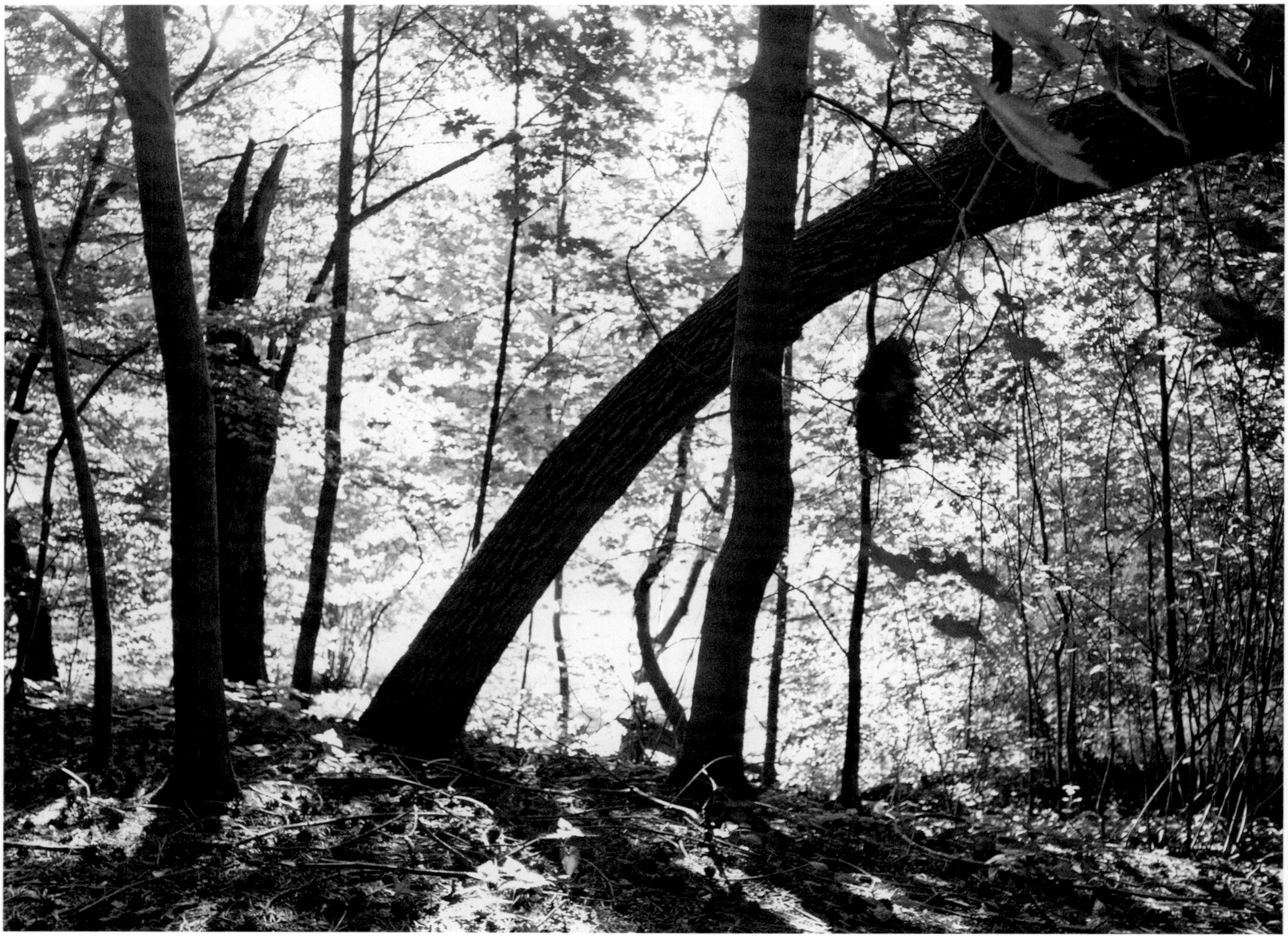

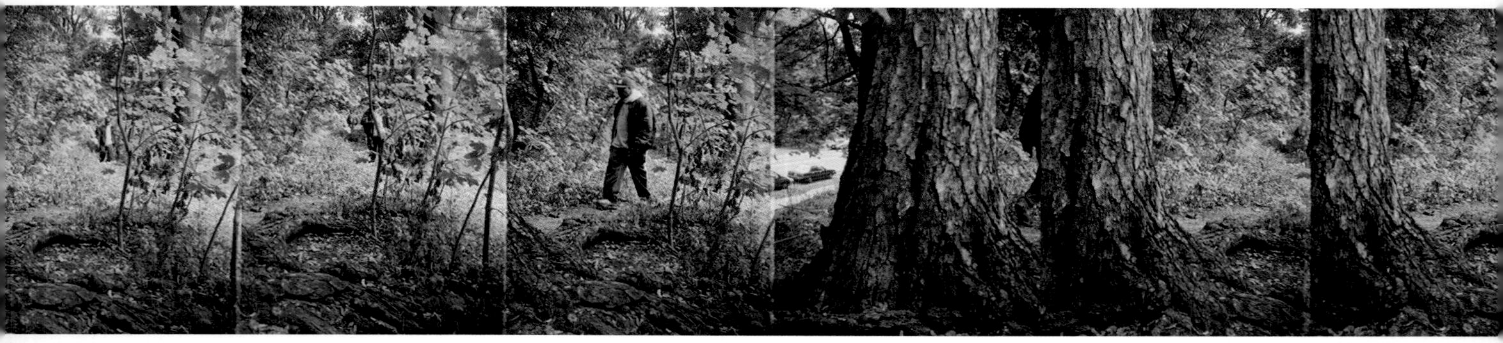

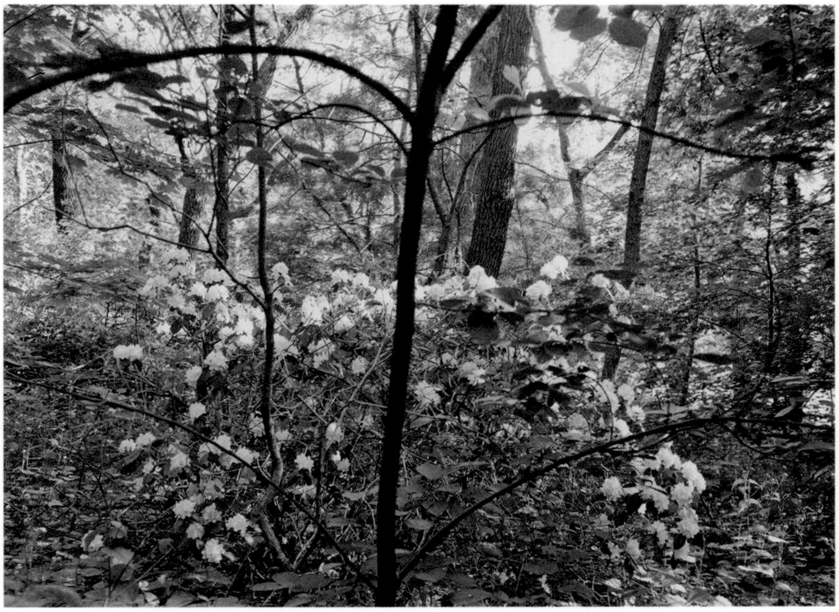

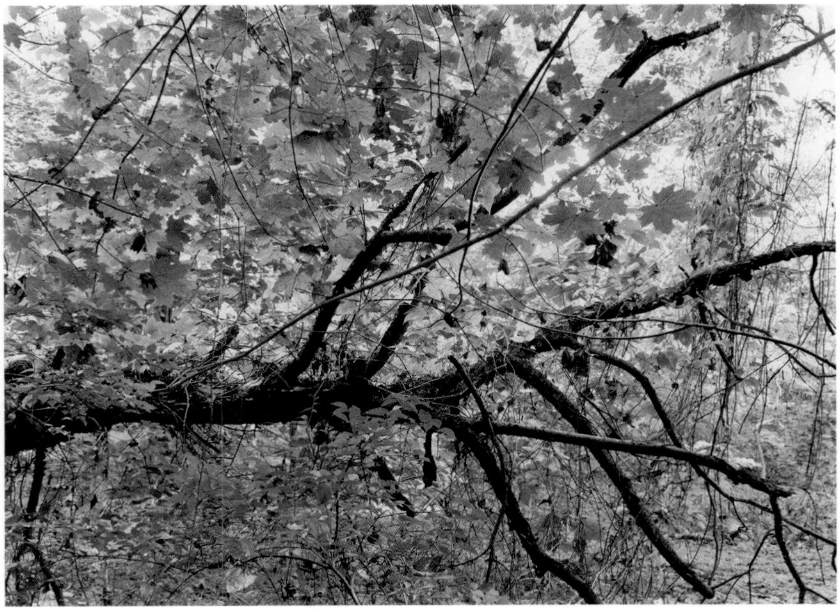

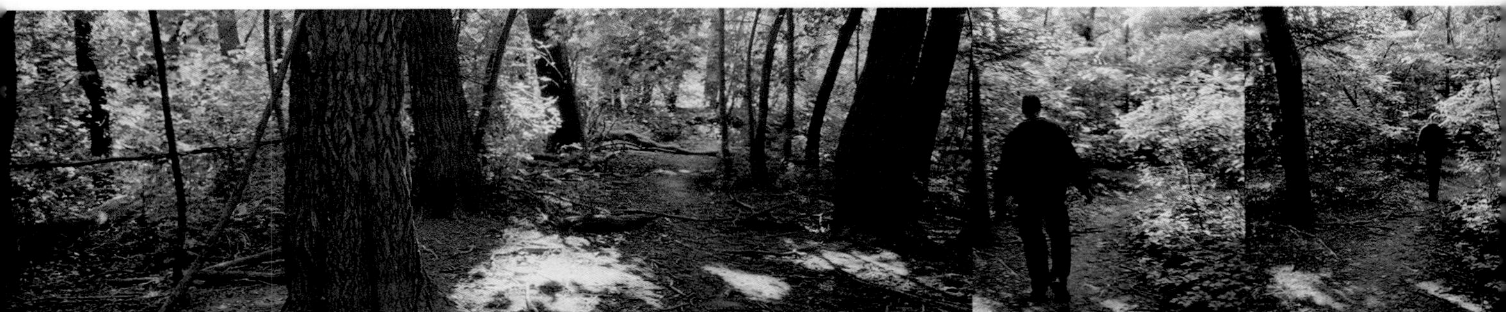

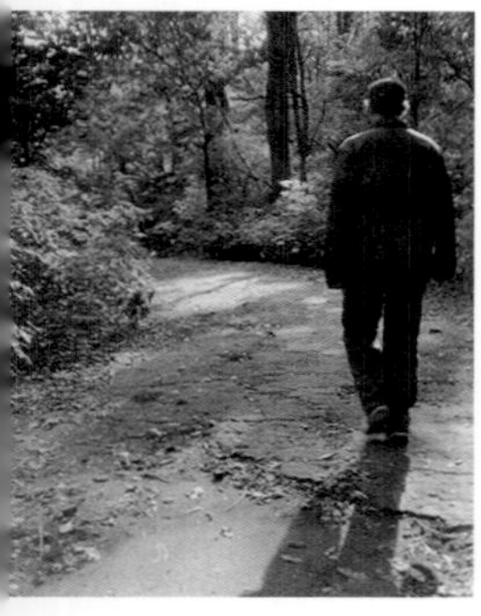

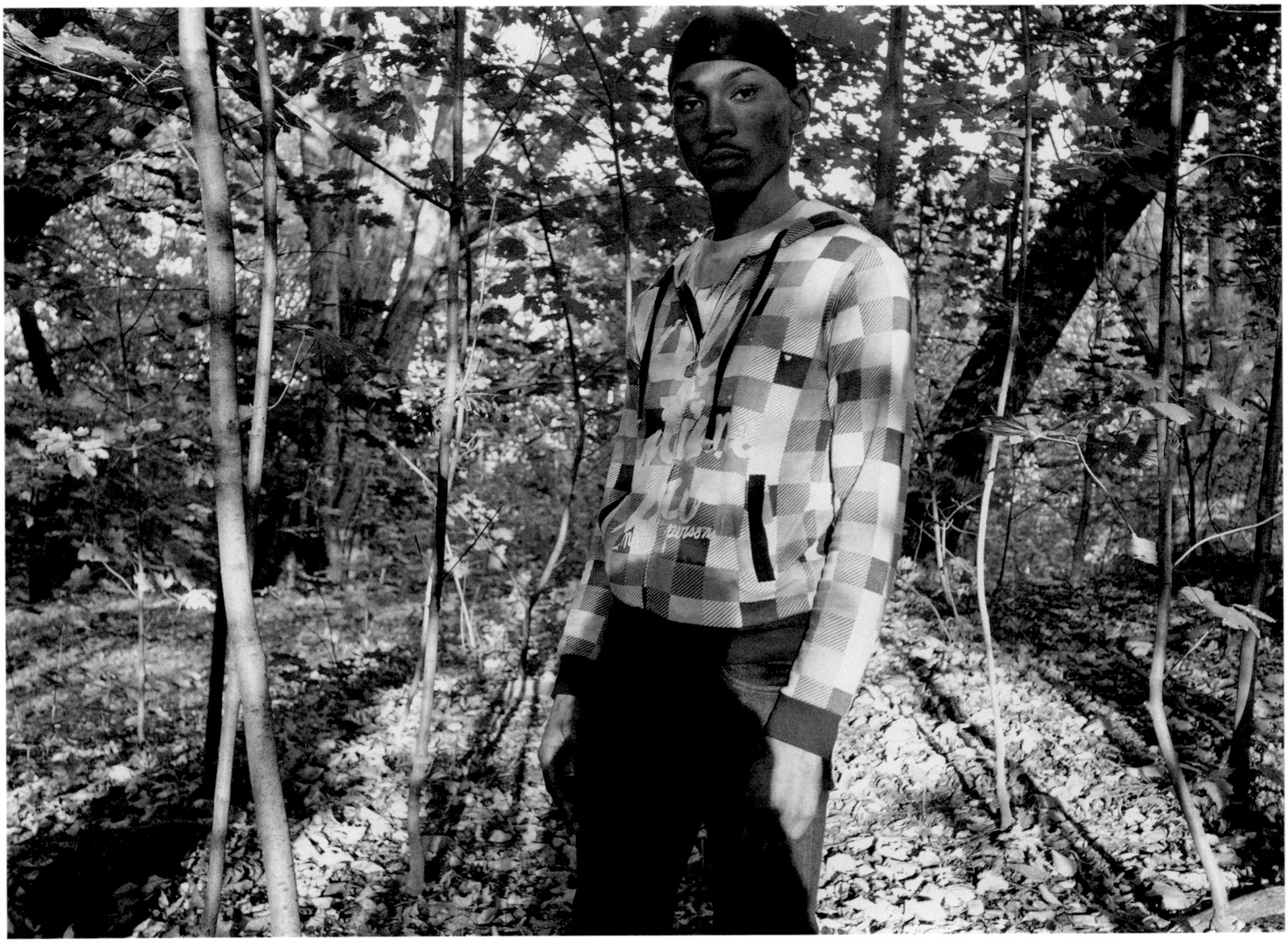

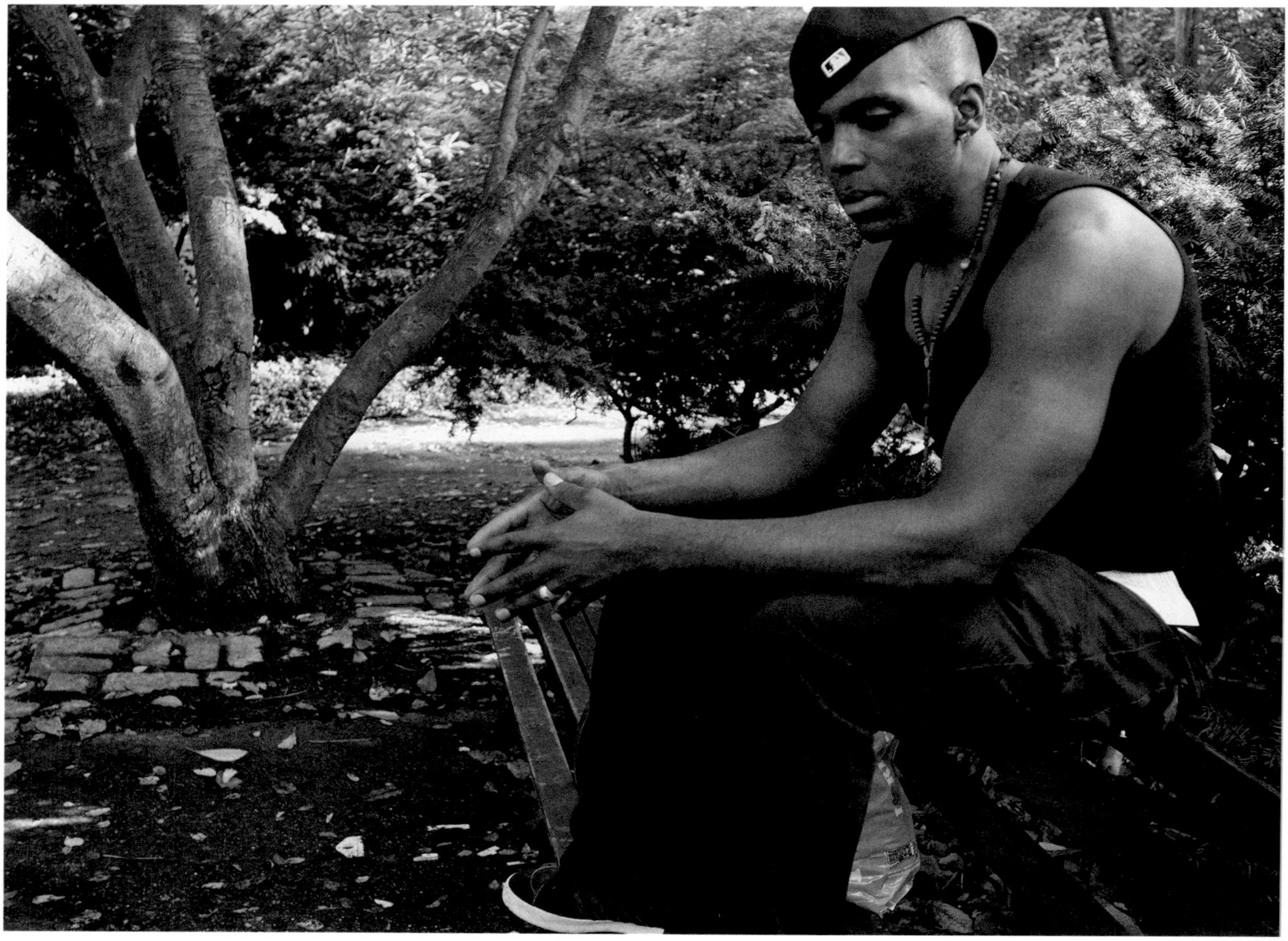

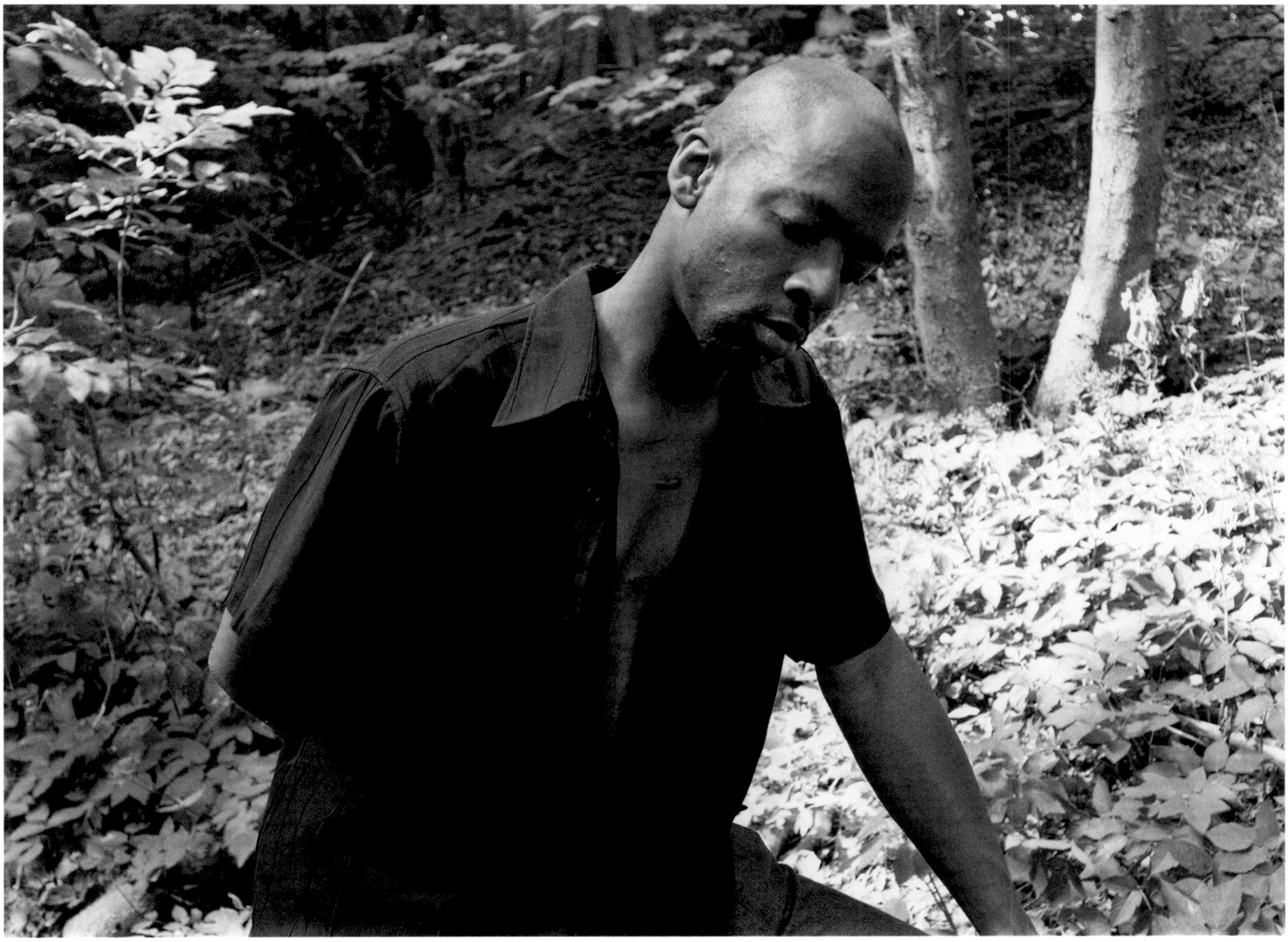

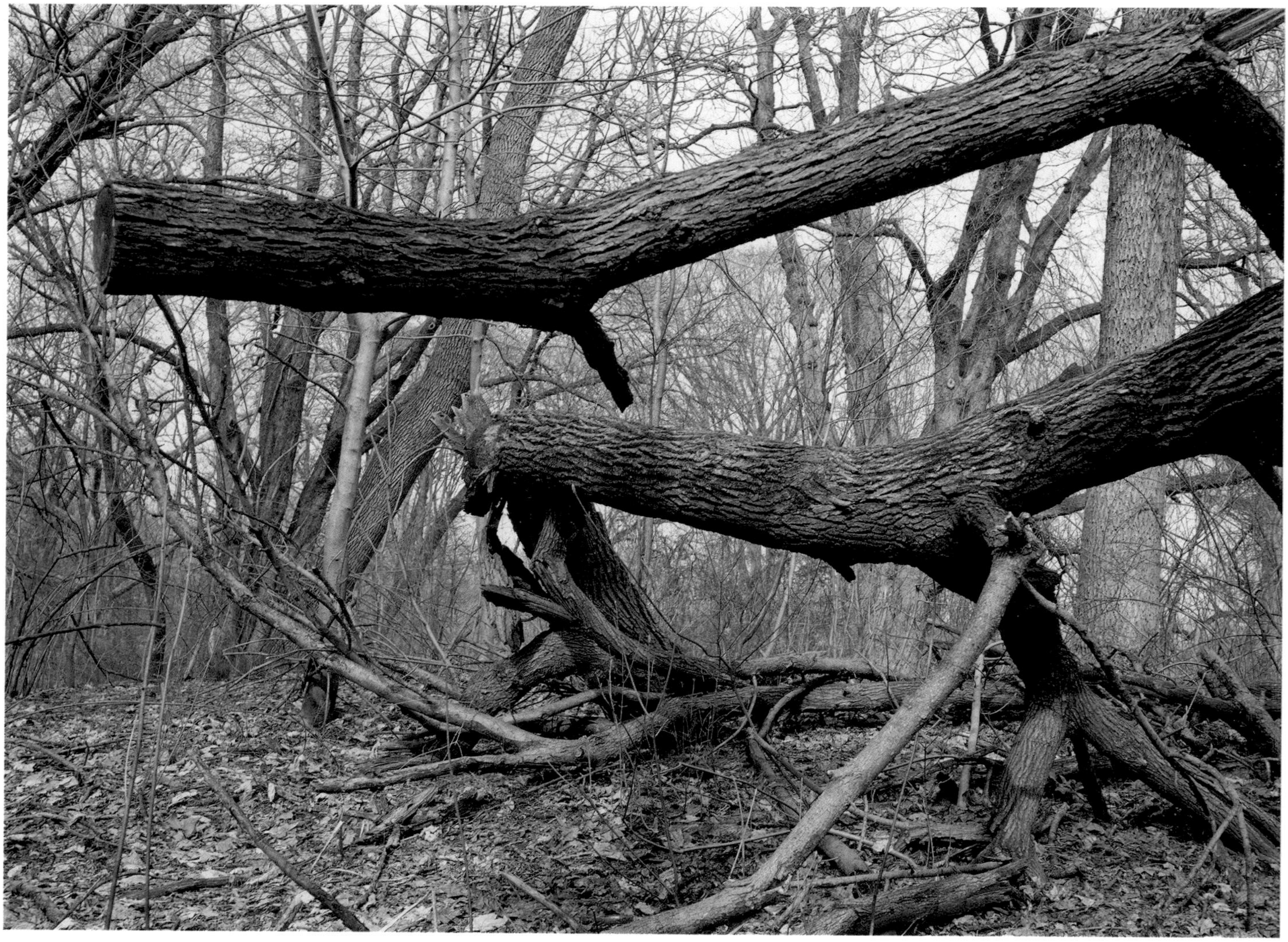

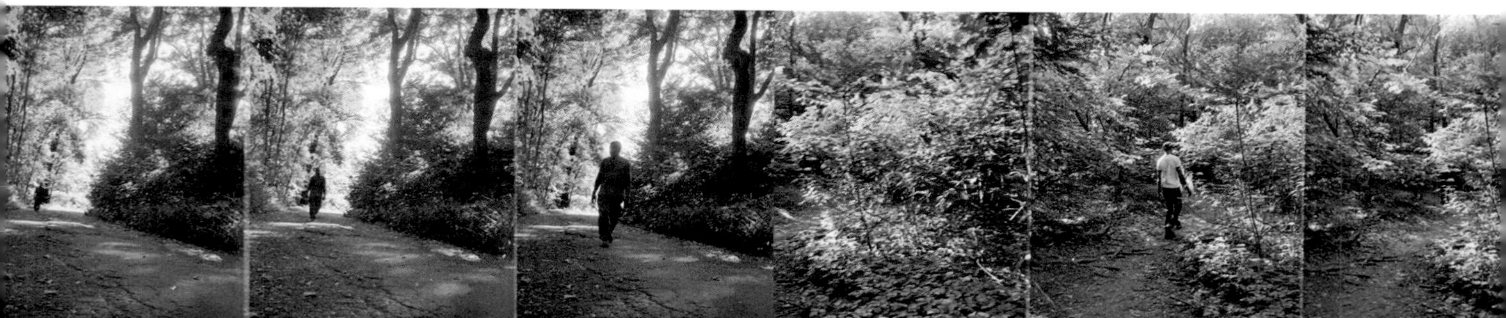

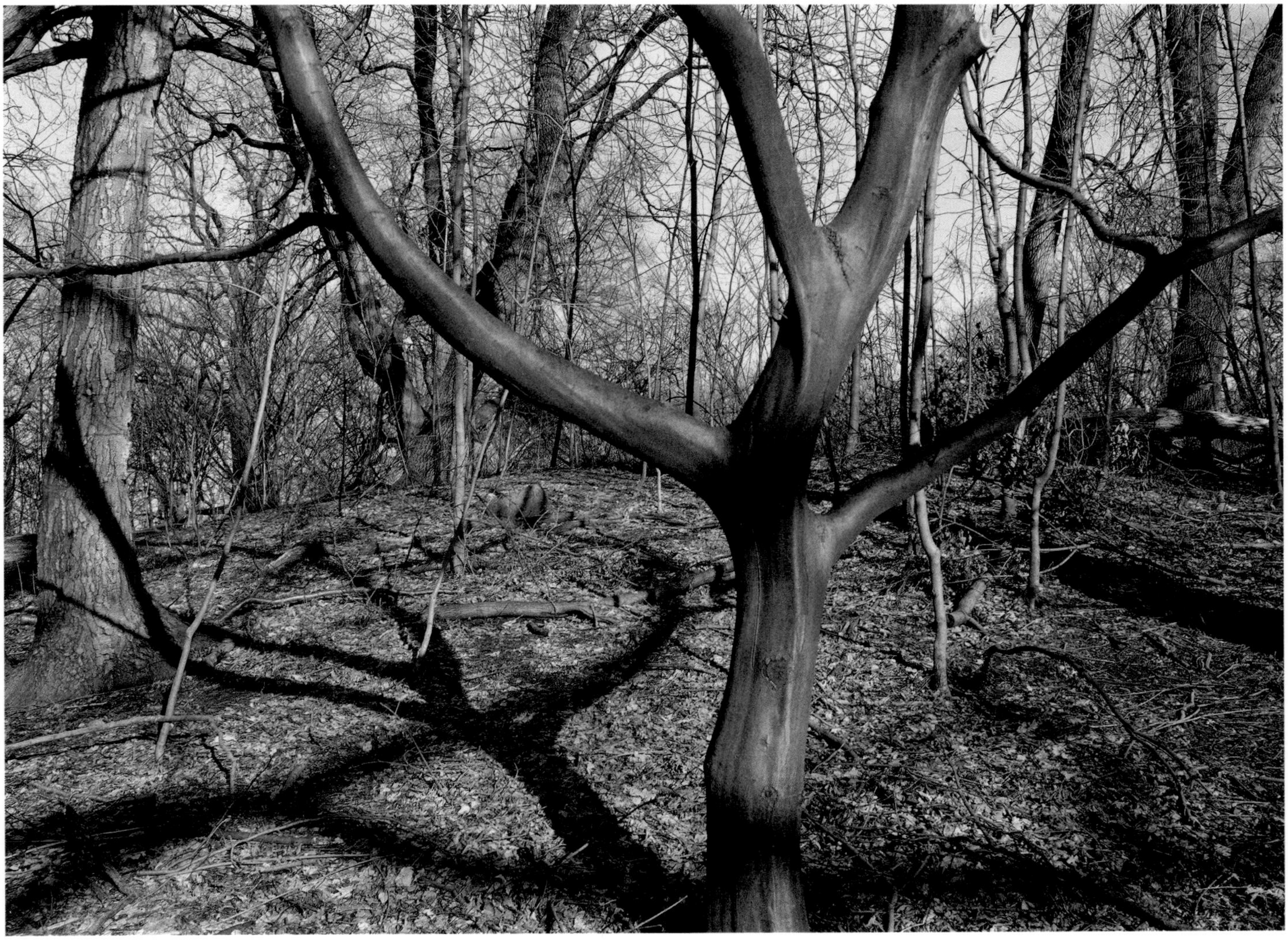

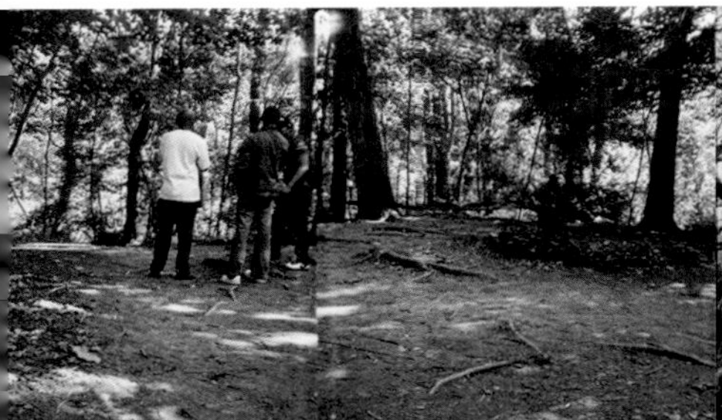

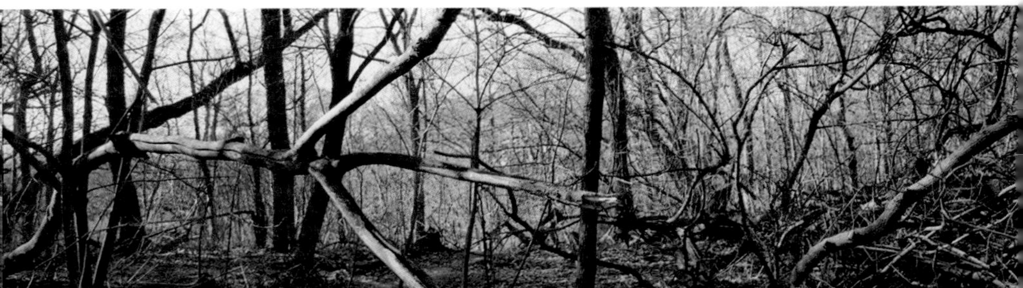

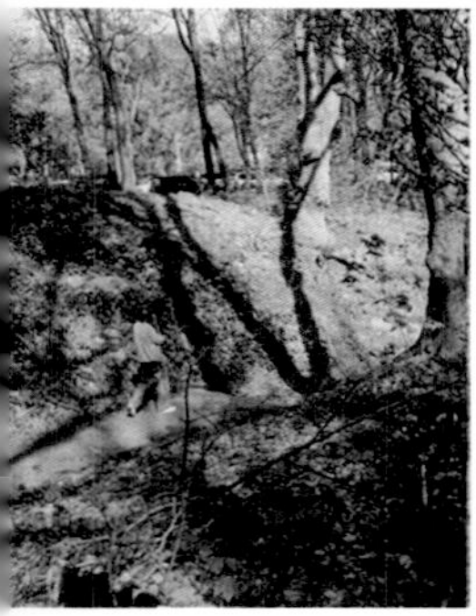

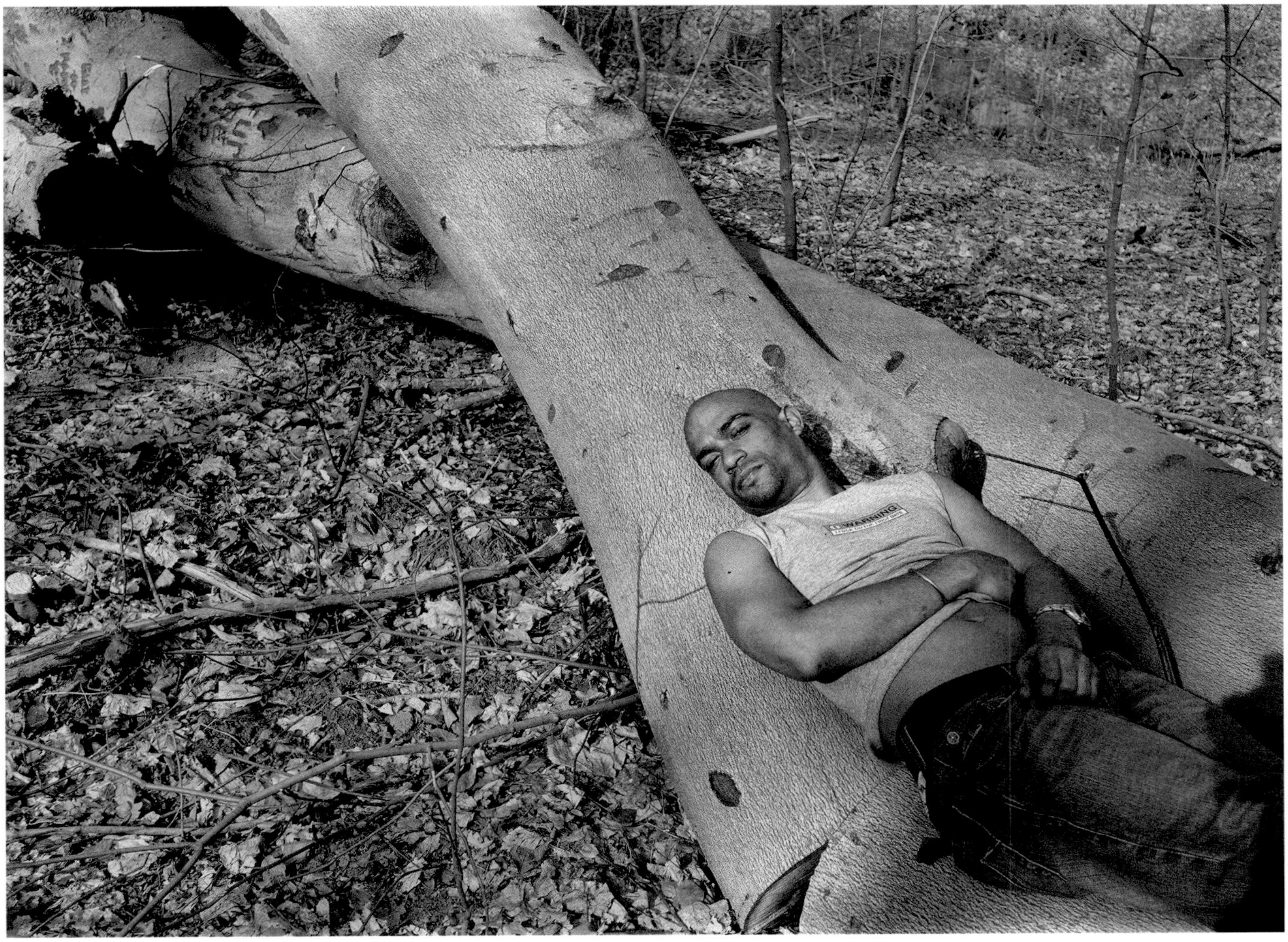
WARNING

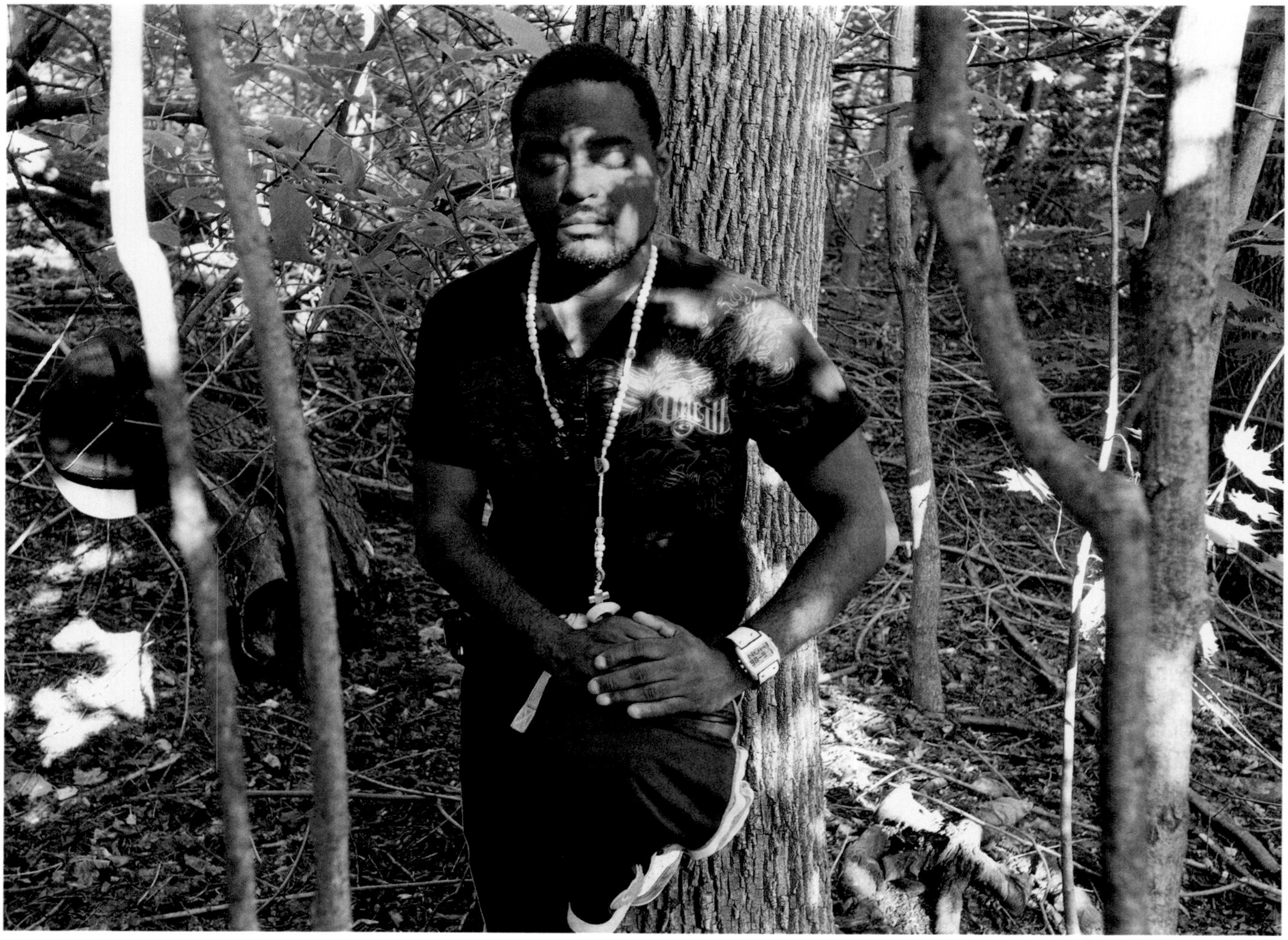

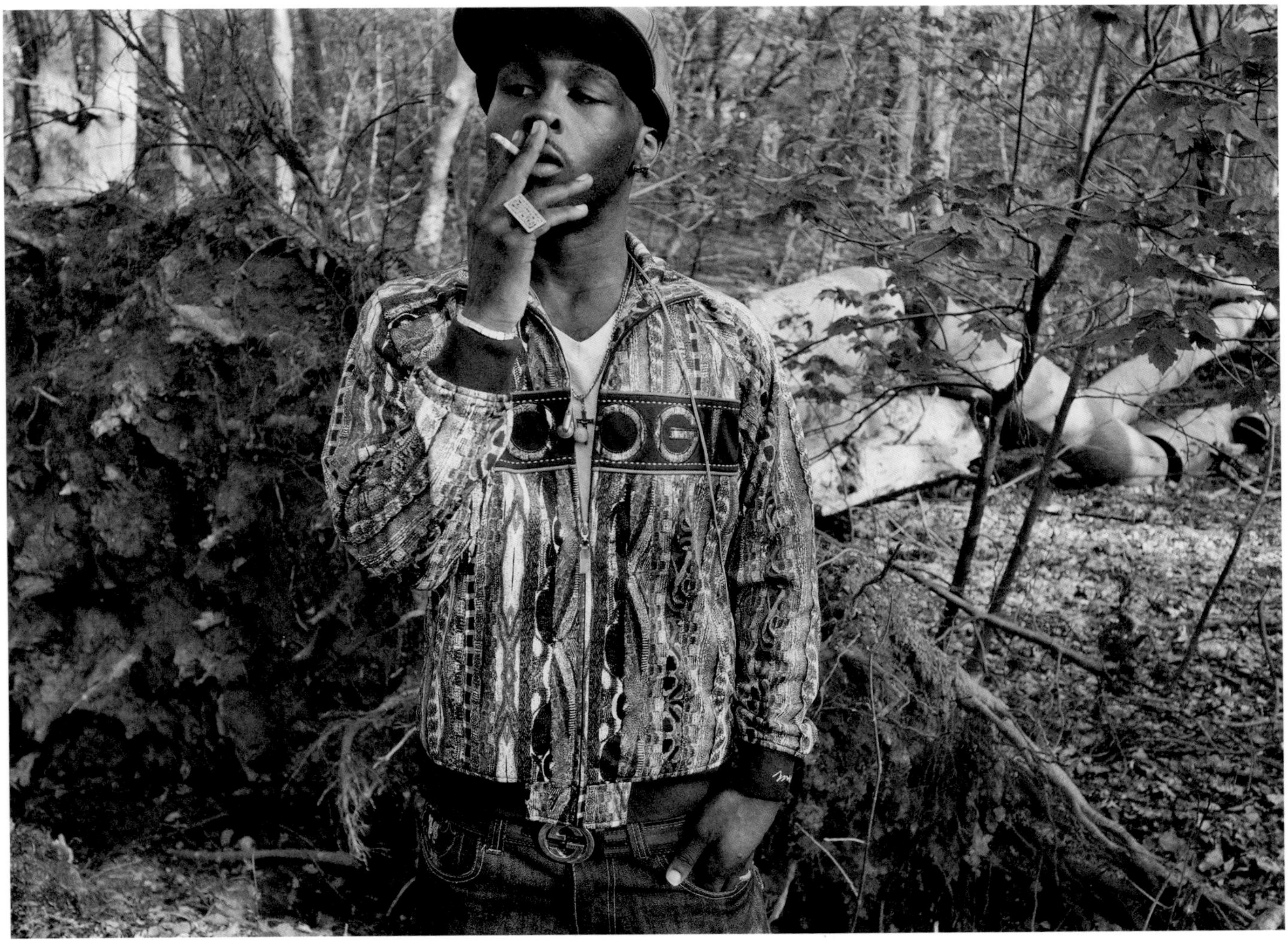

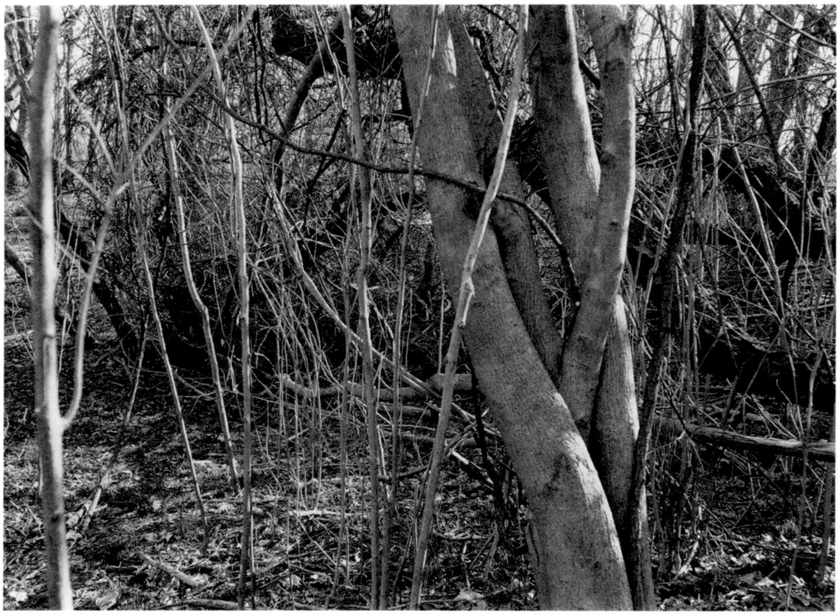

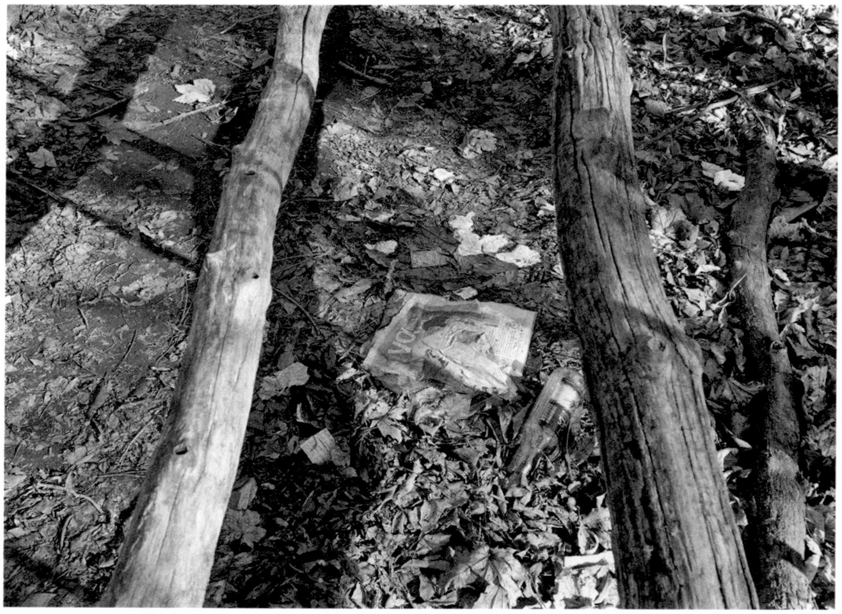

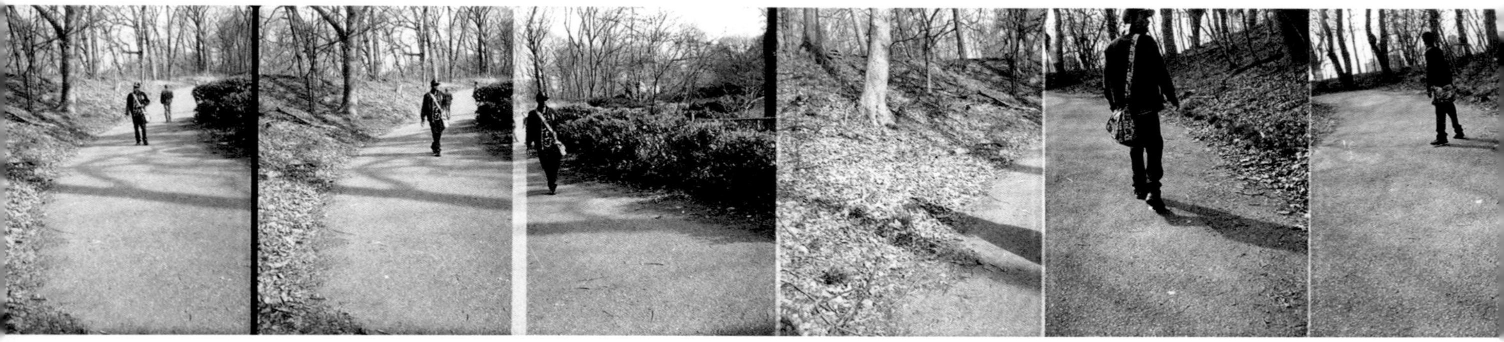

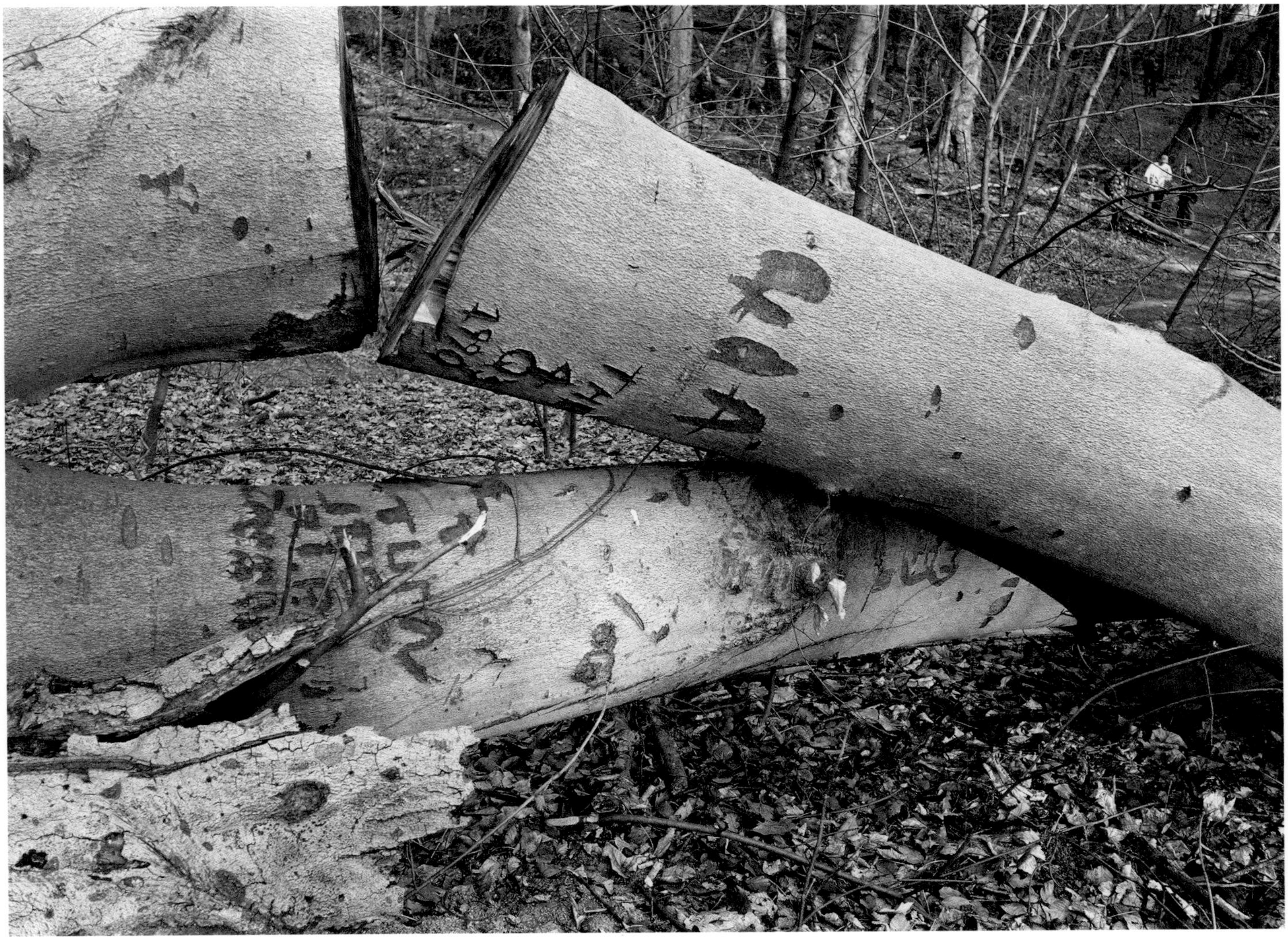

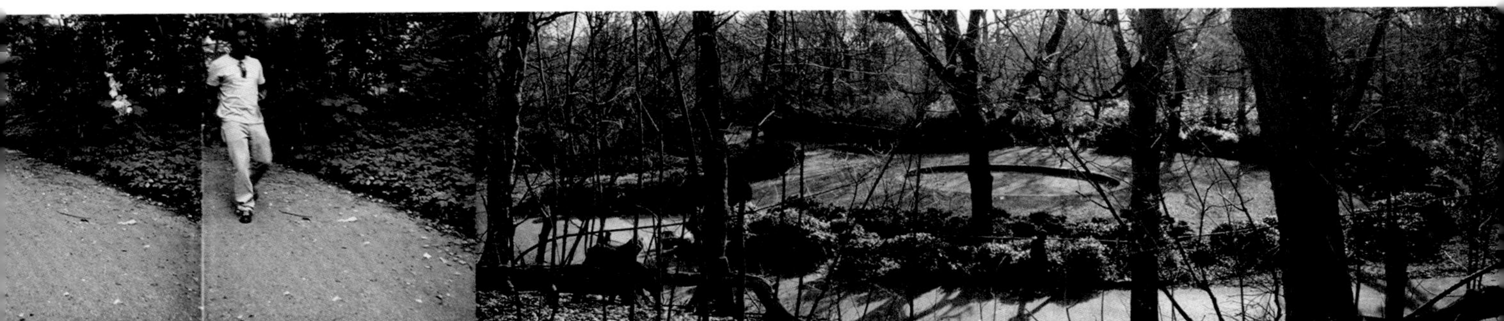

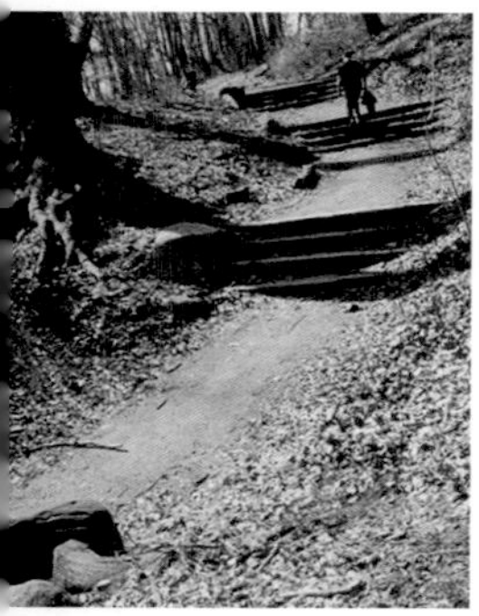

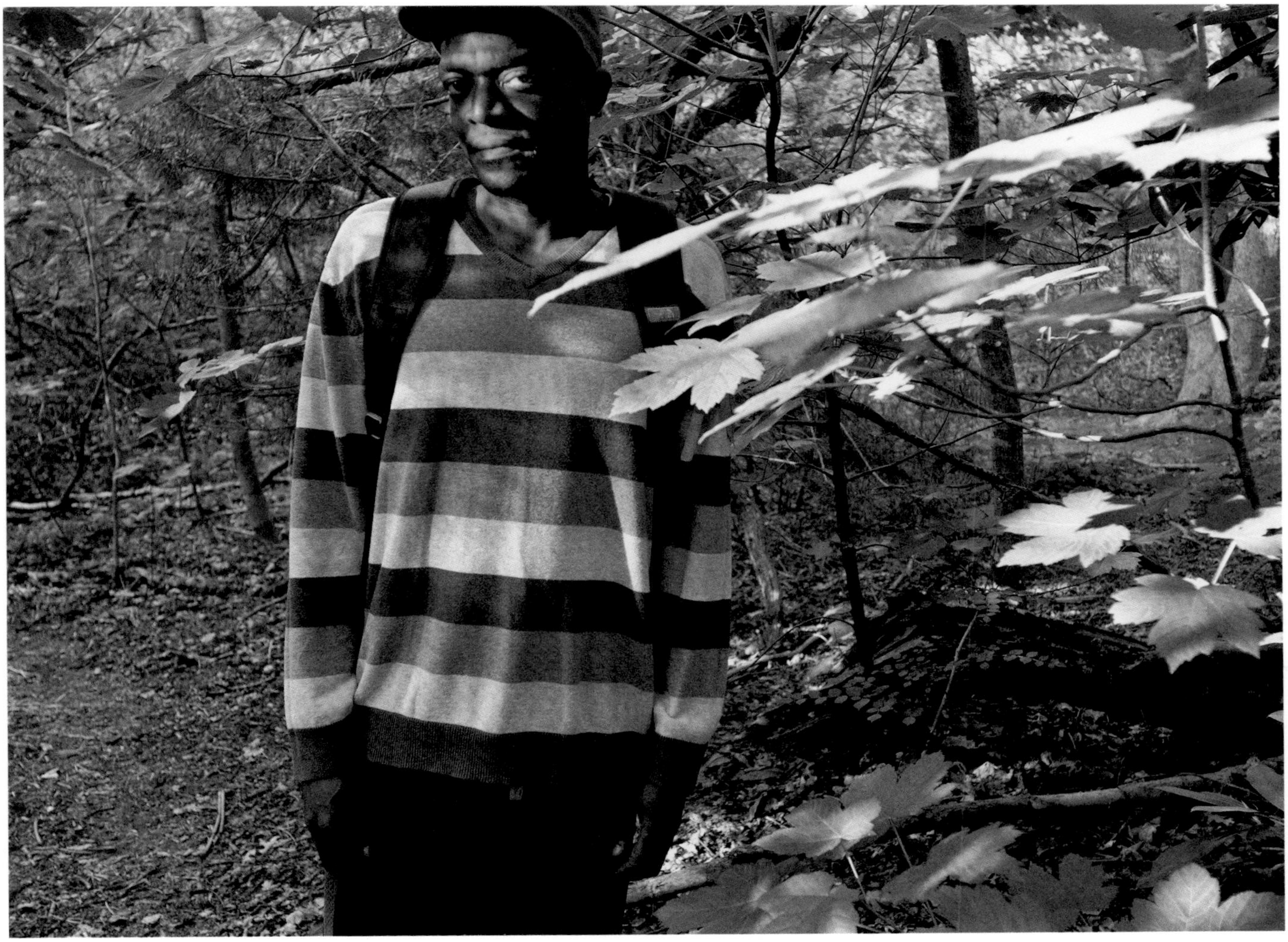

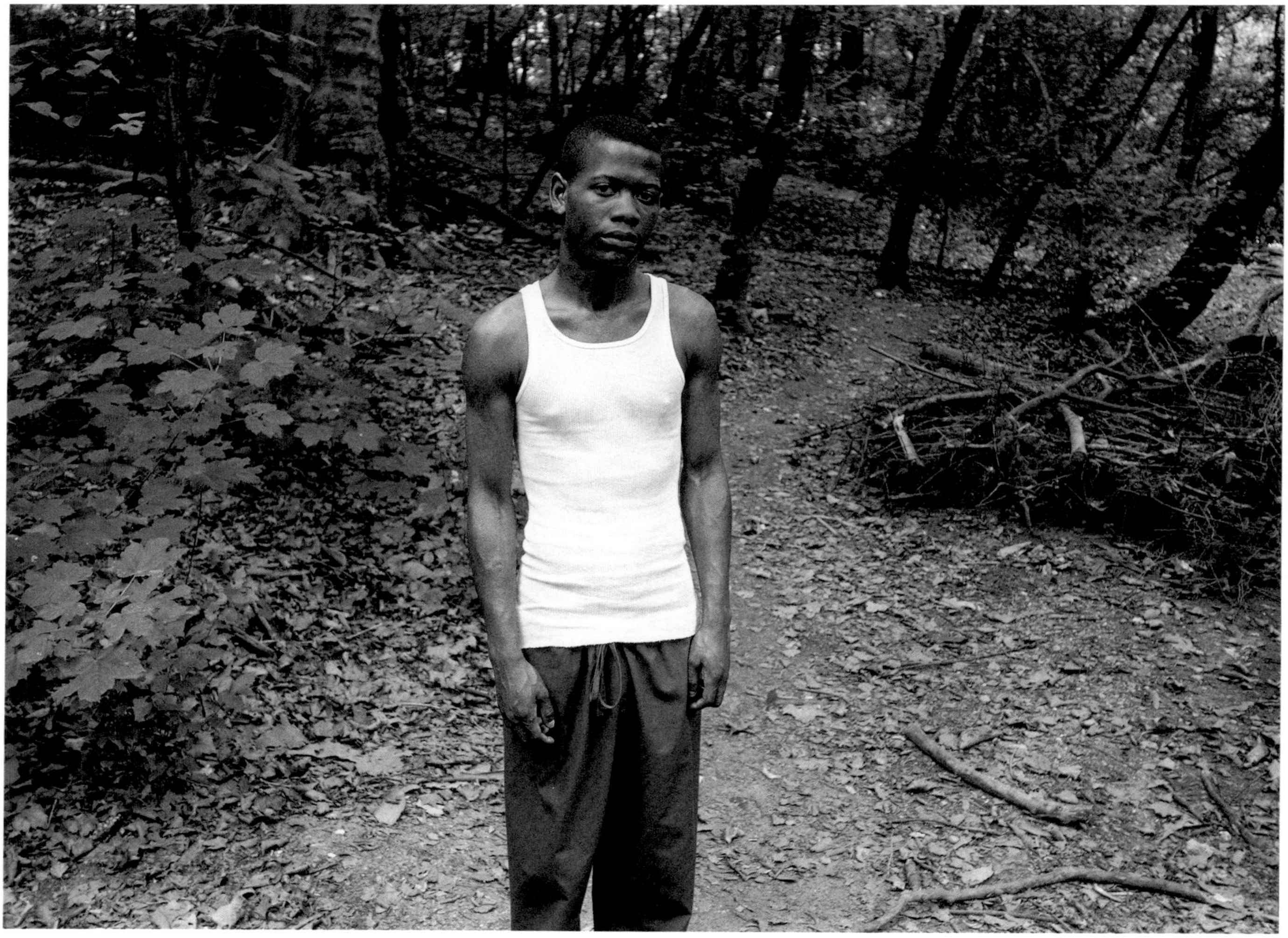

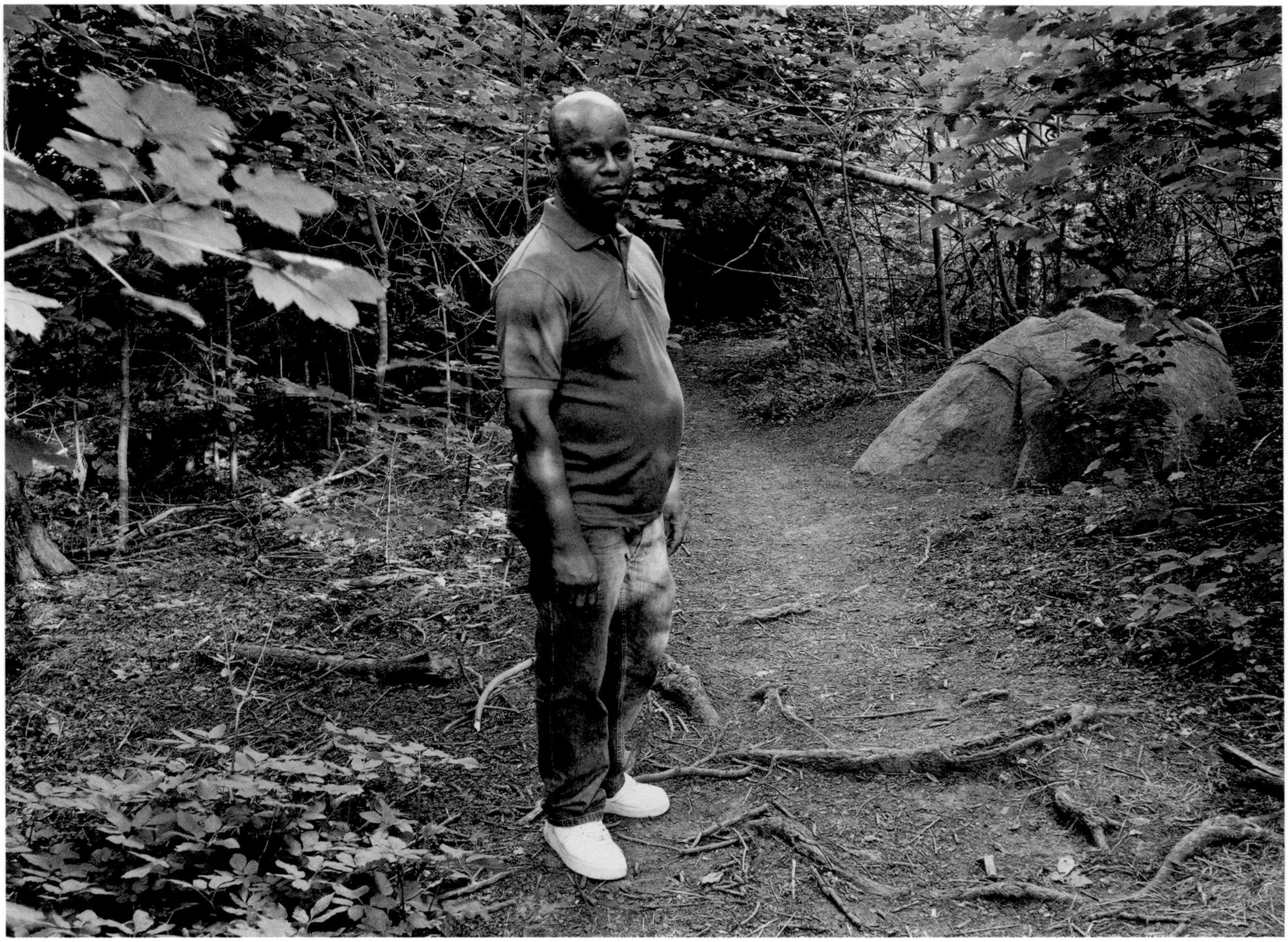

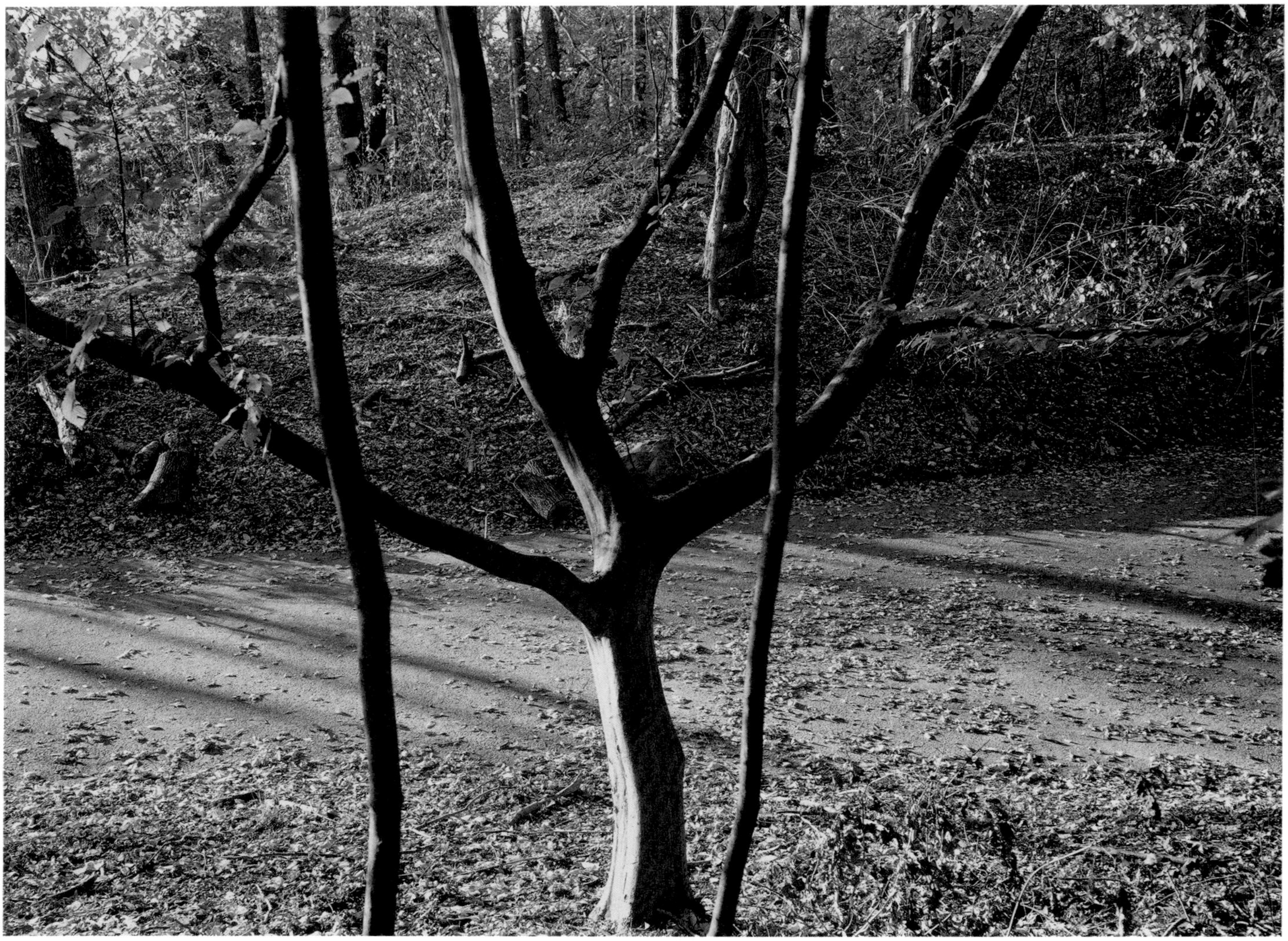

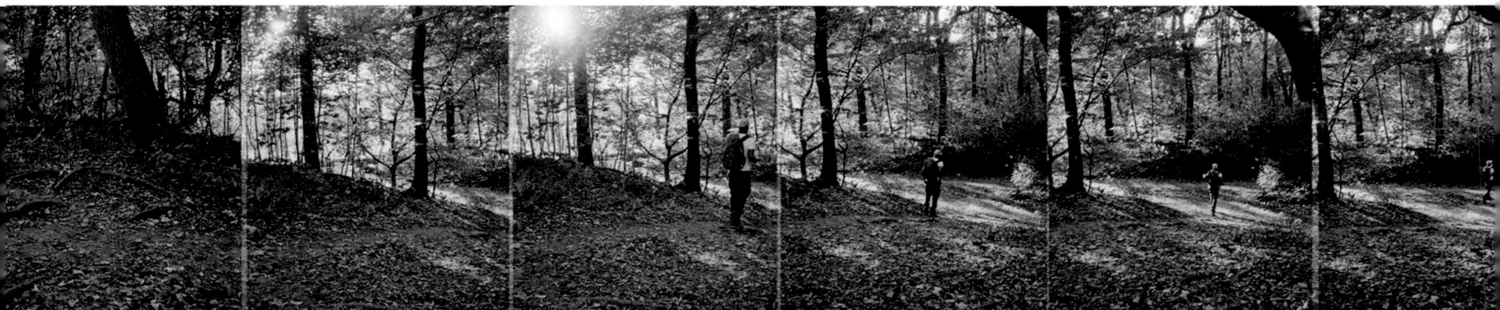

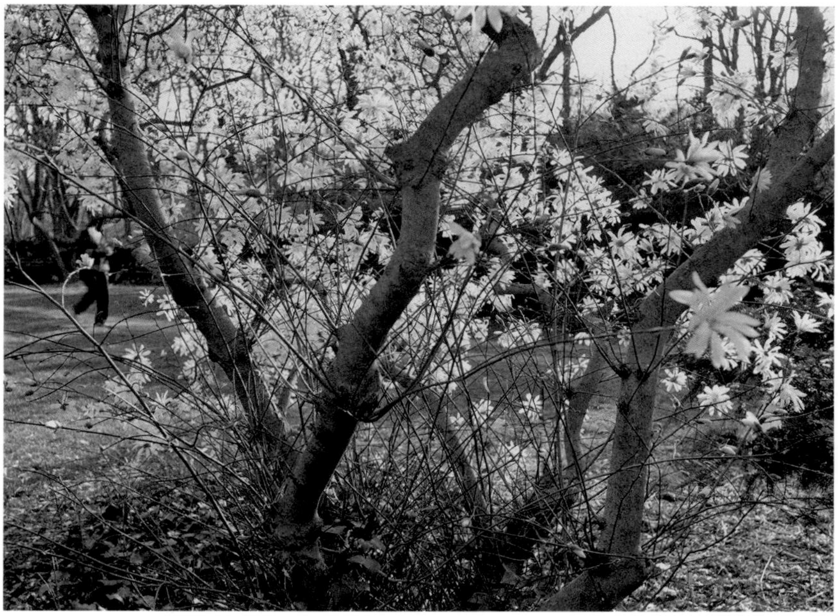

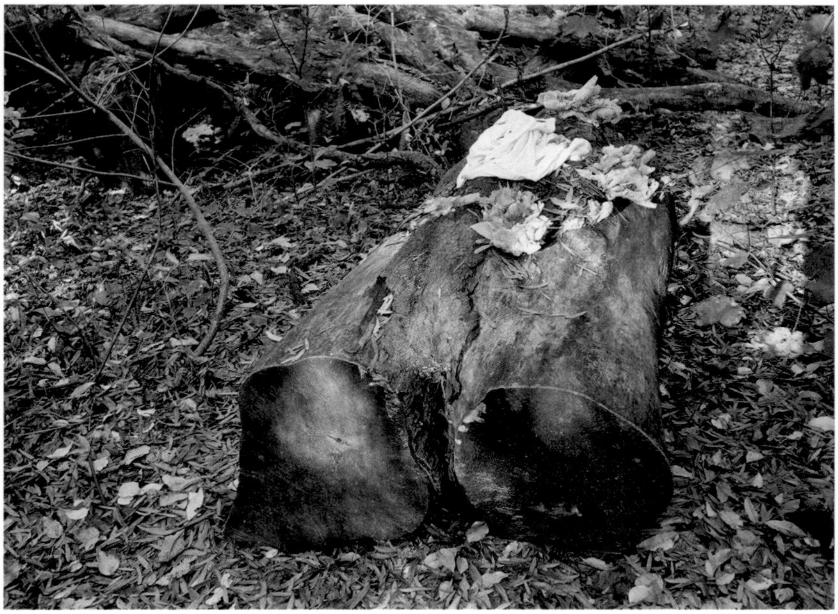

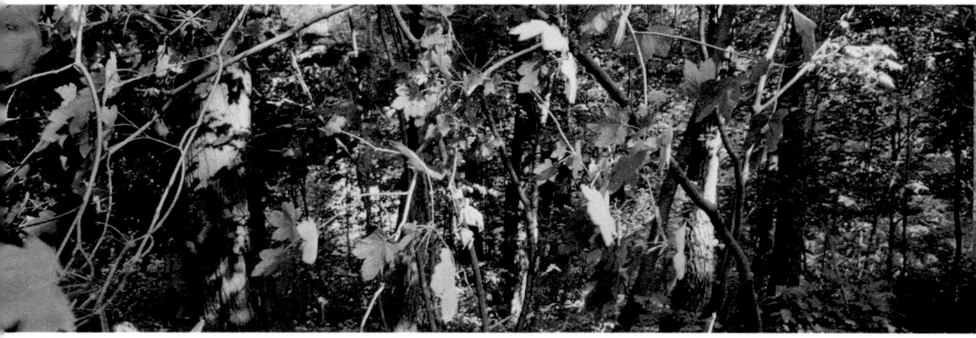

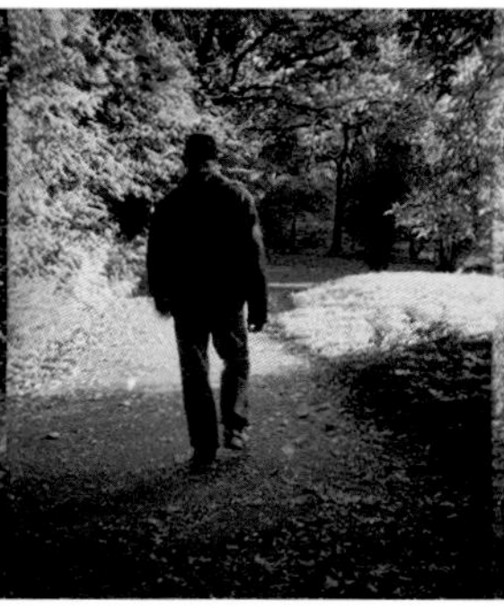

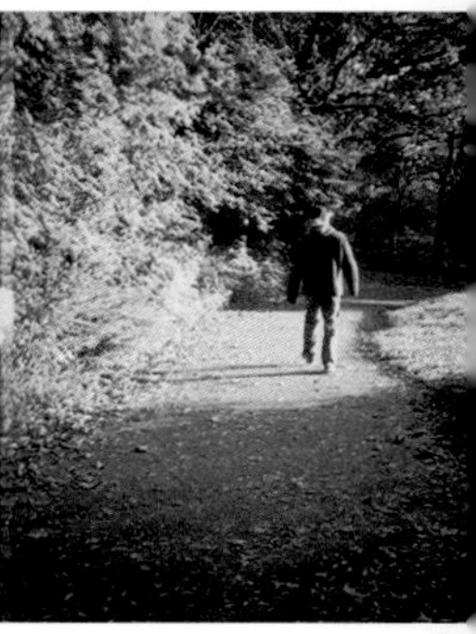

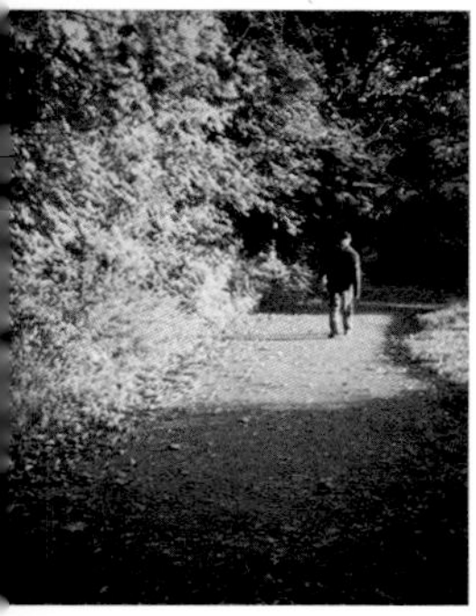

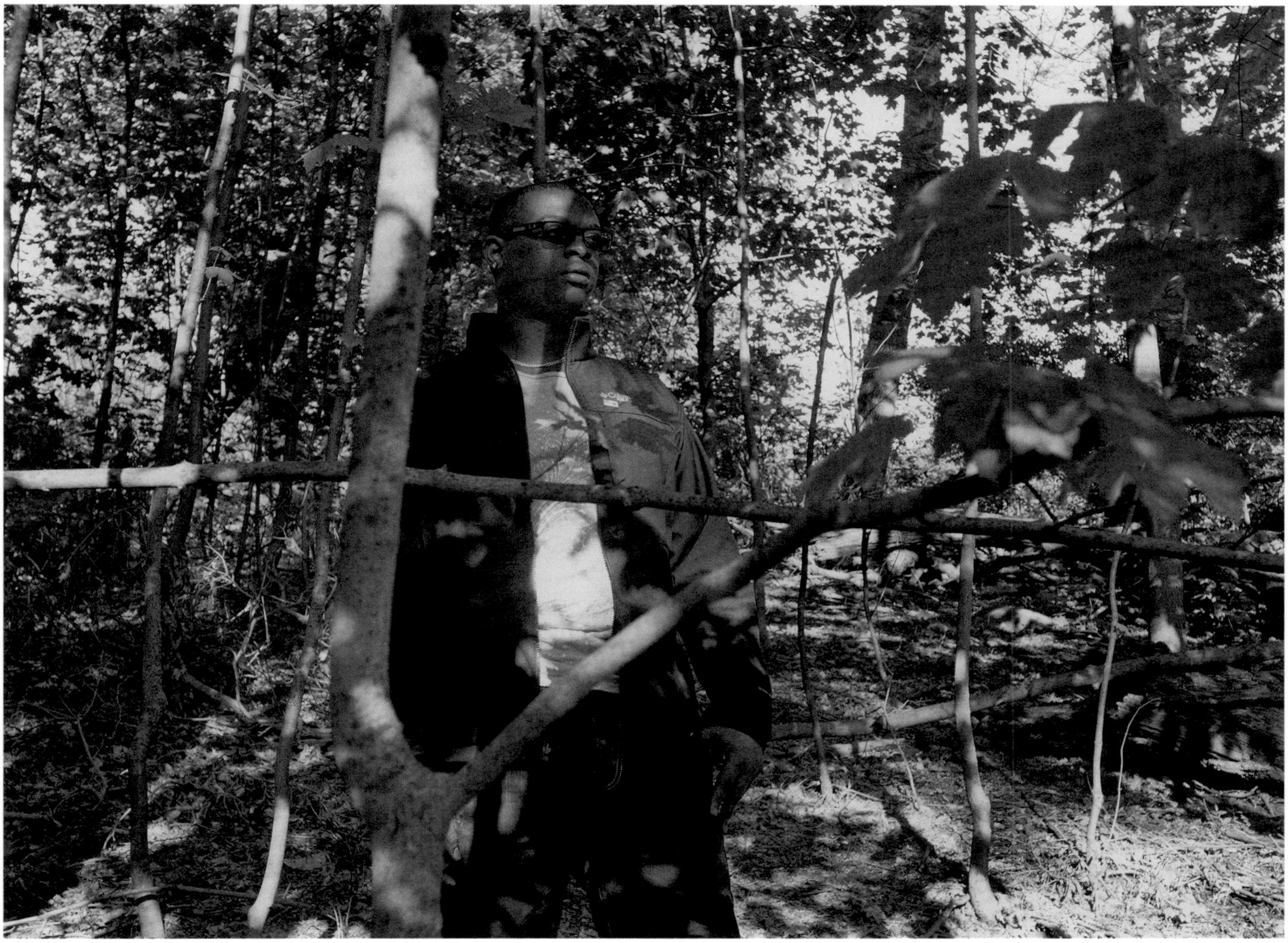

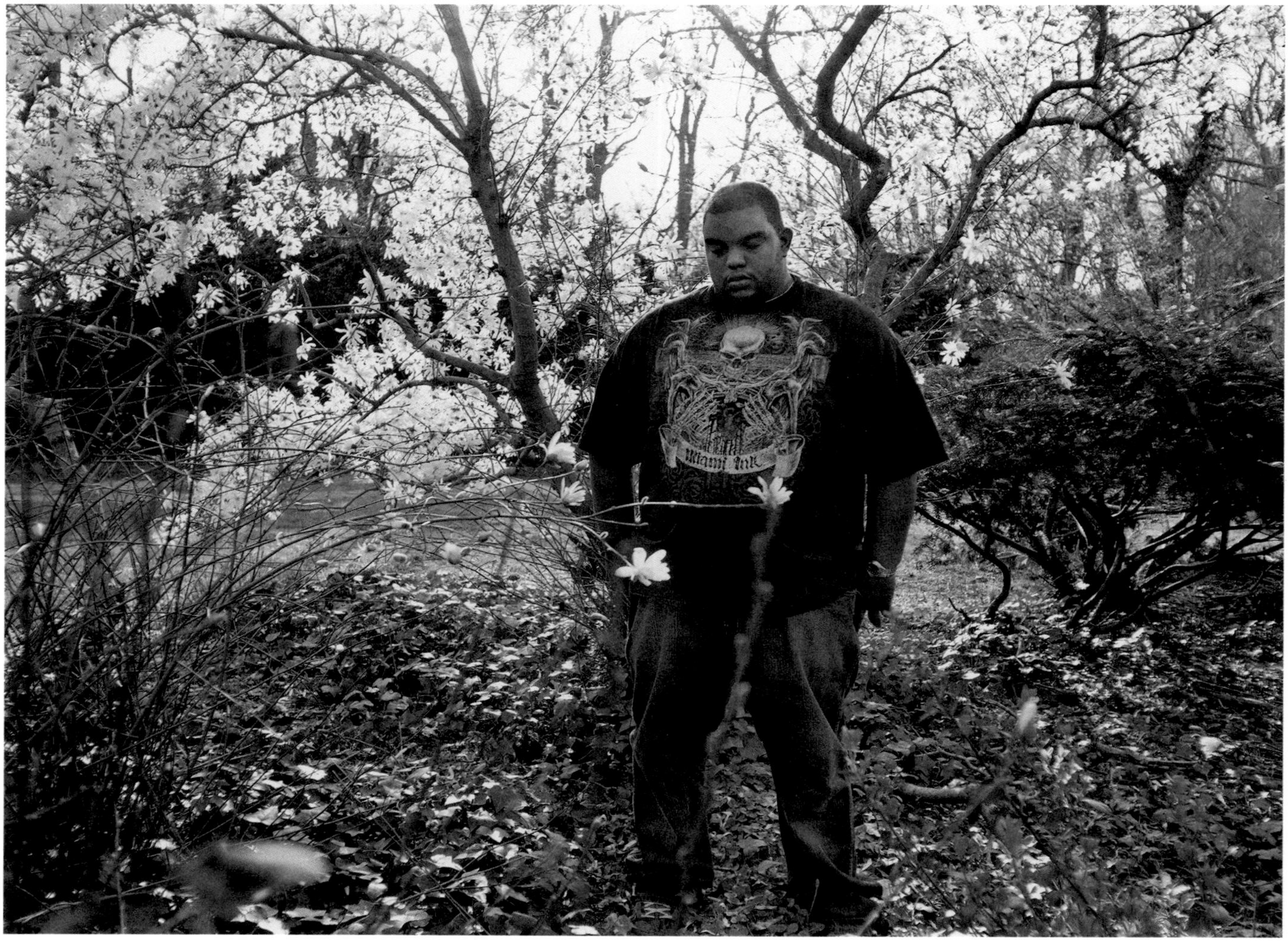

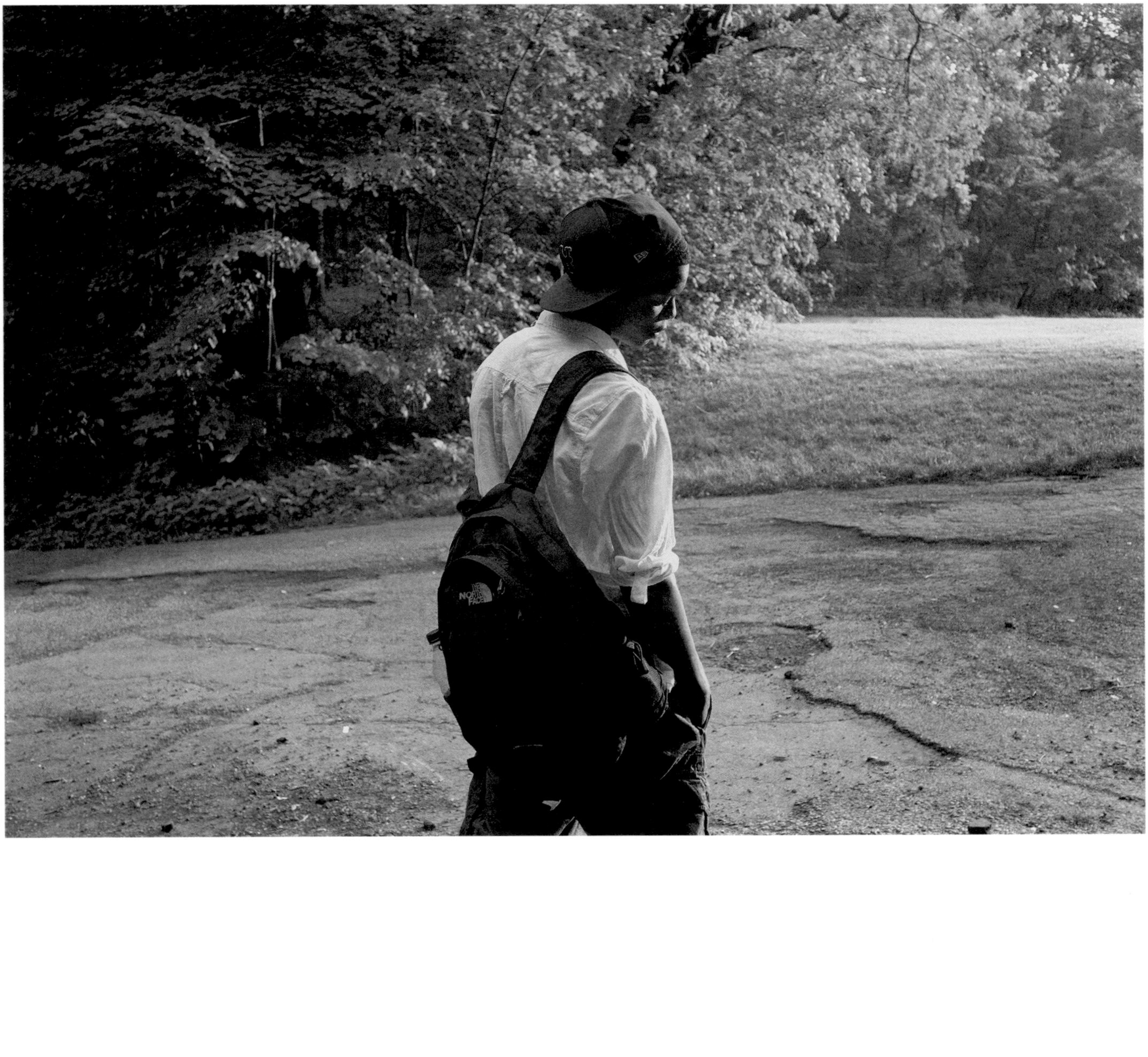
THE NORTH FACE

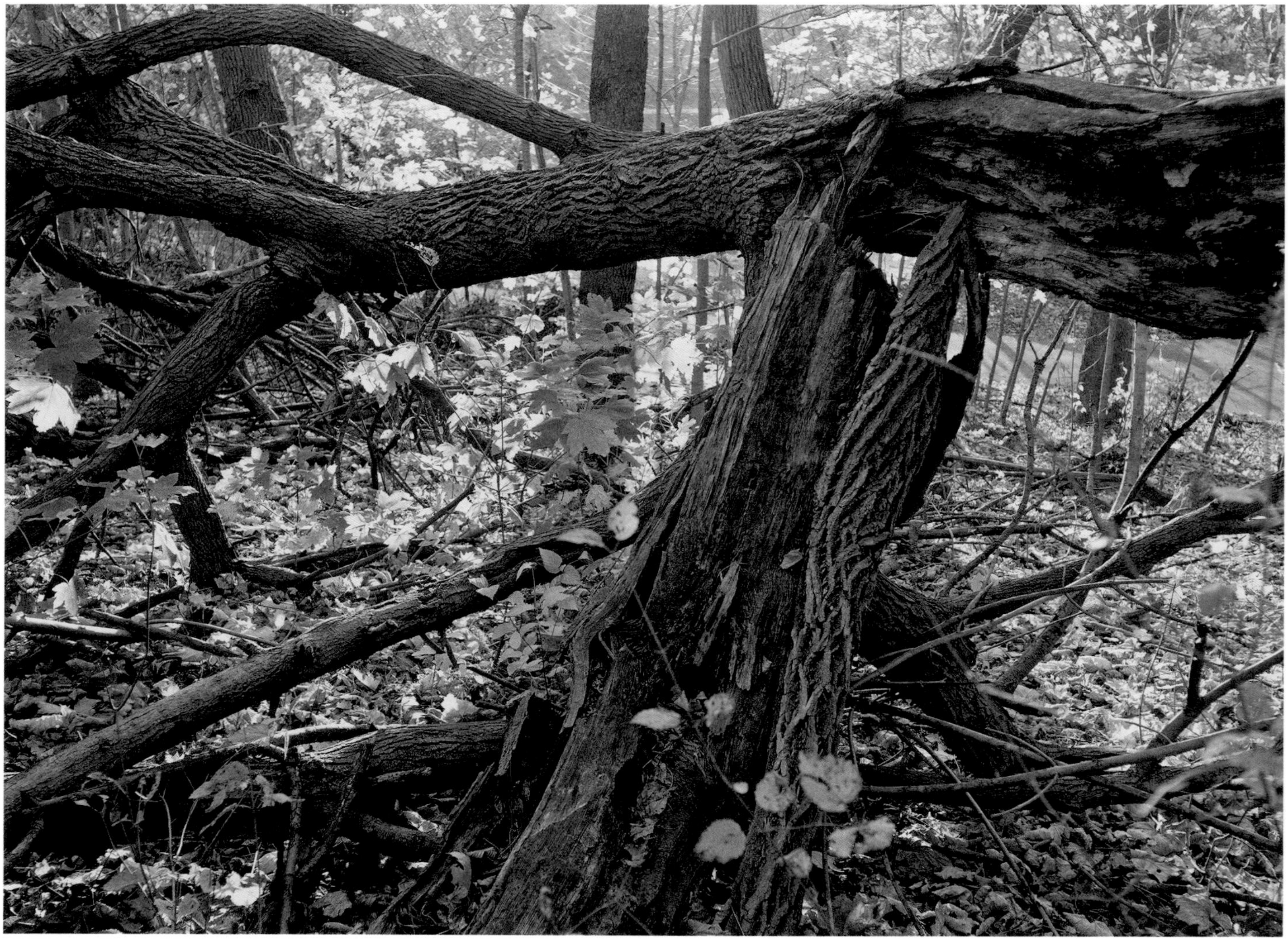

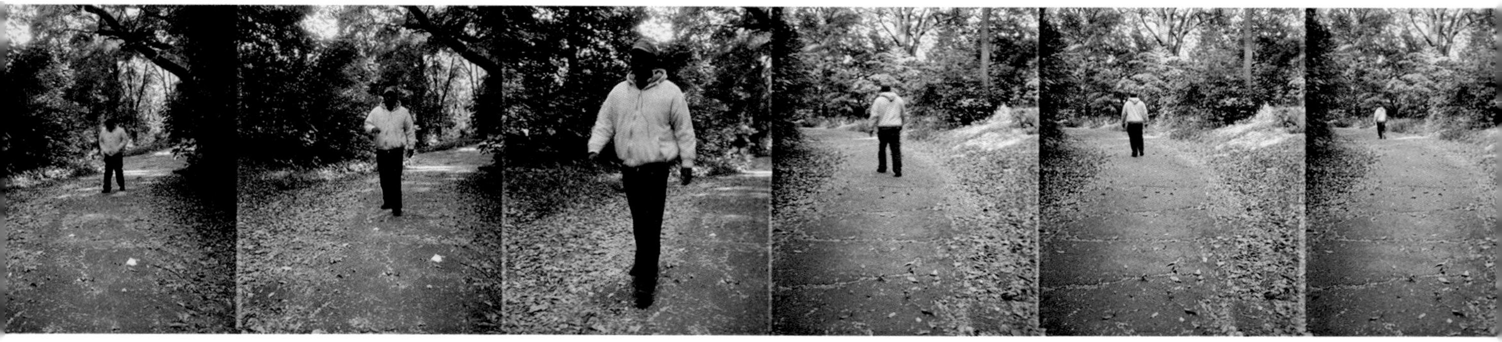

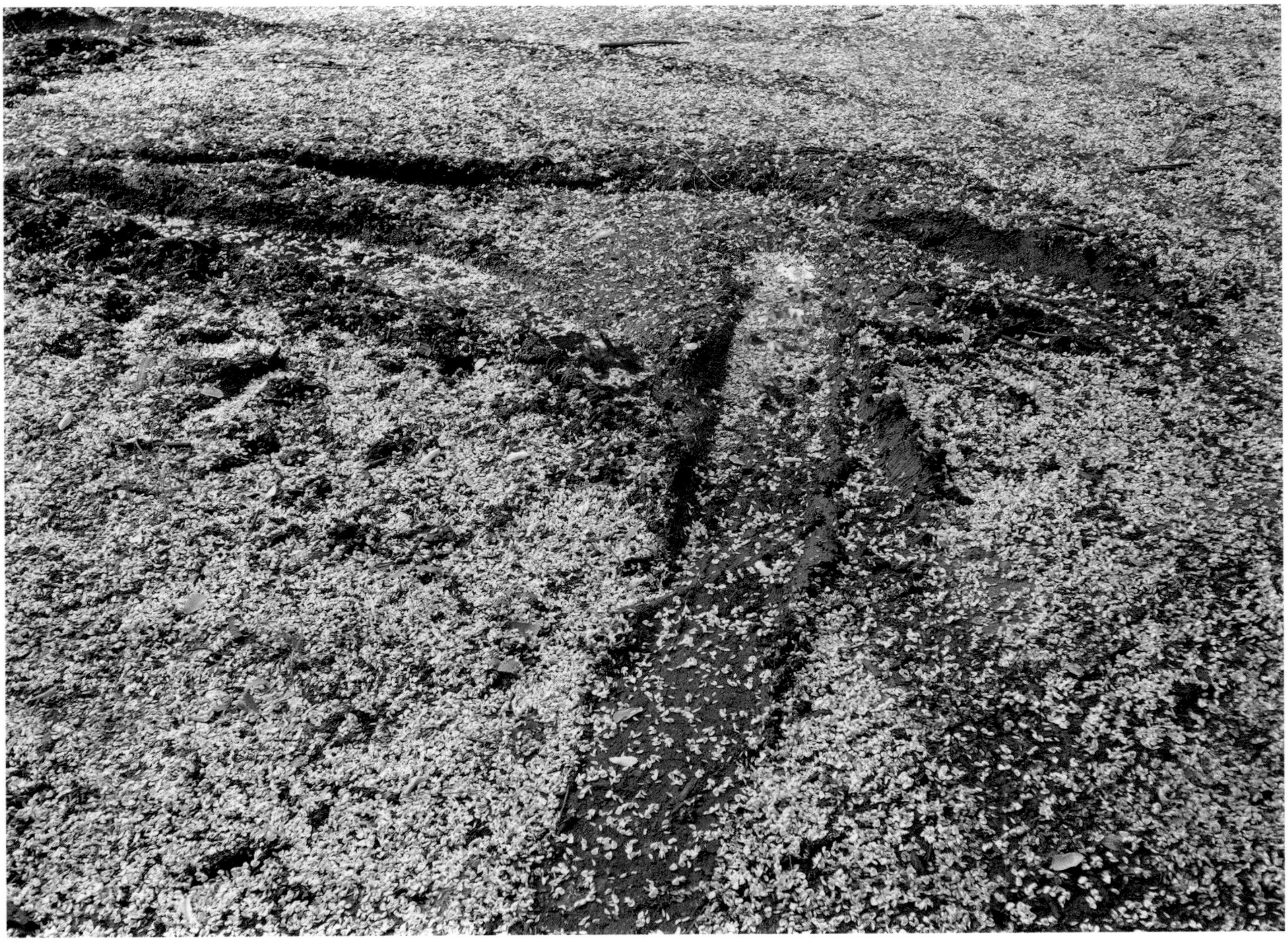

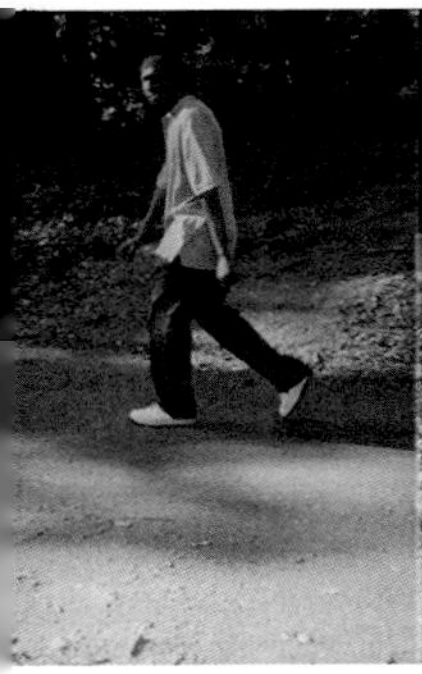

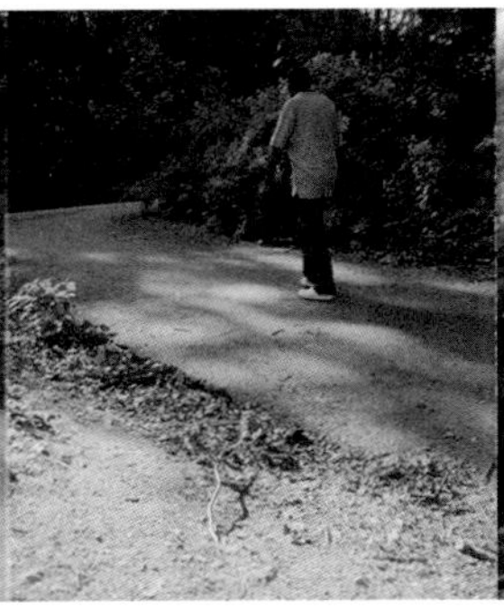

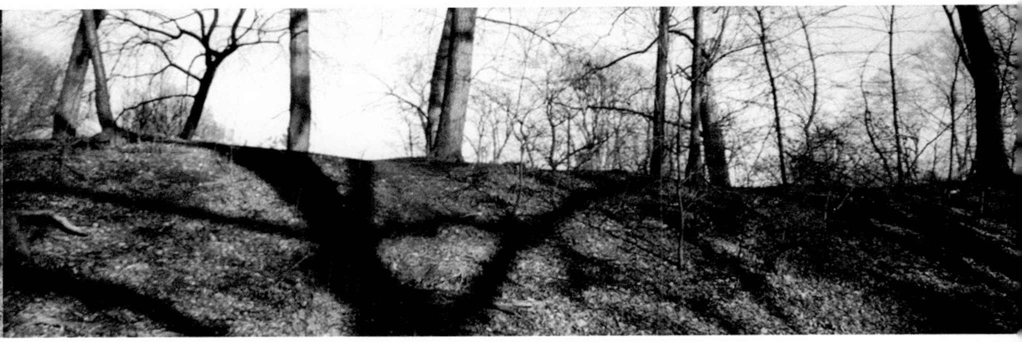

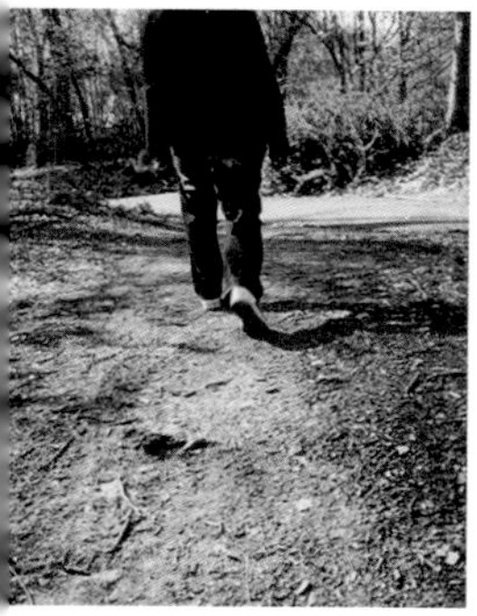

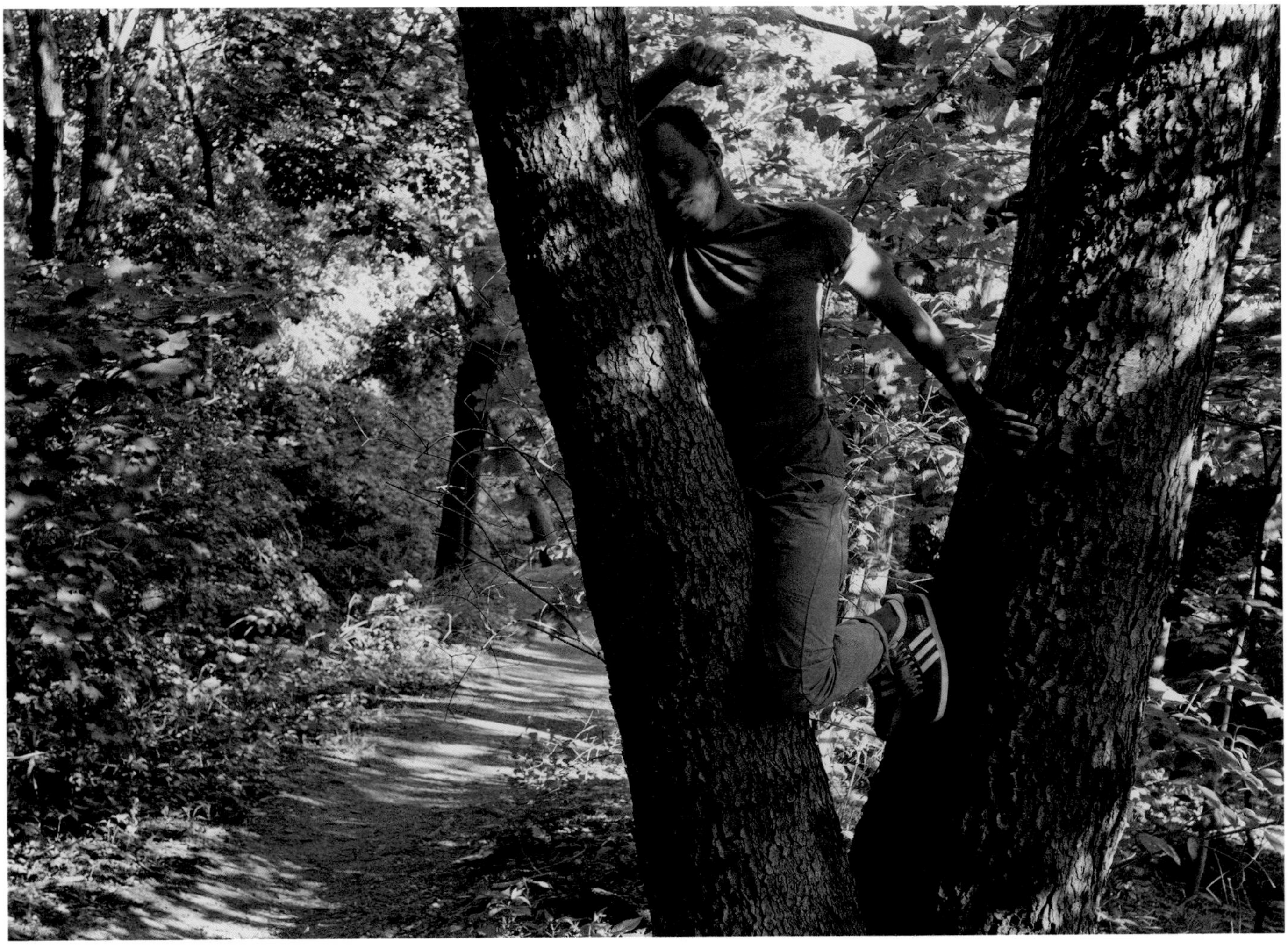

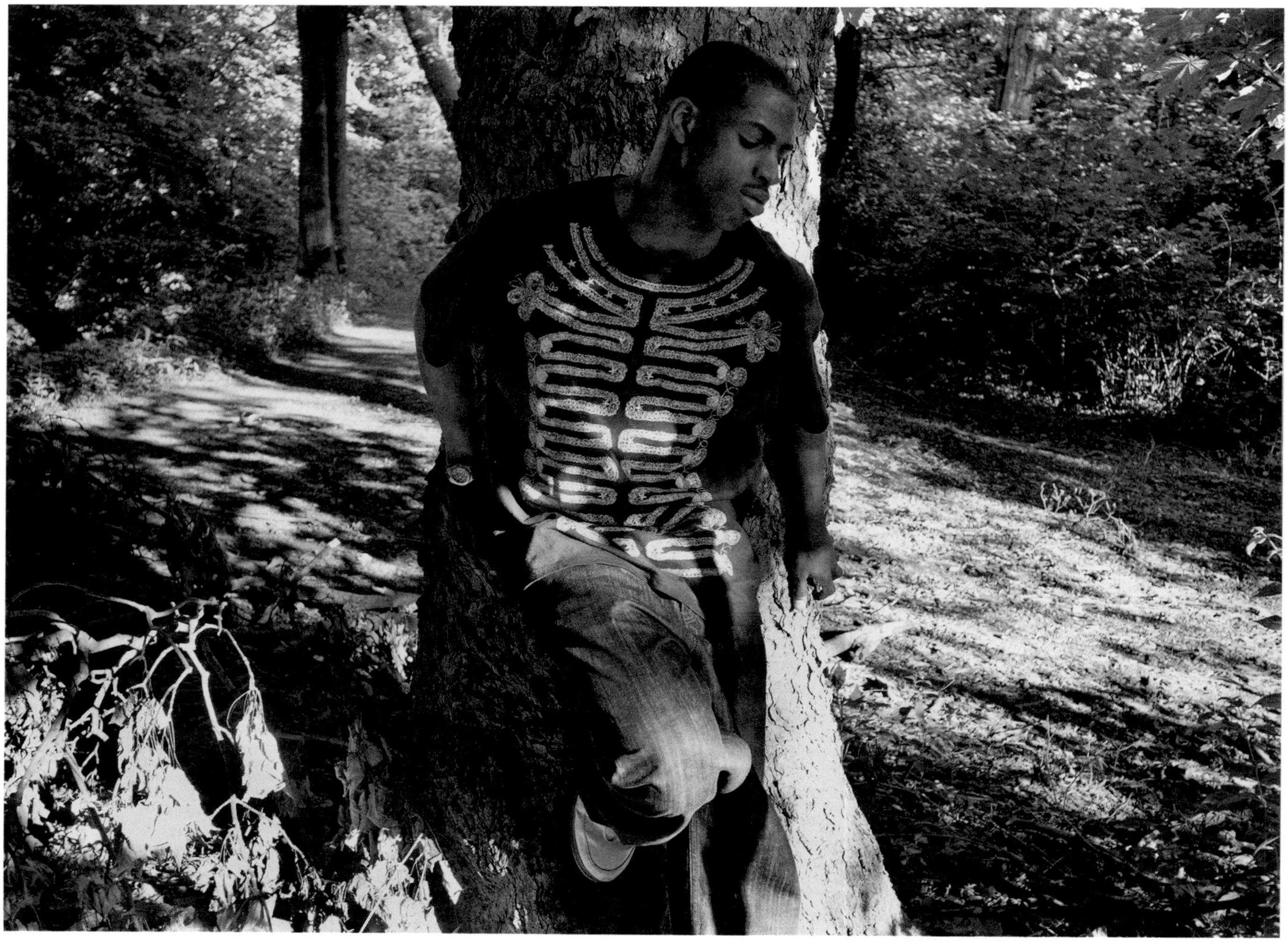

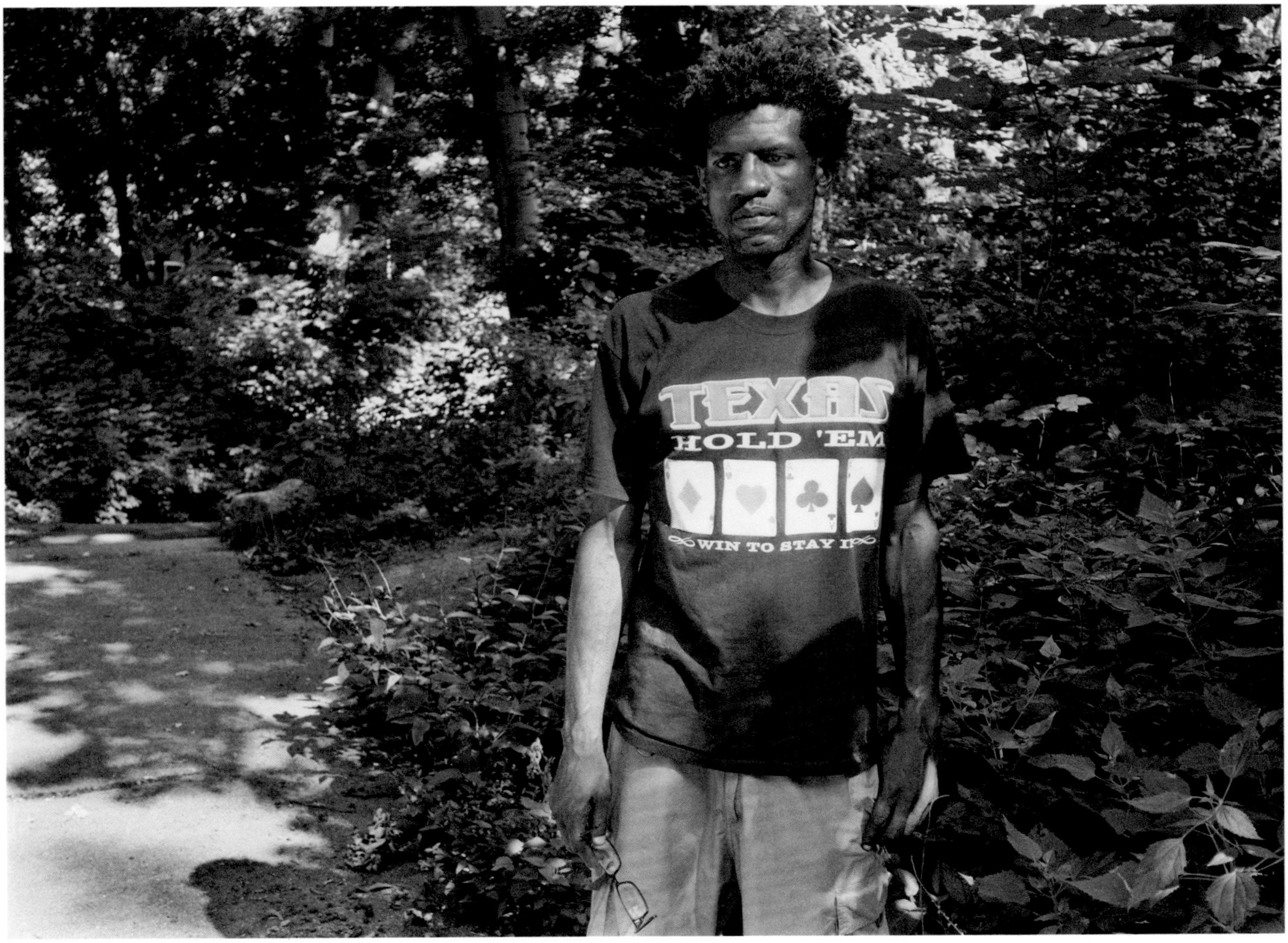
TEXAS
HOLD 'EM
WIN TO STAY

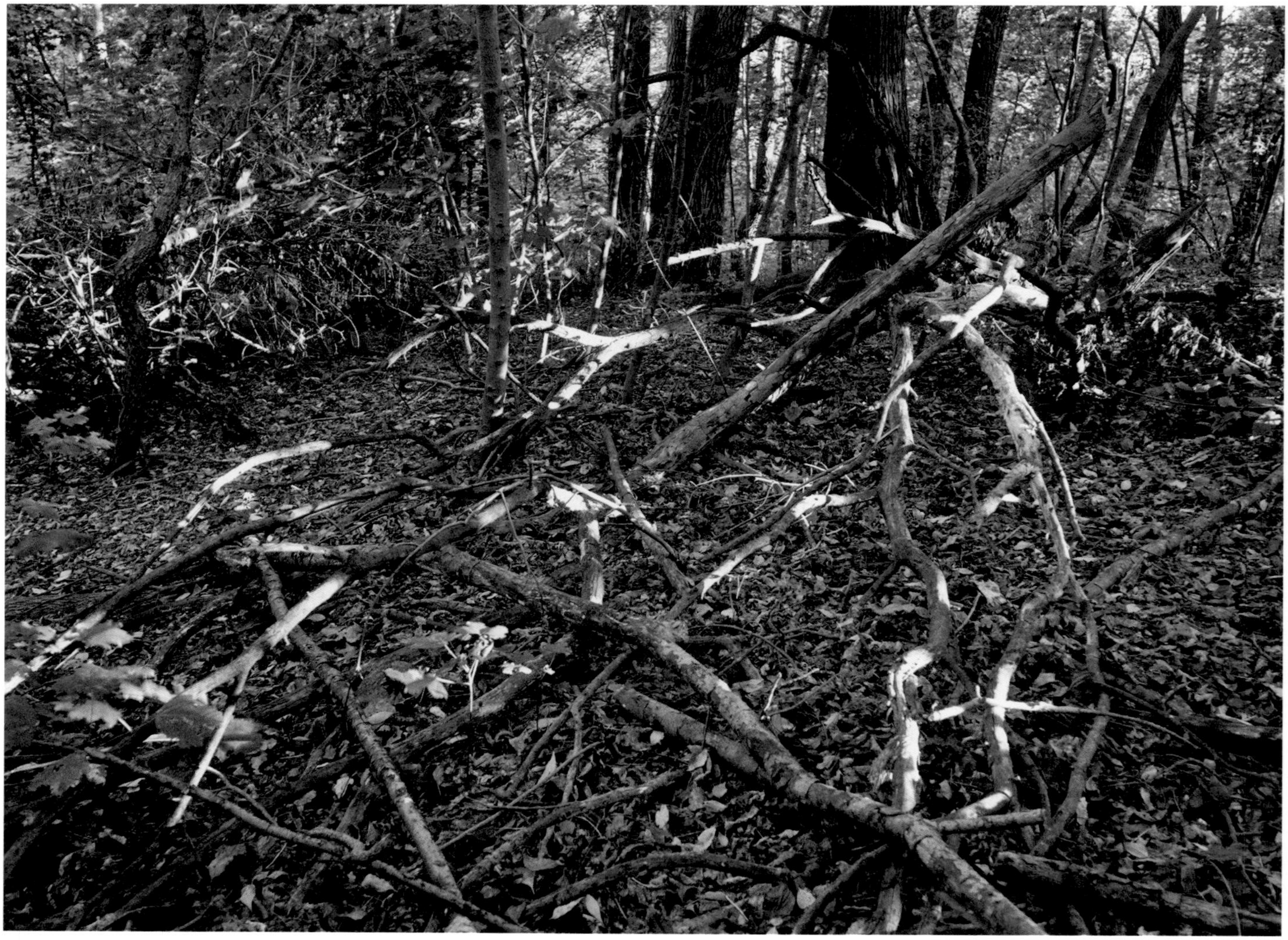

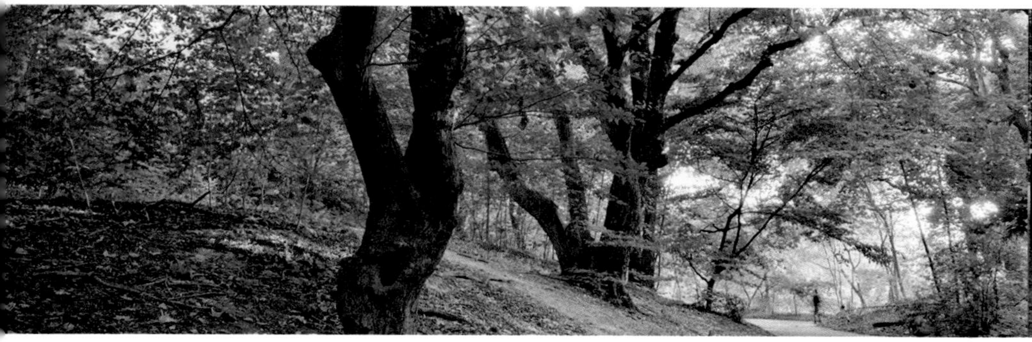

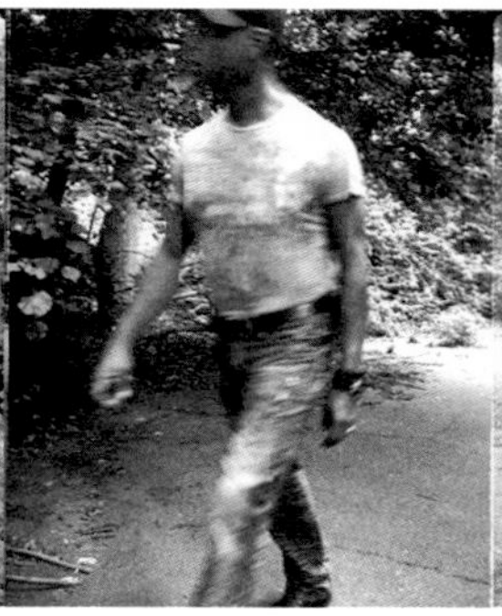

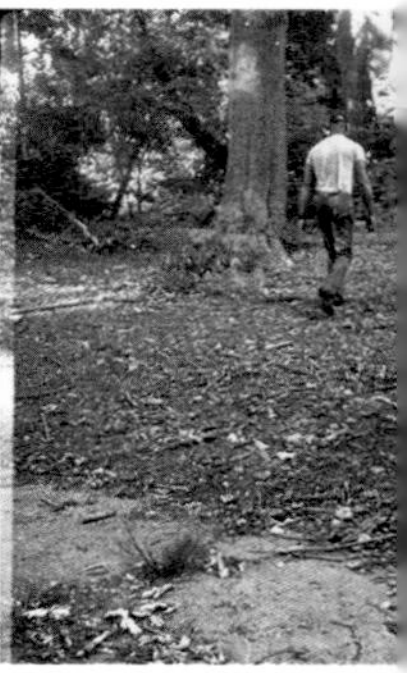

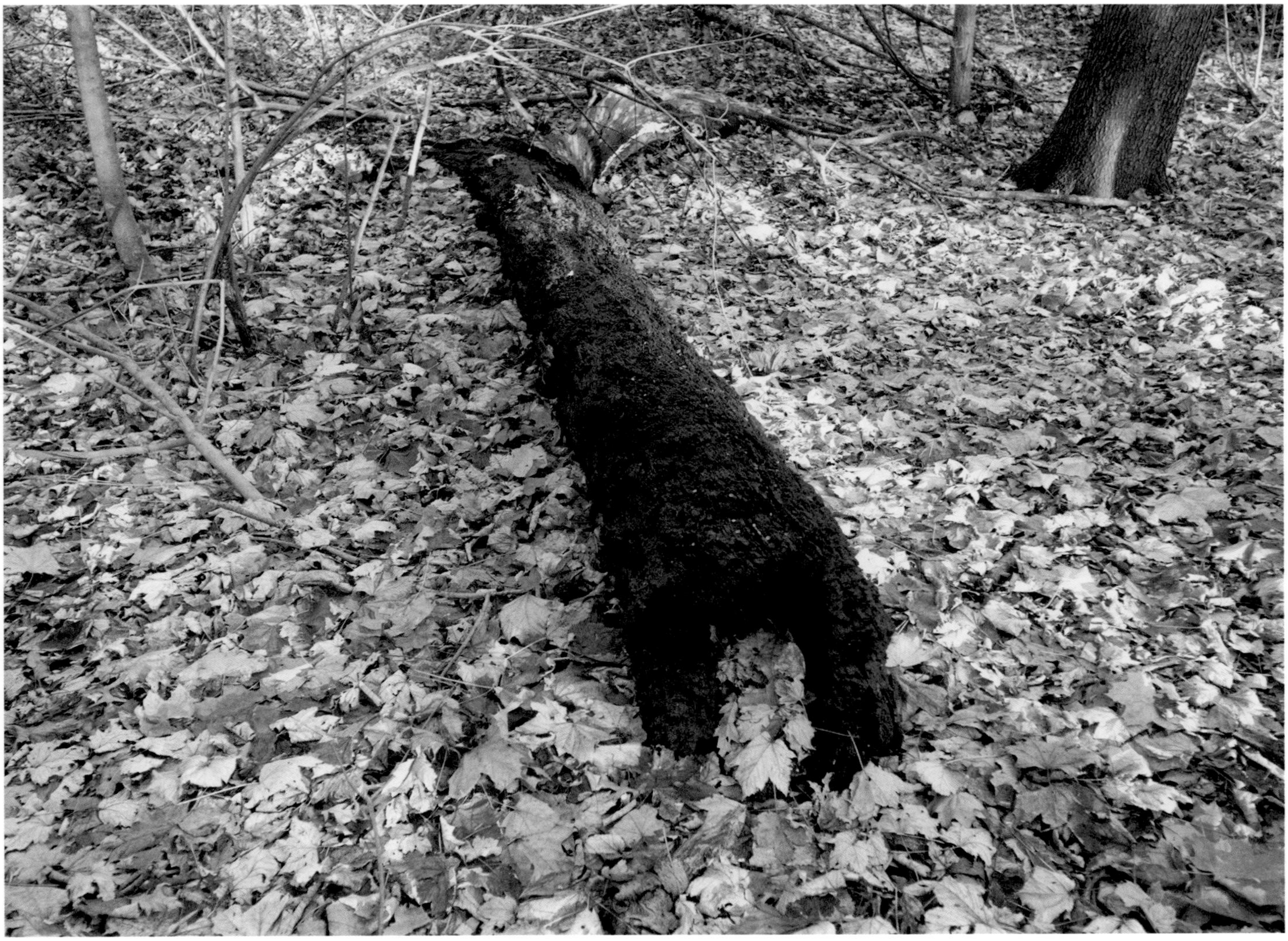

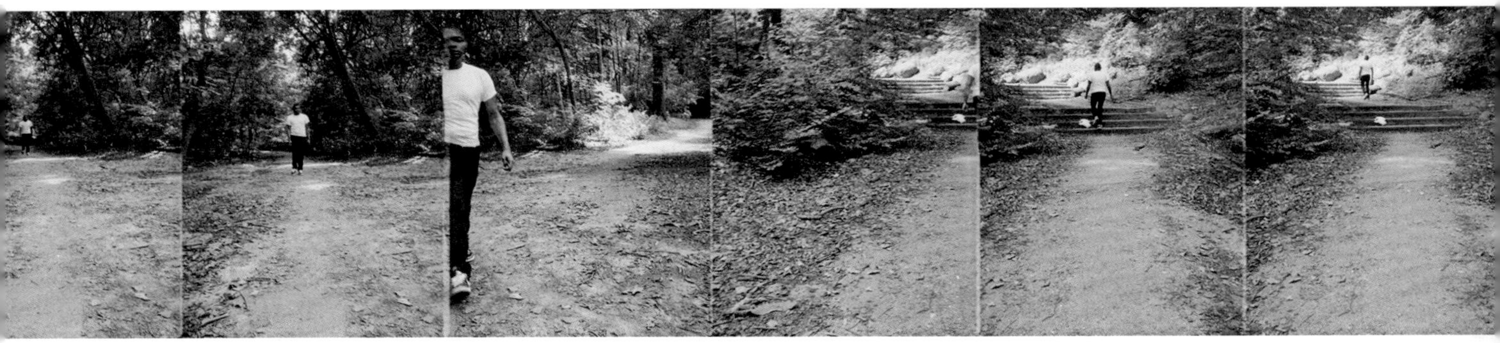

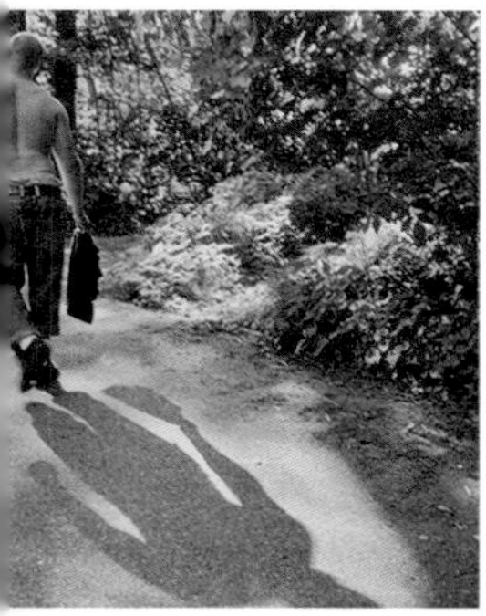

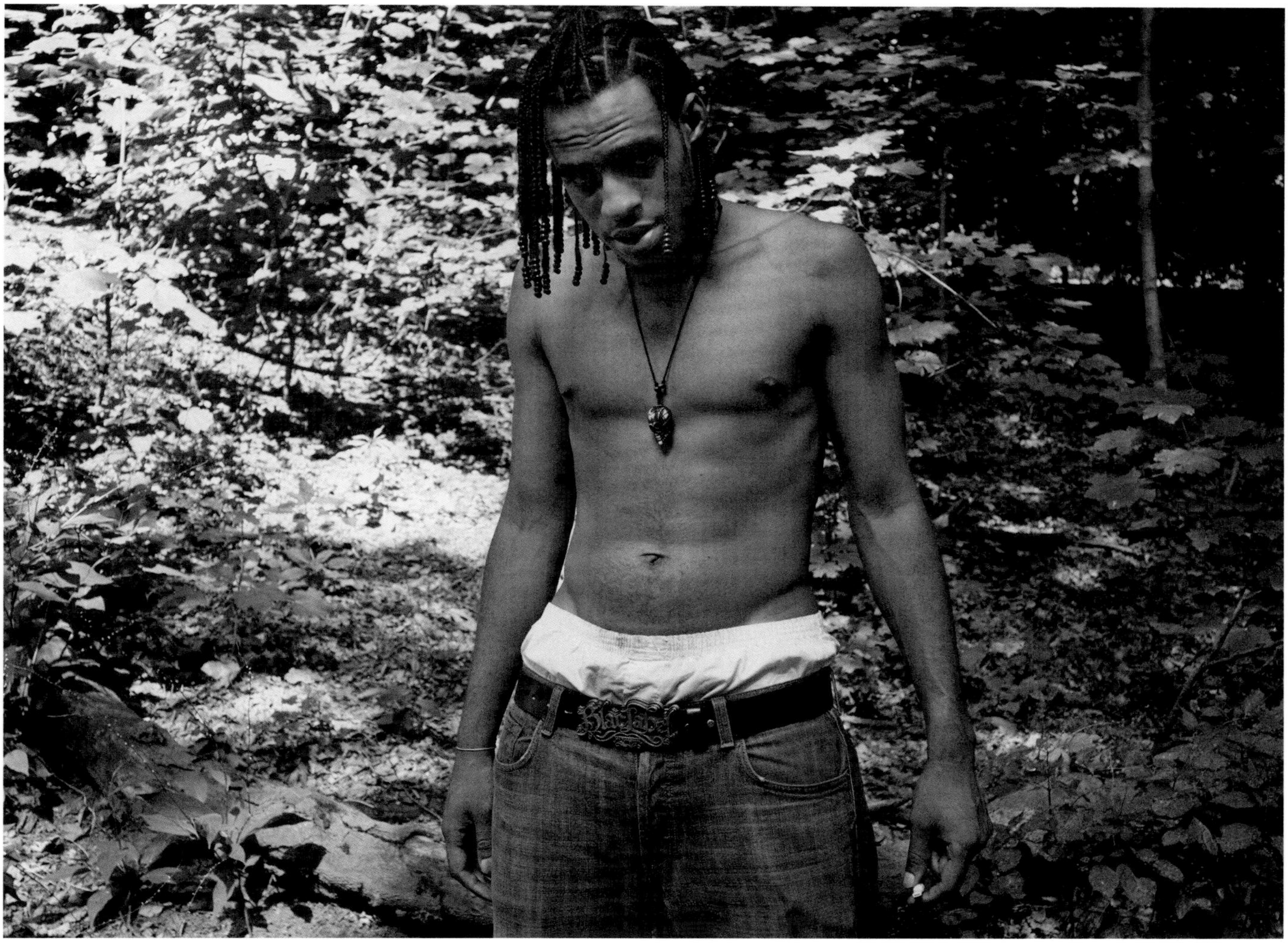

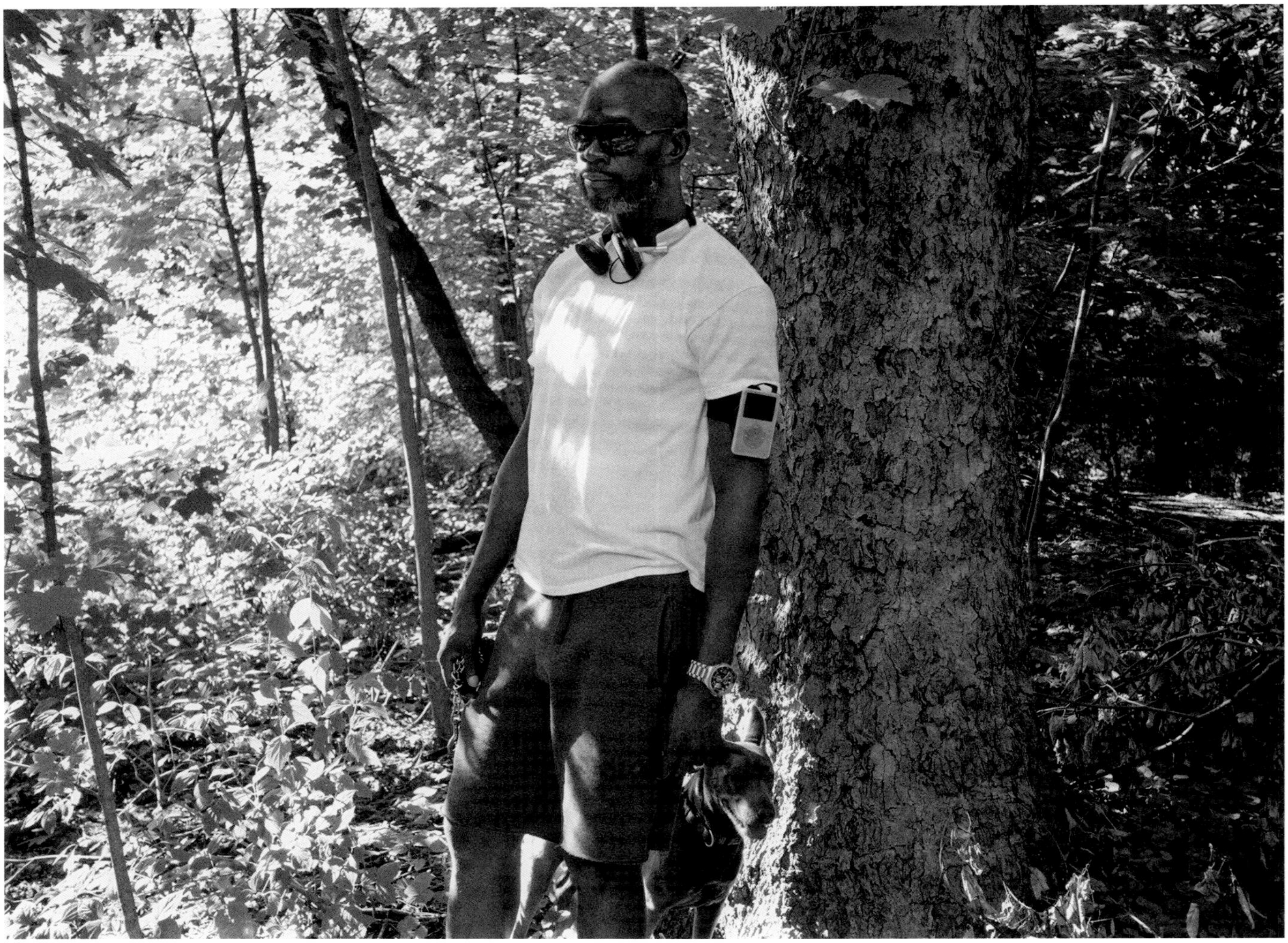

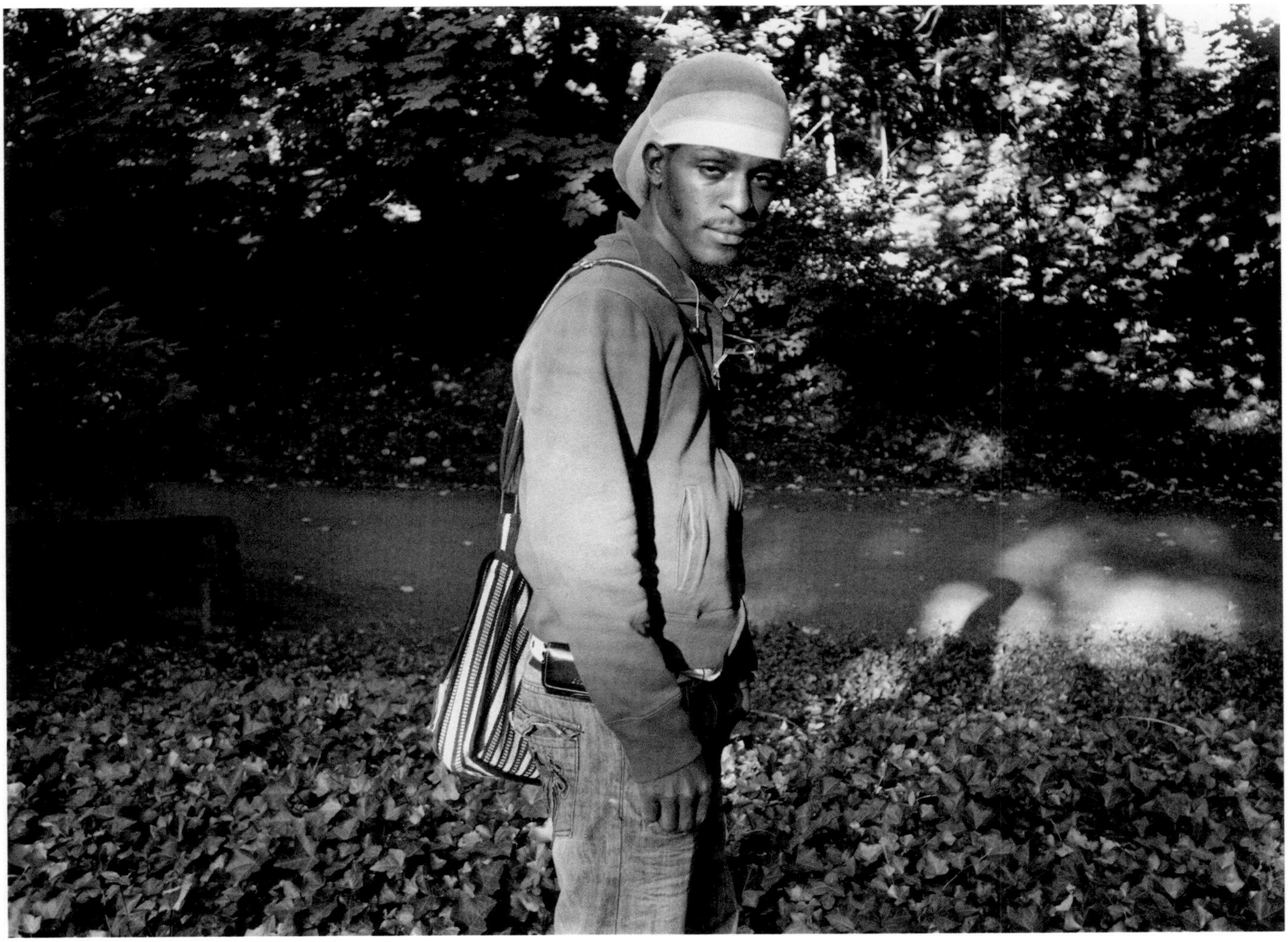

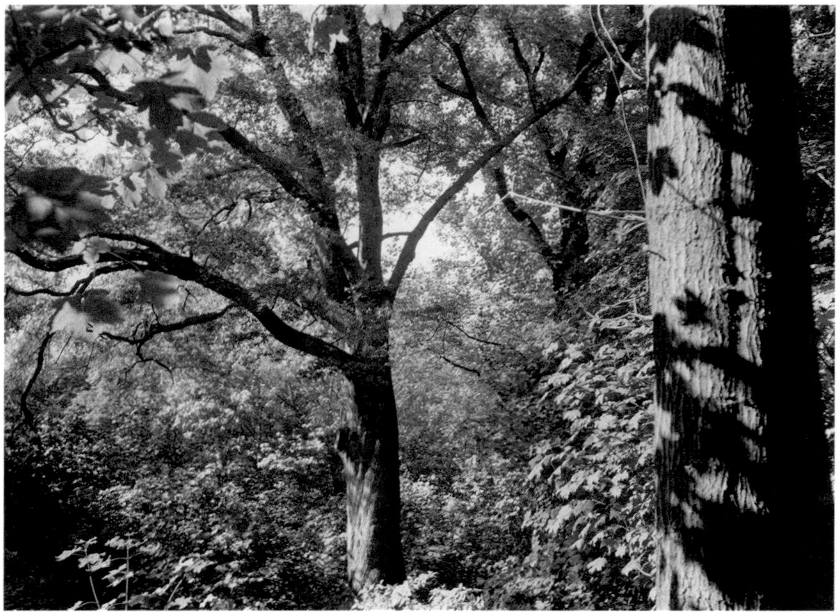

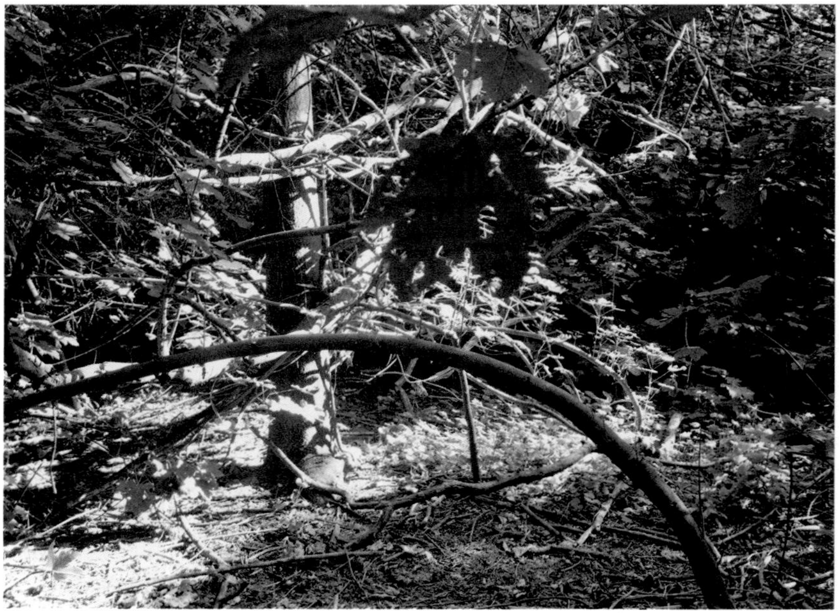

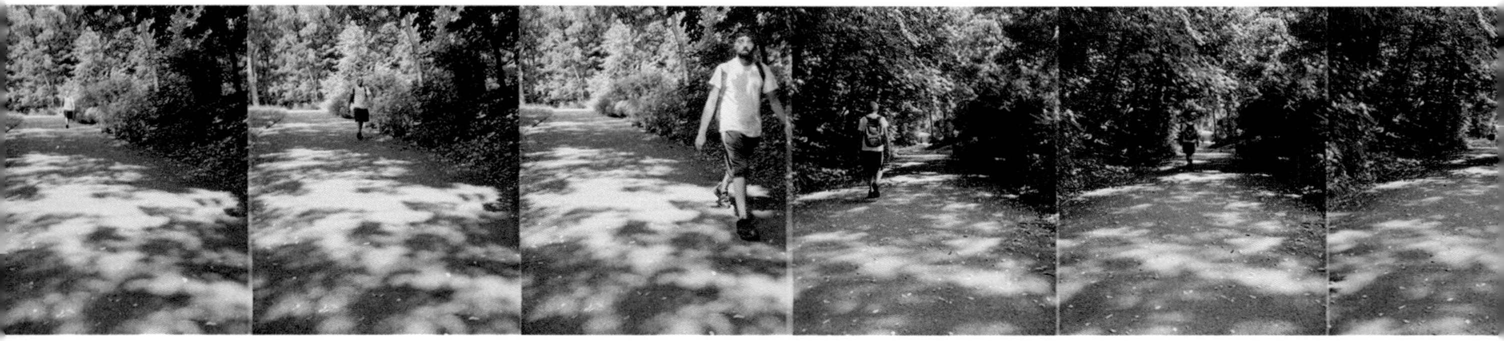

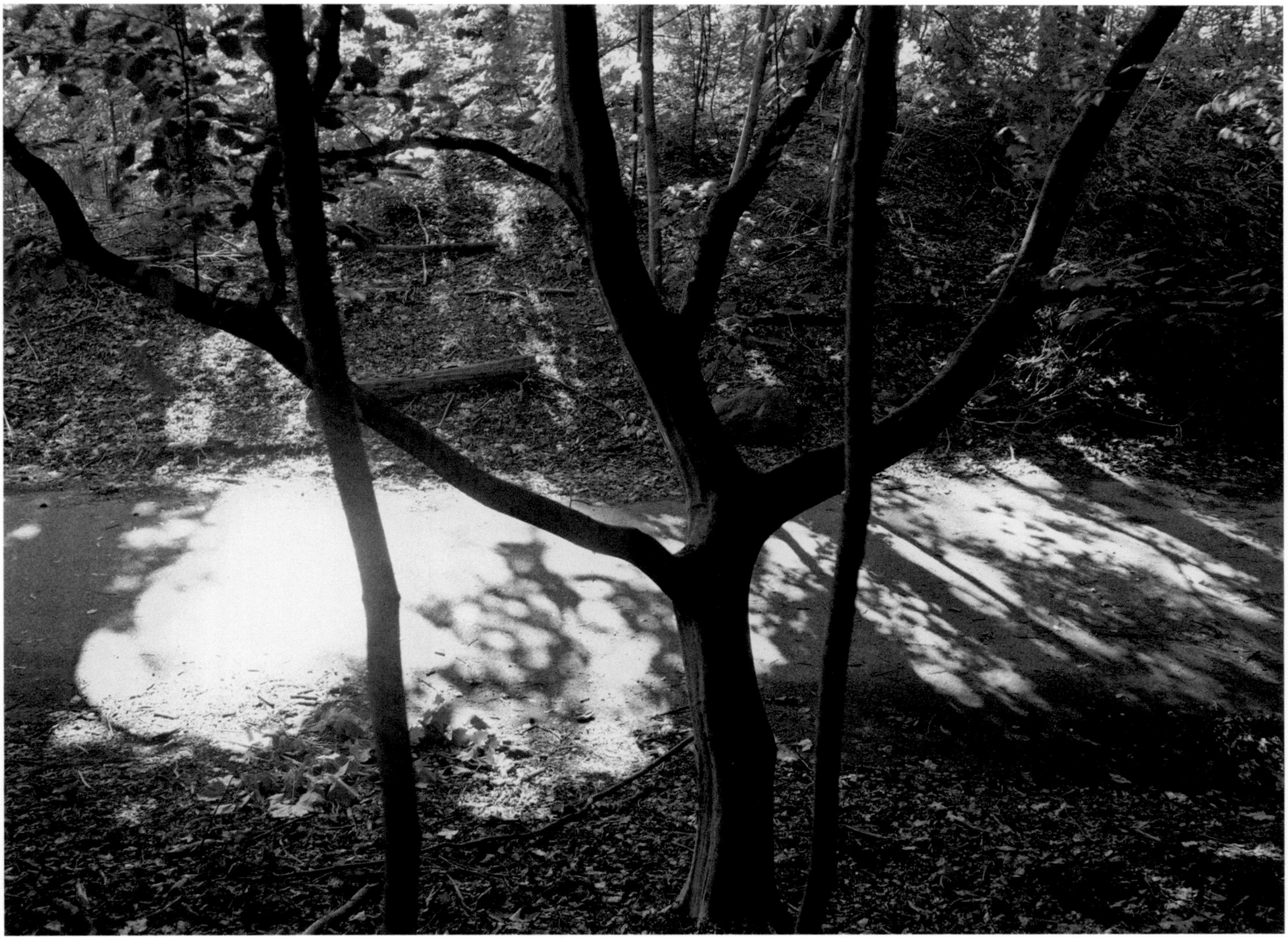

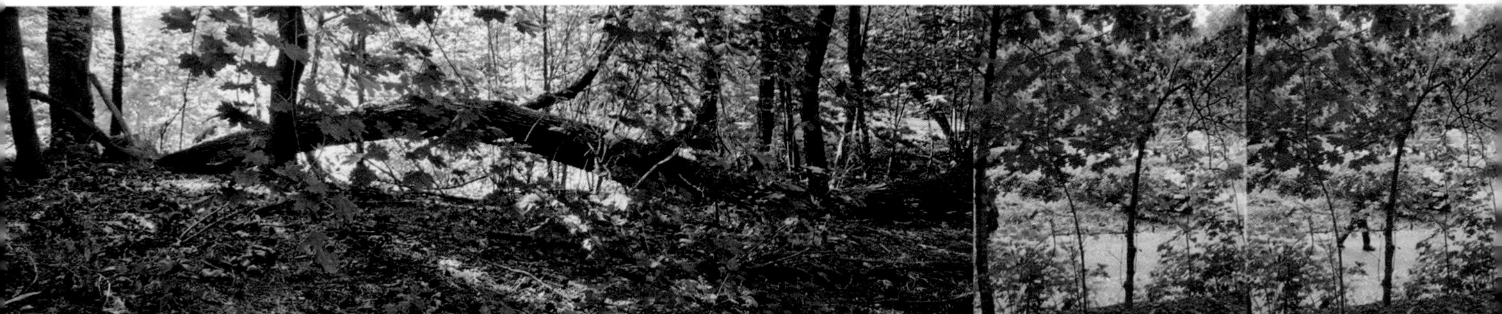

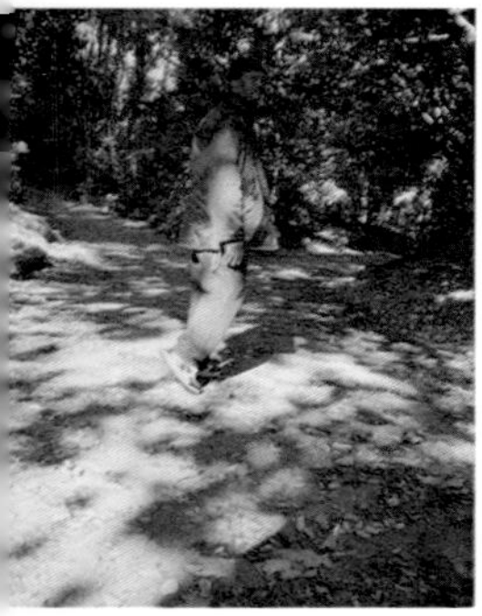

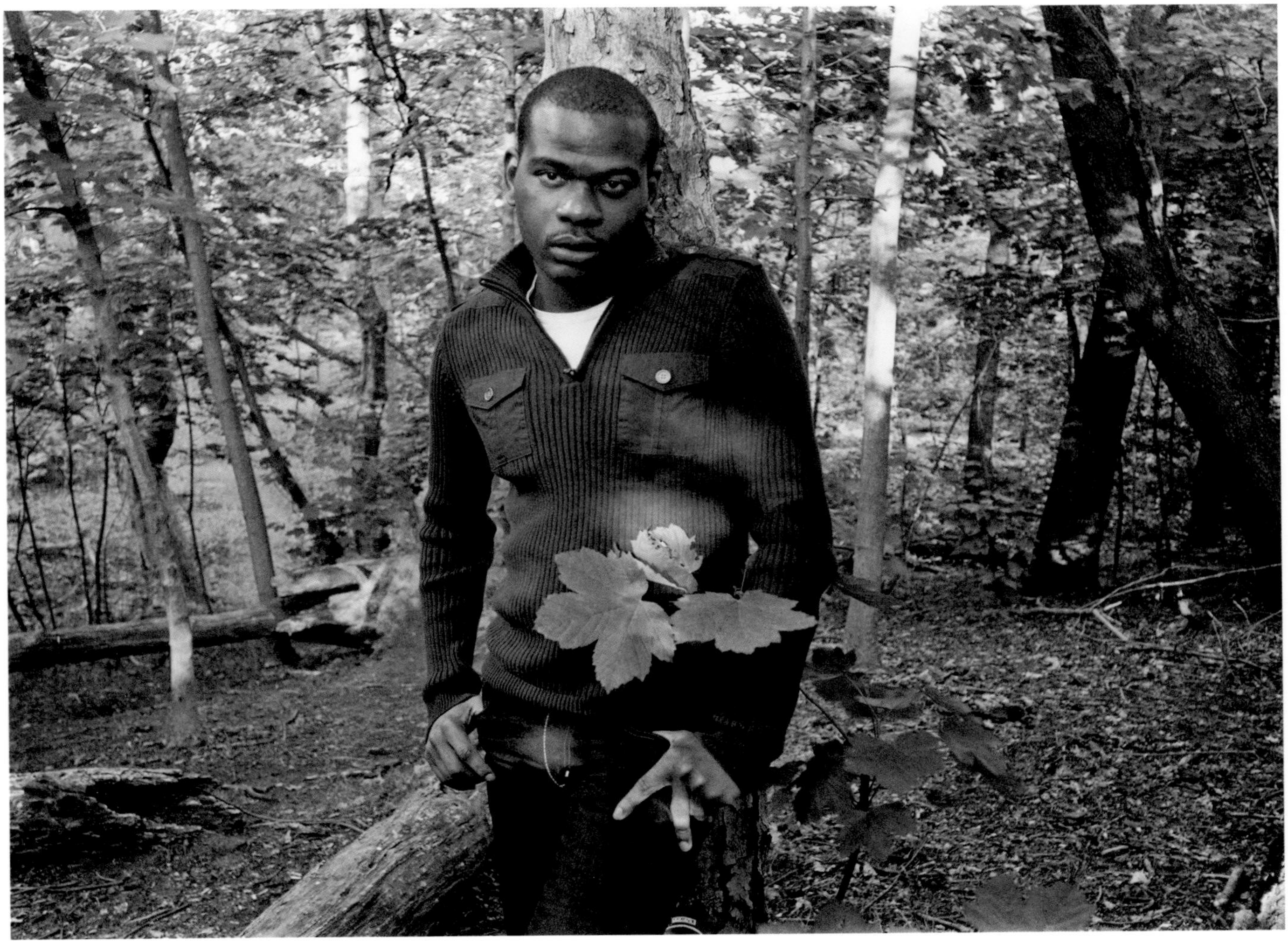

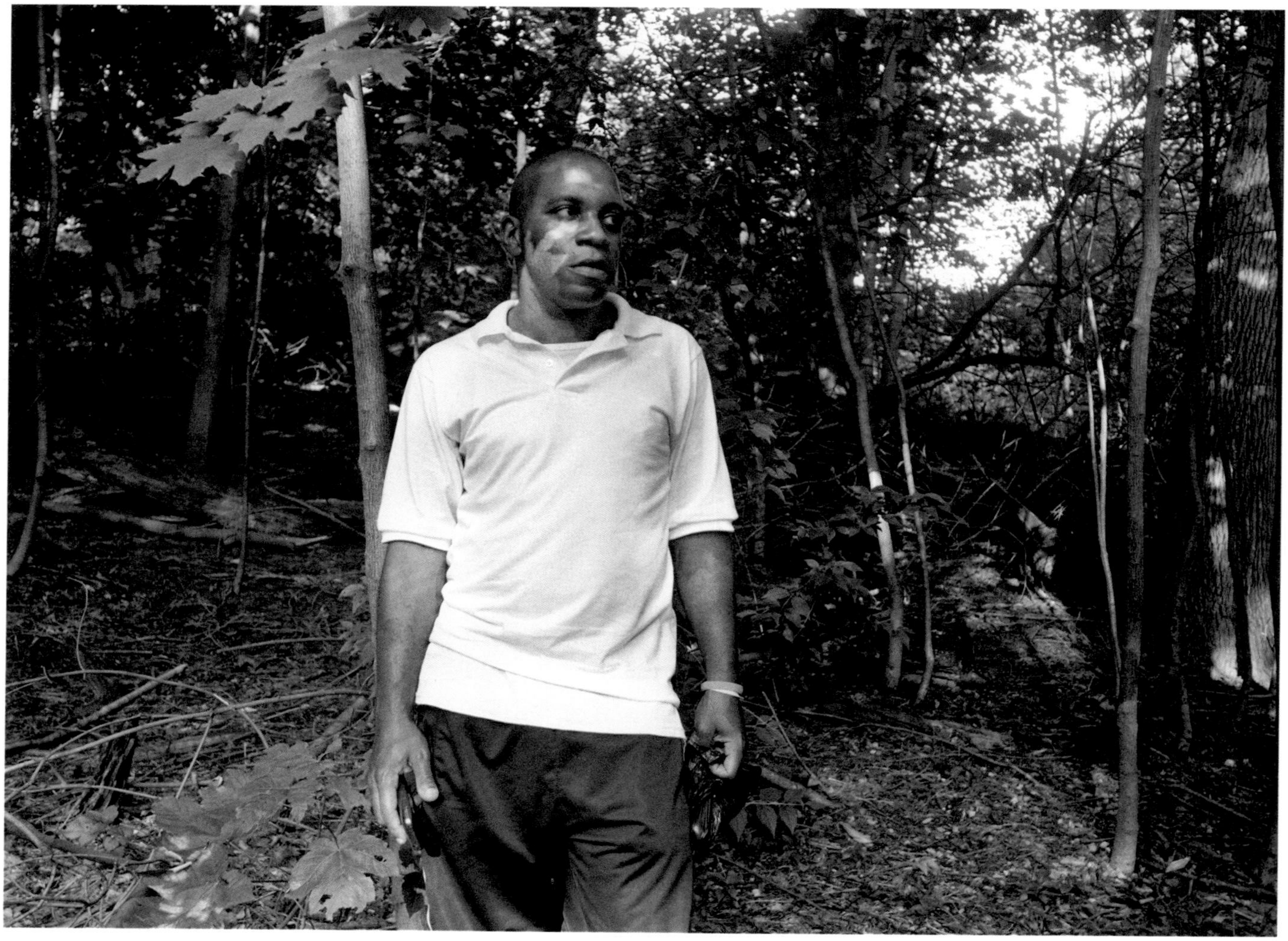

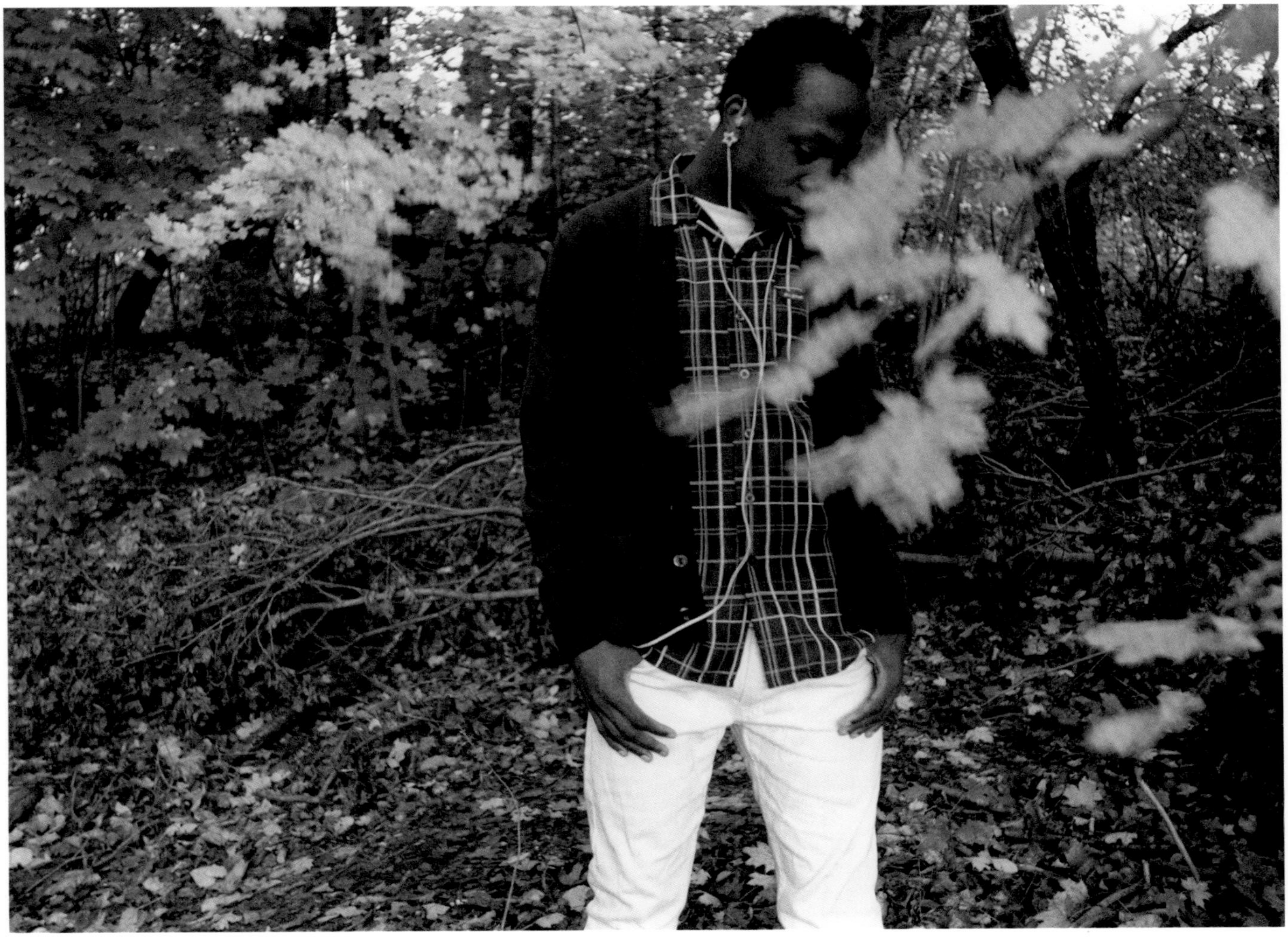

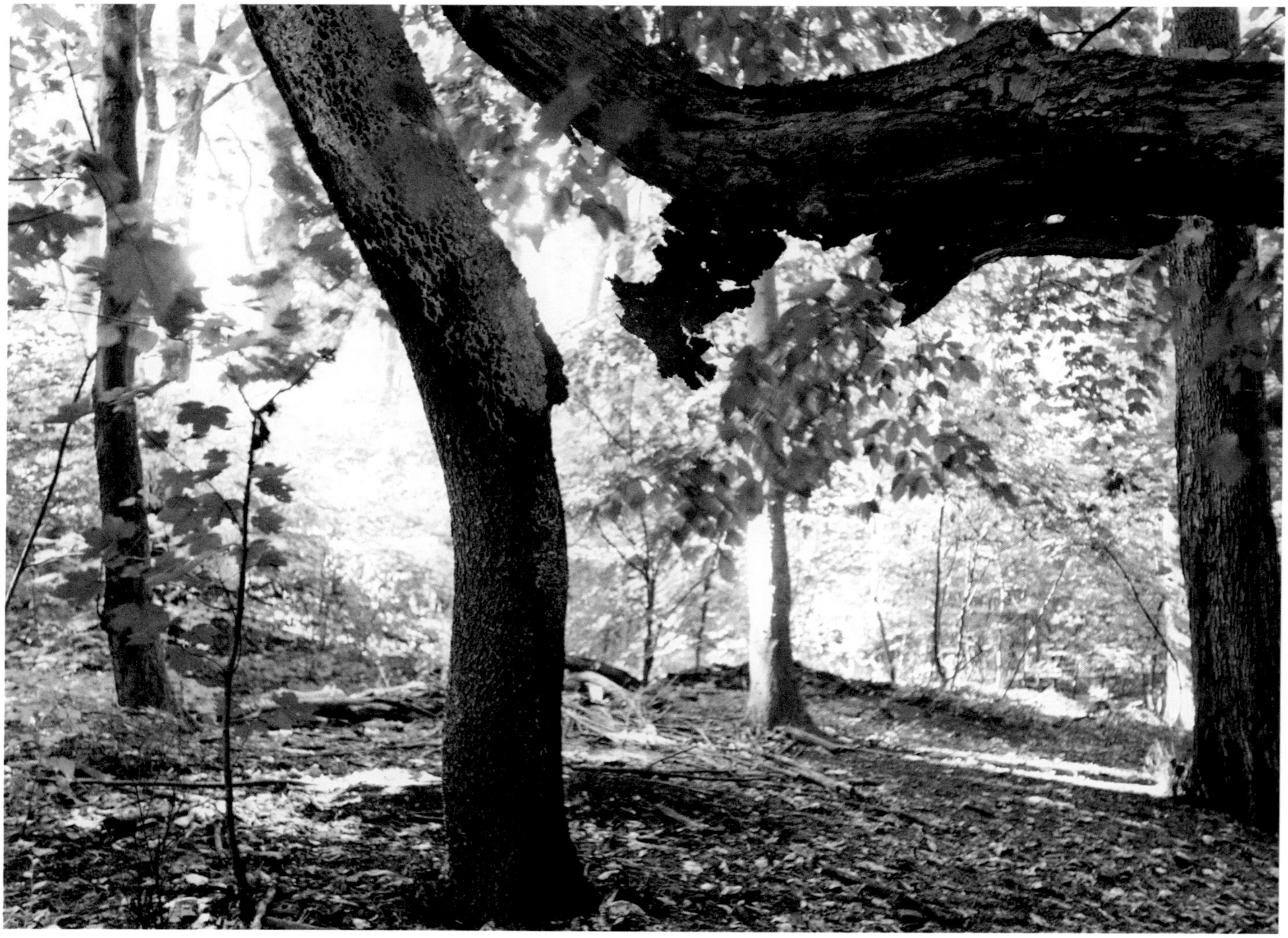

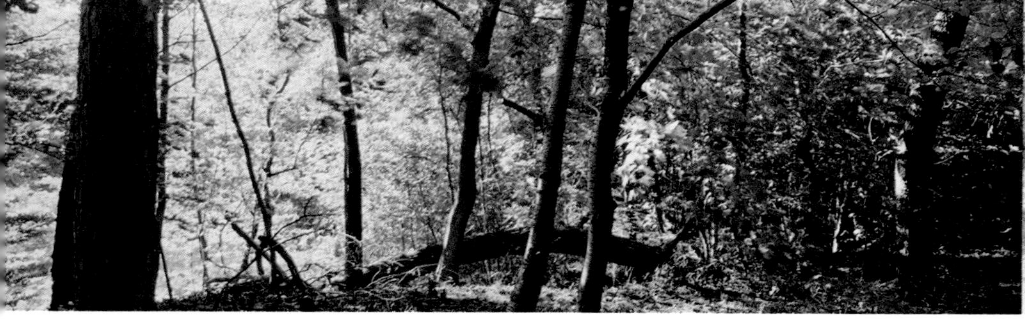

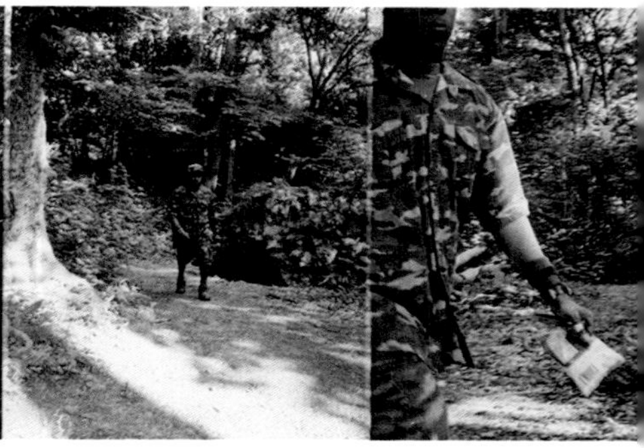

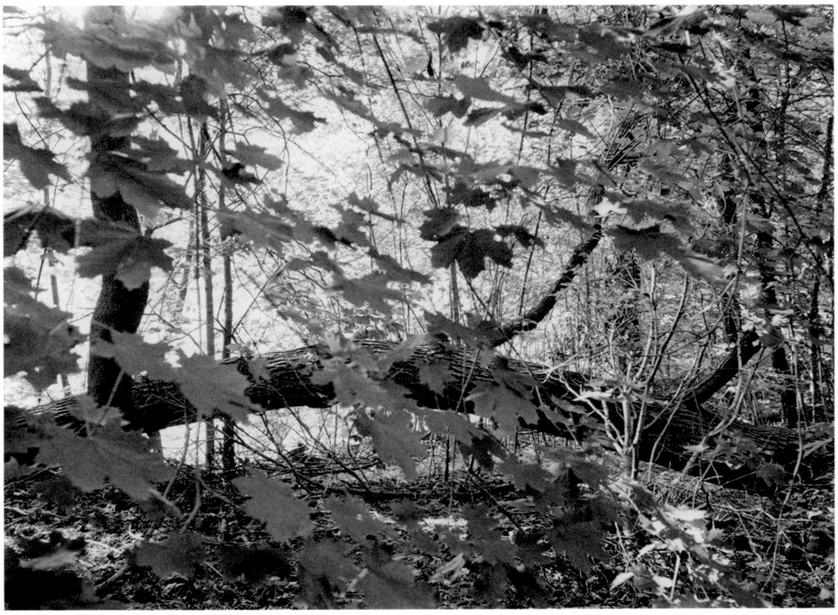

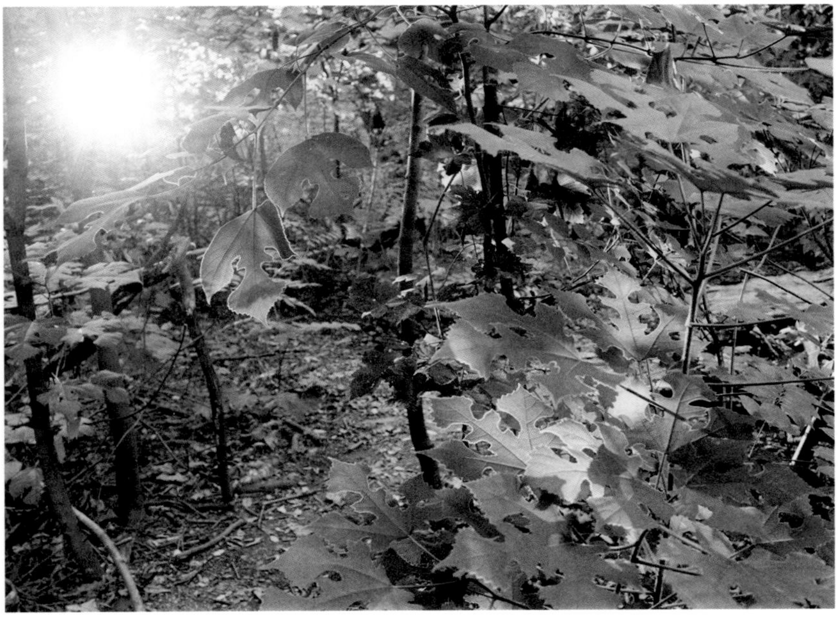

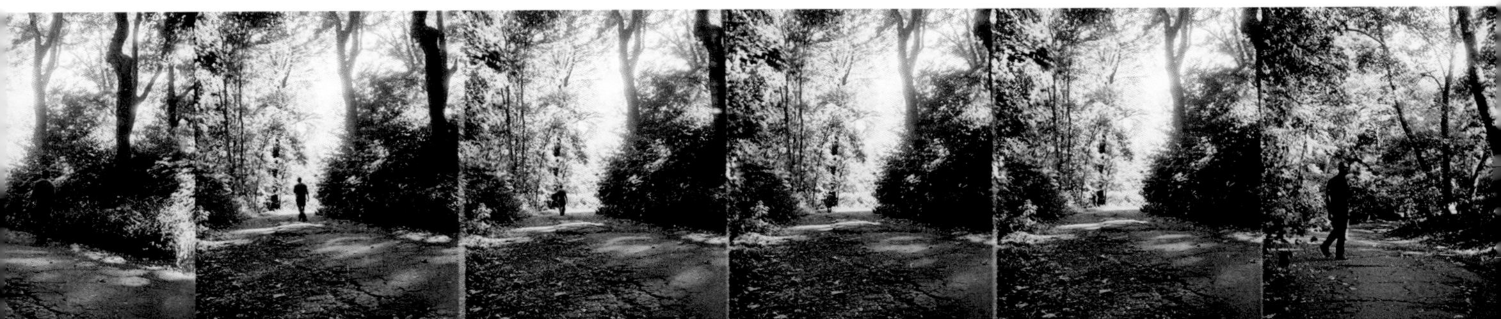

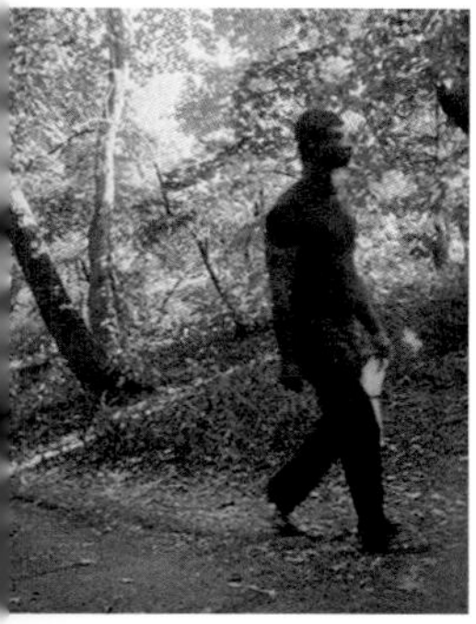

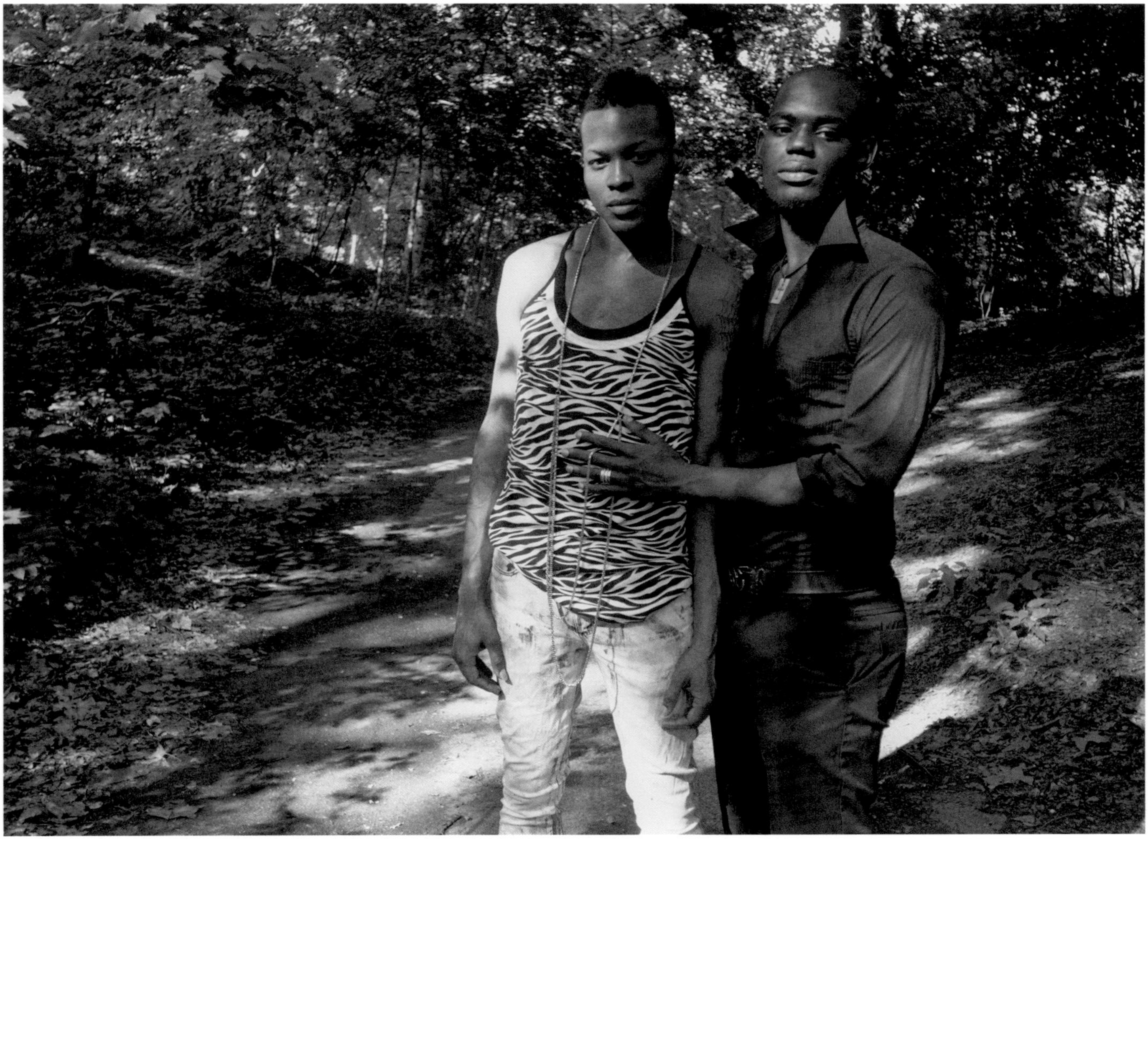

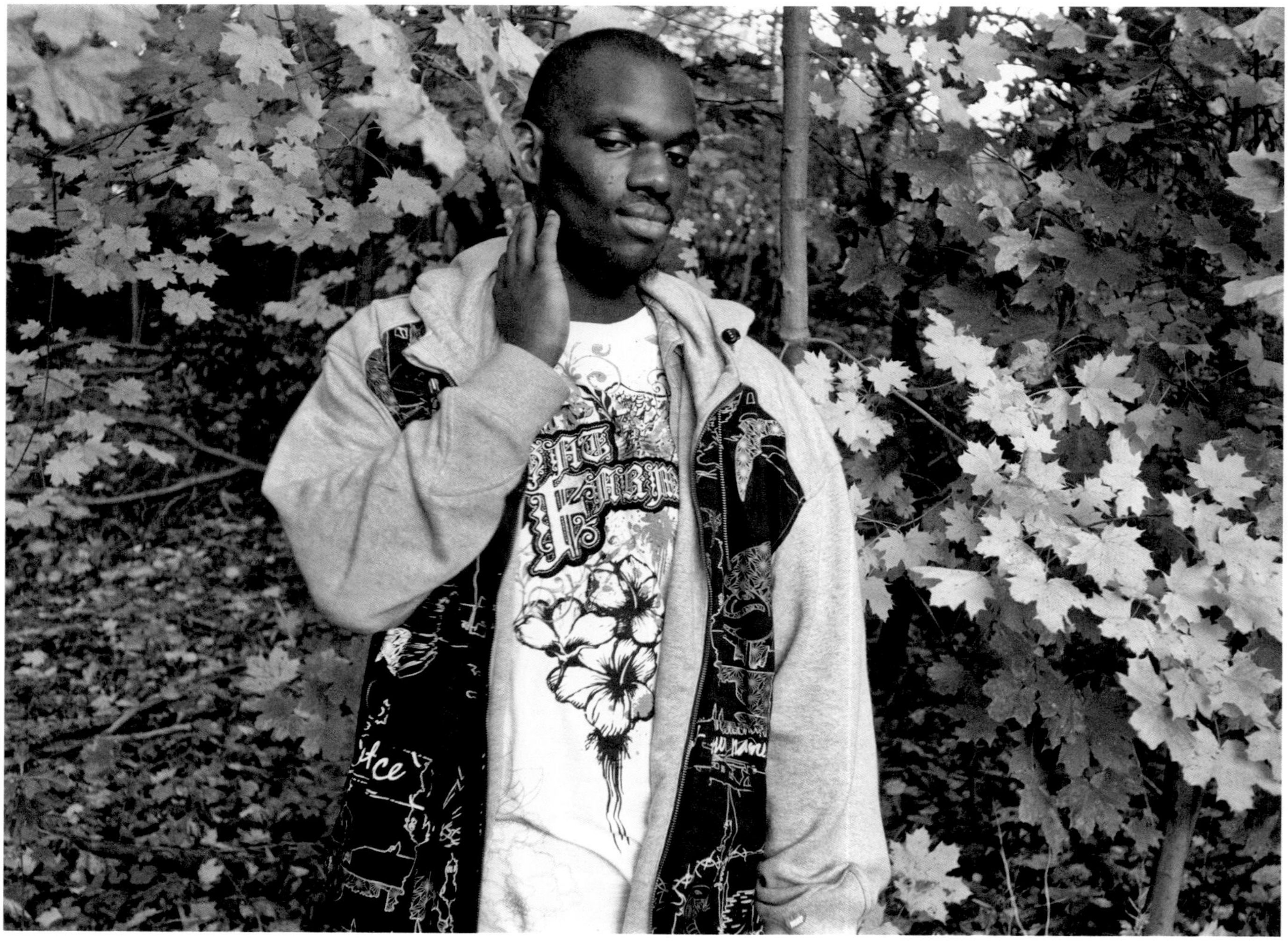

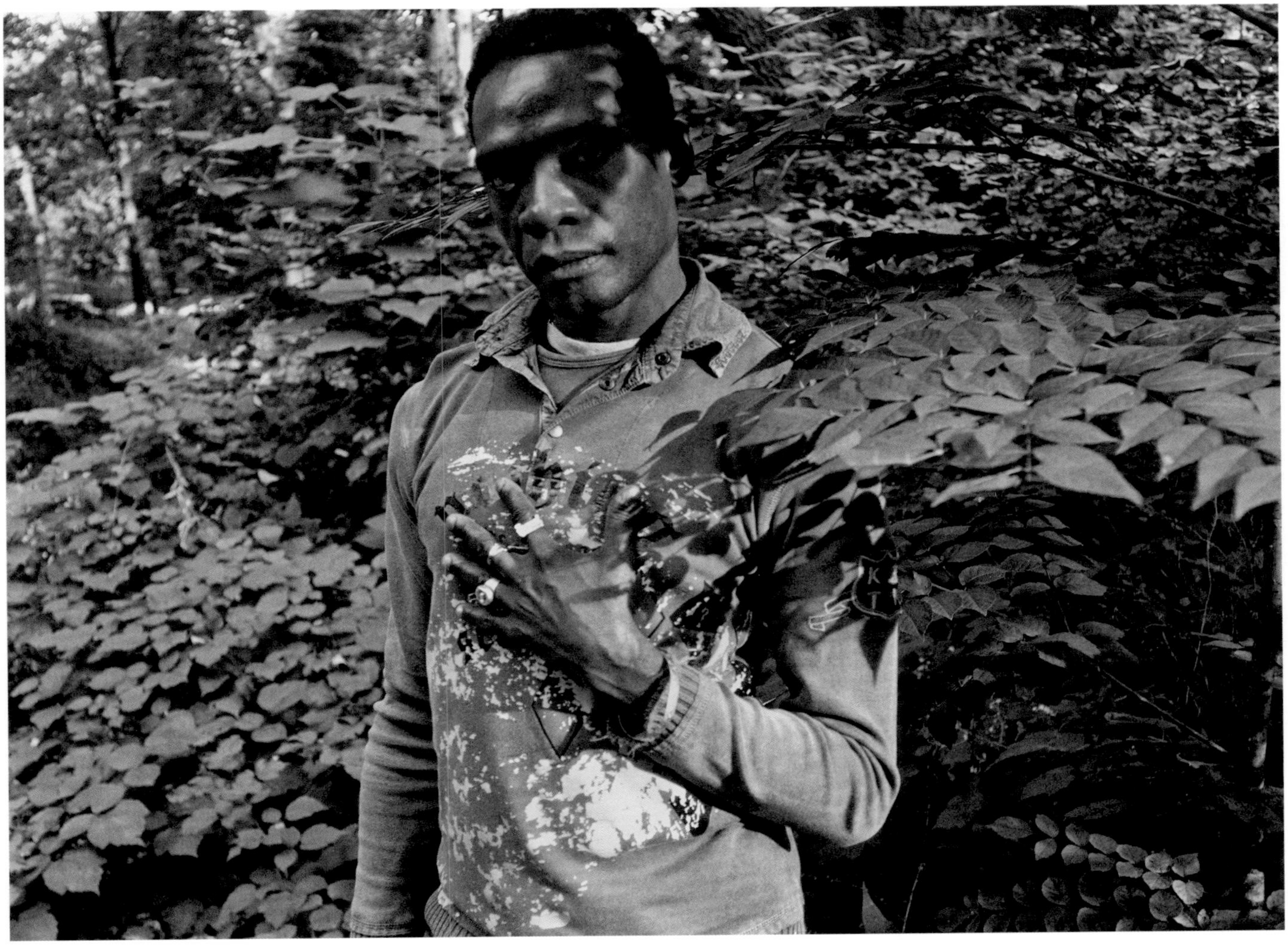

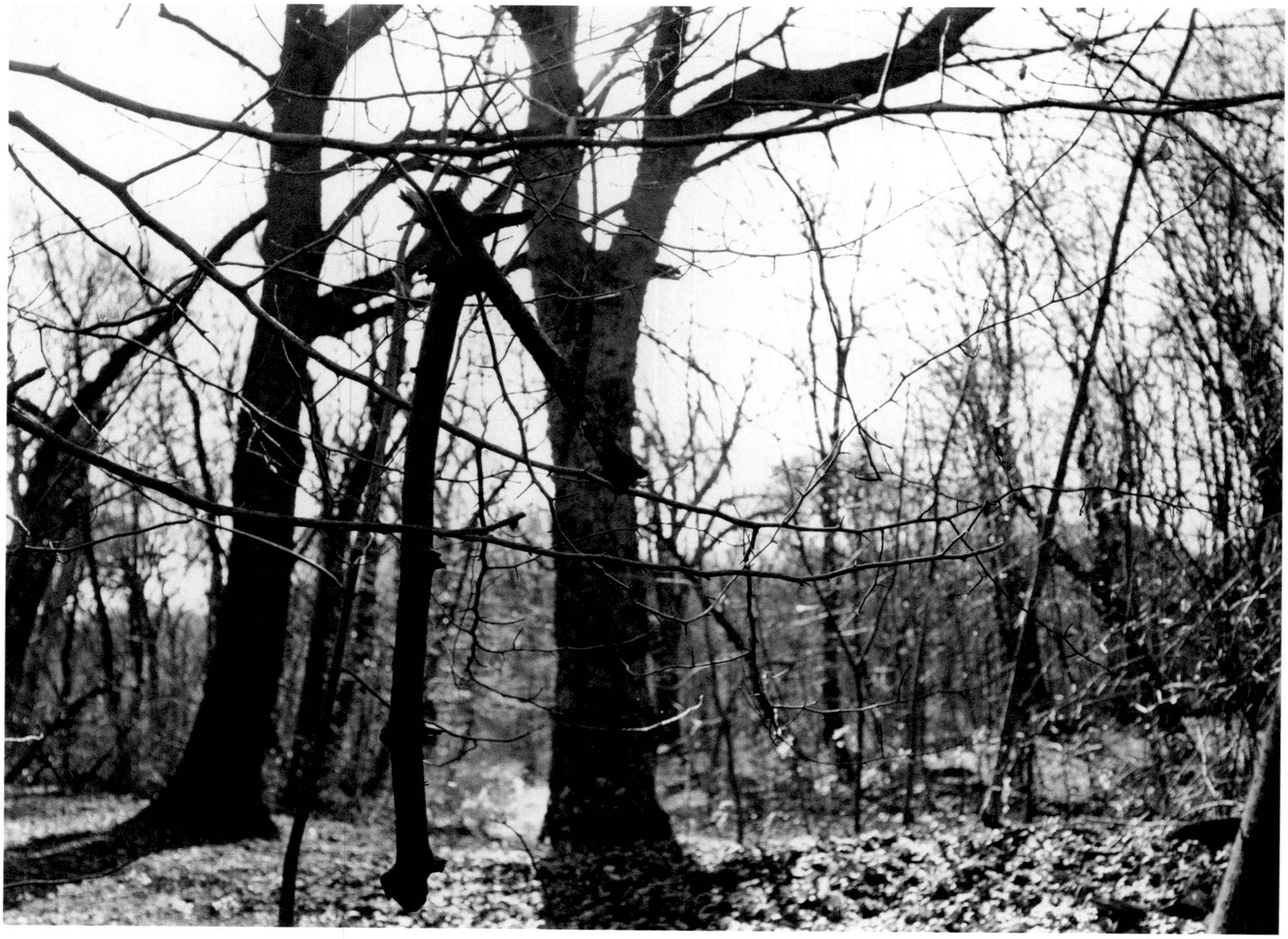

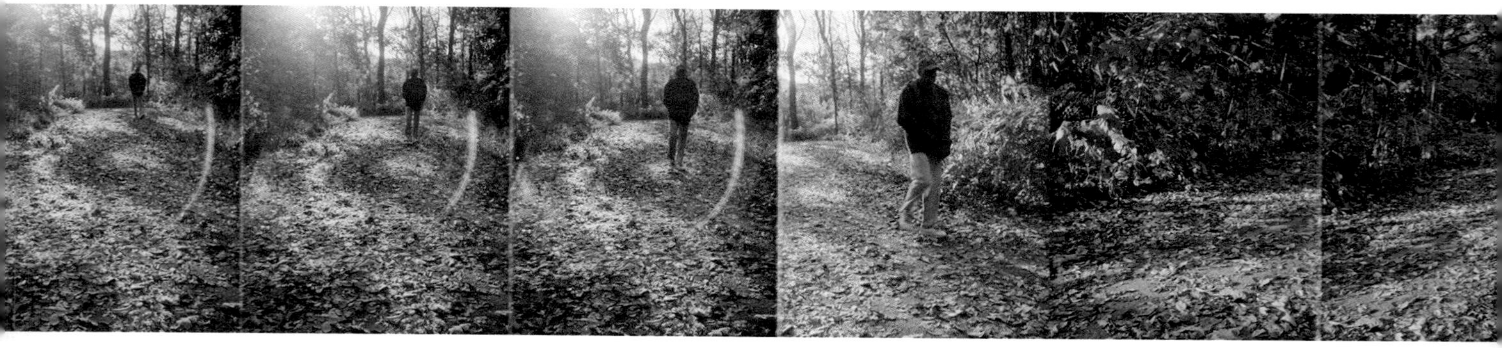

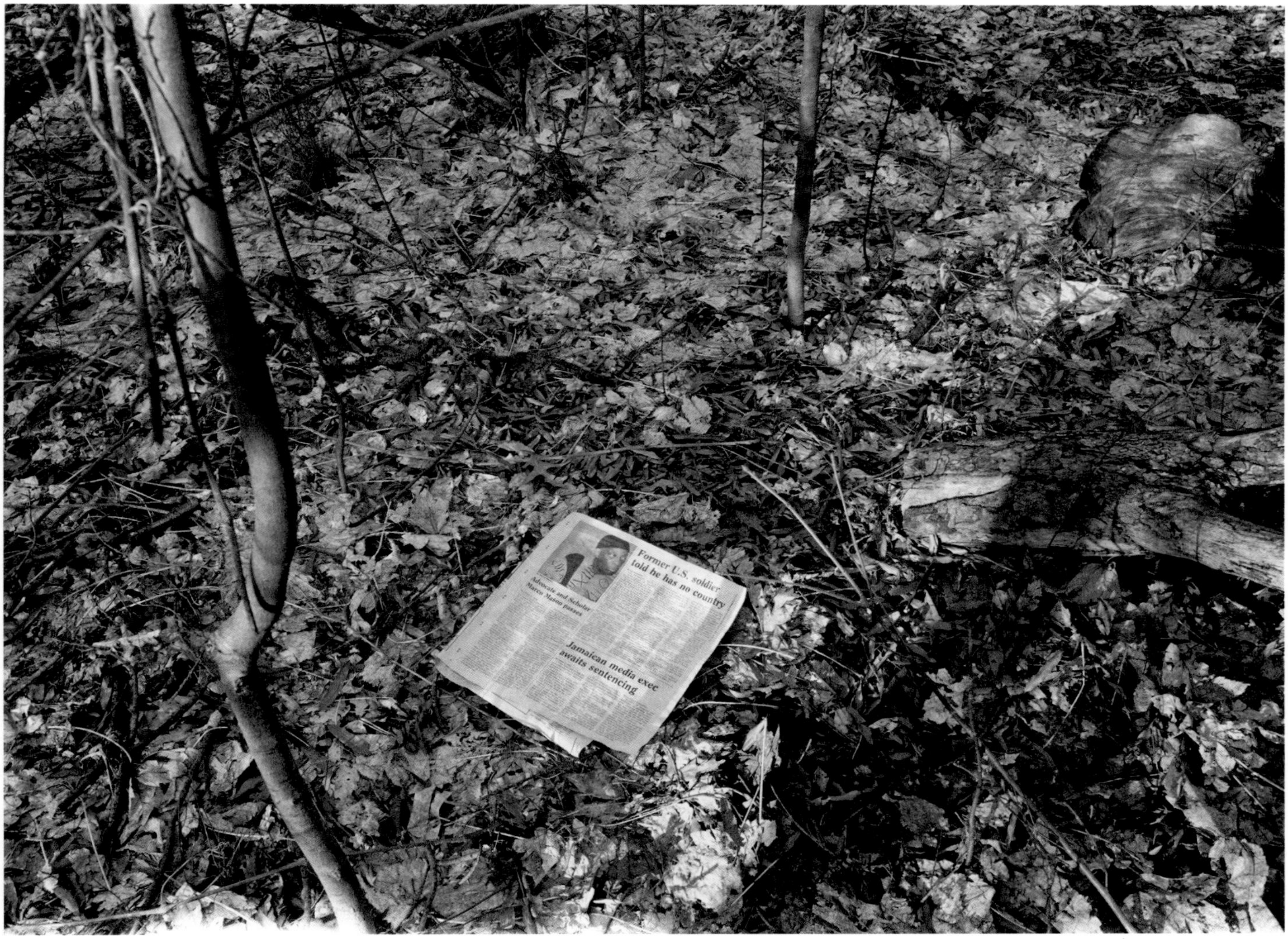
Former U.S. soldier told he has no country
Advocate and Scholar Marcu Mason passes
Jamaican media exec awaits sentencing

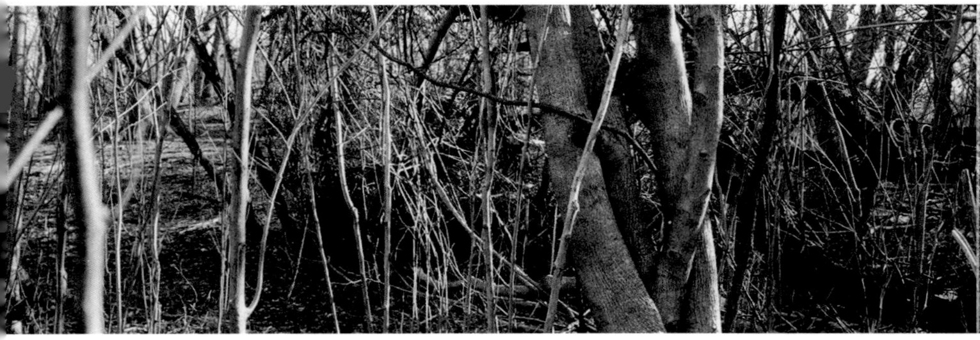

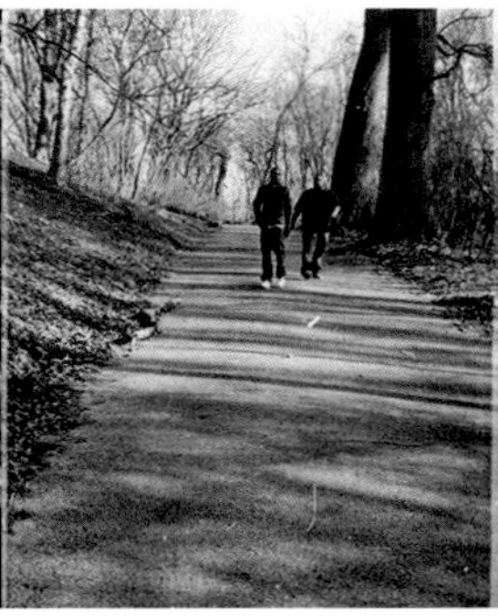

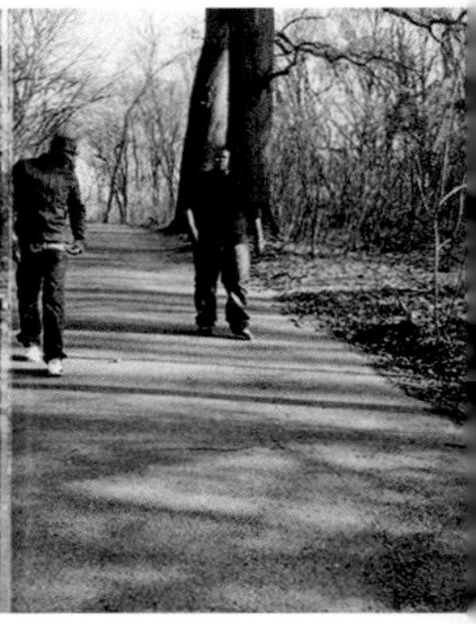

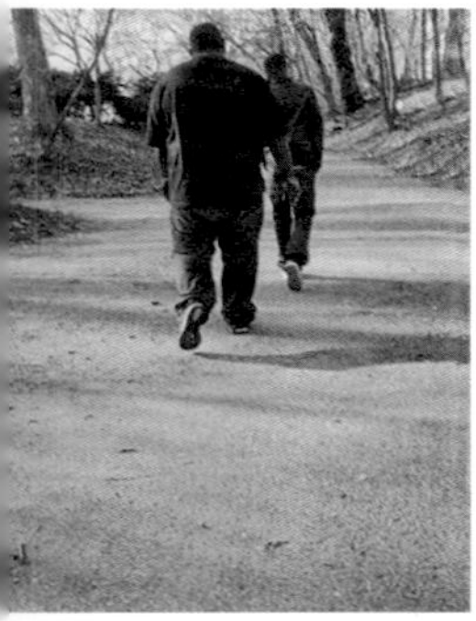

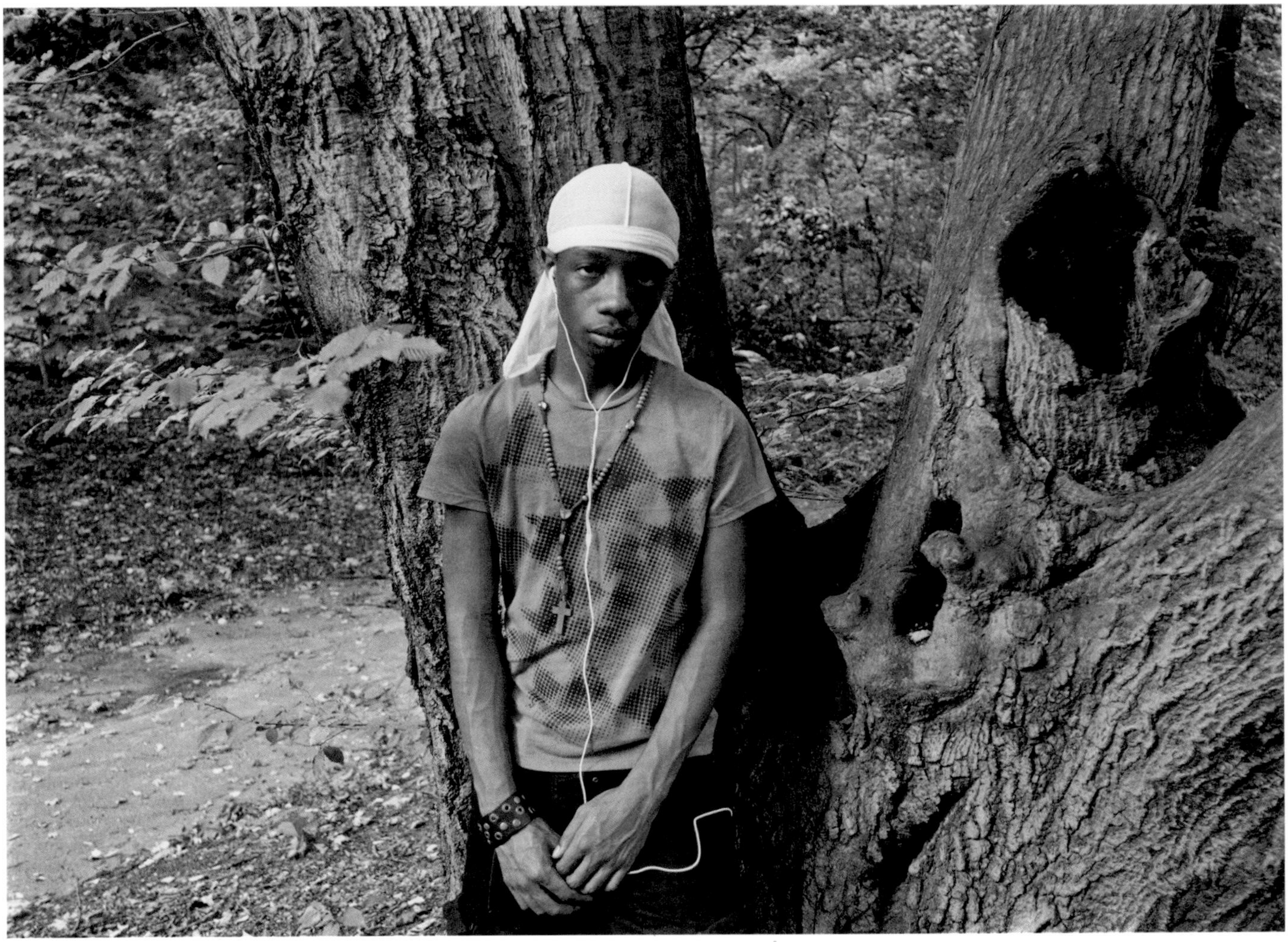

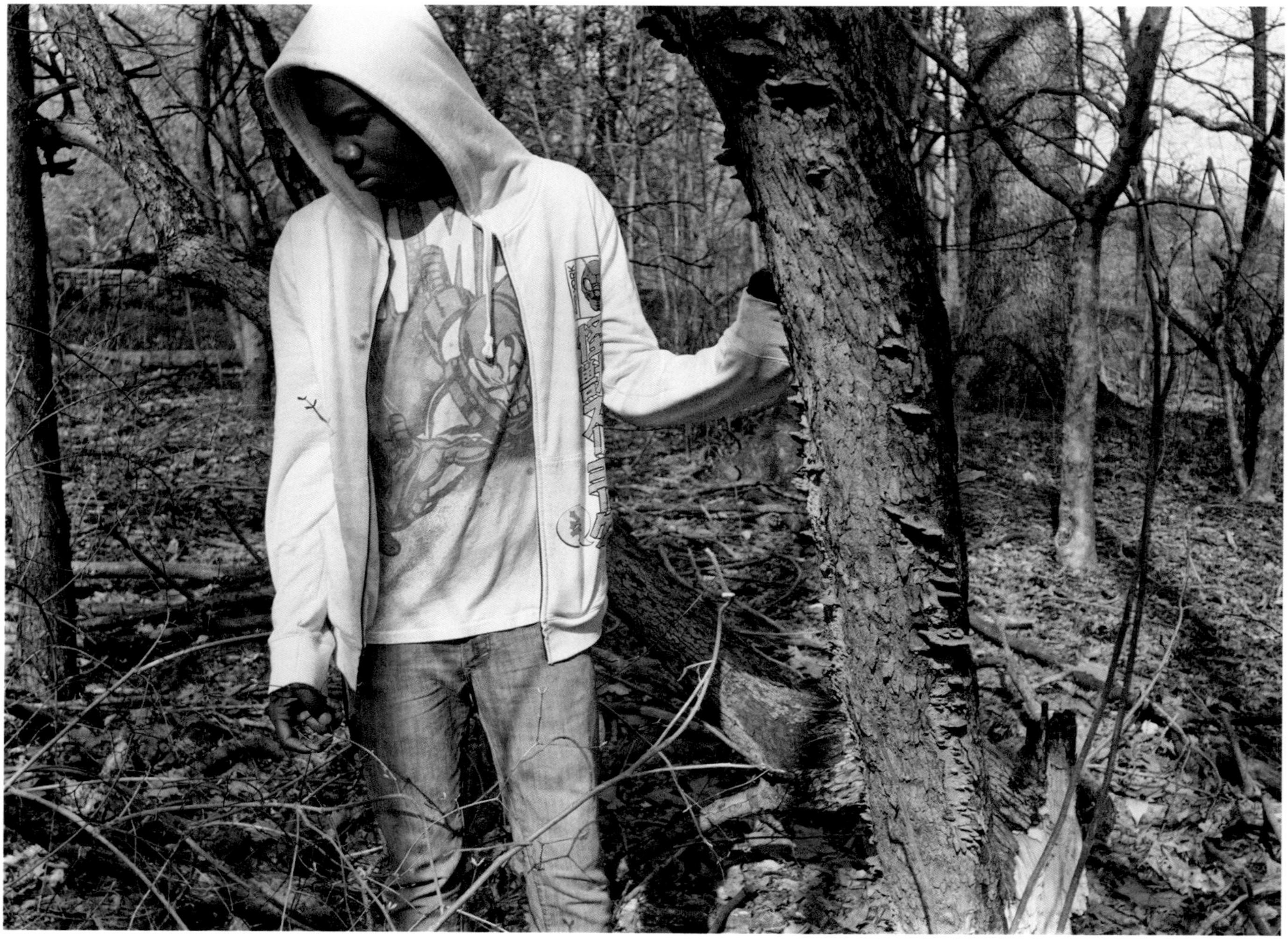

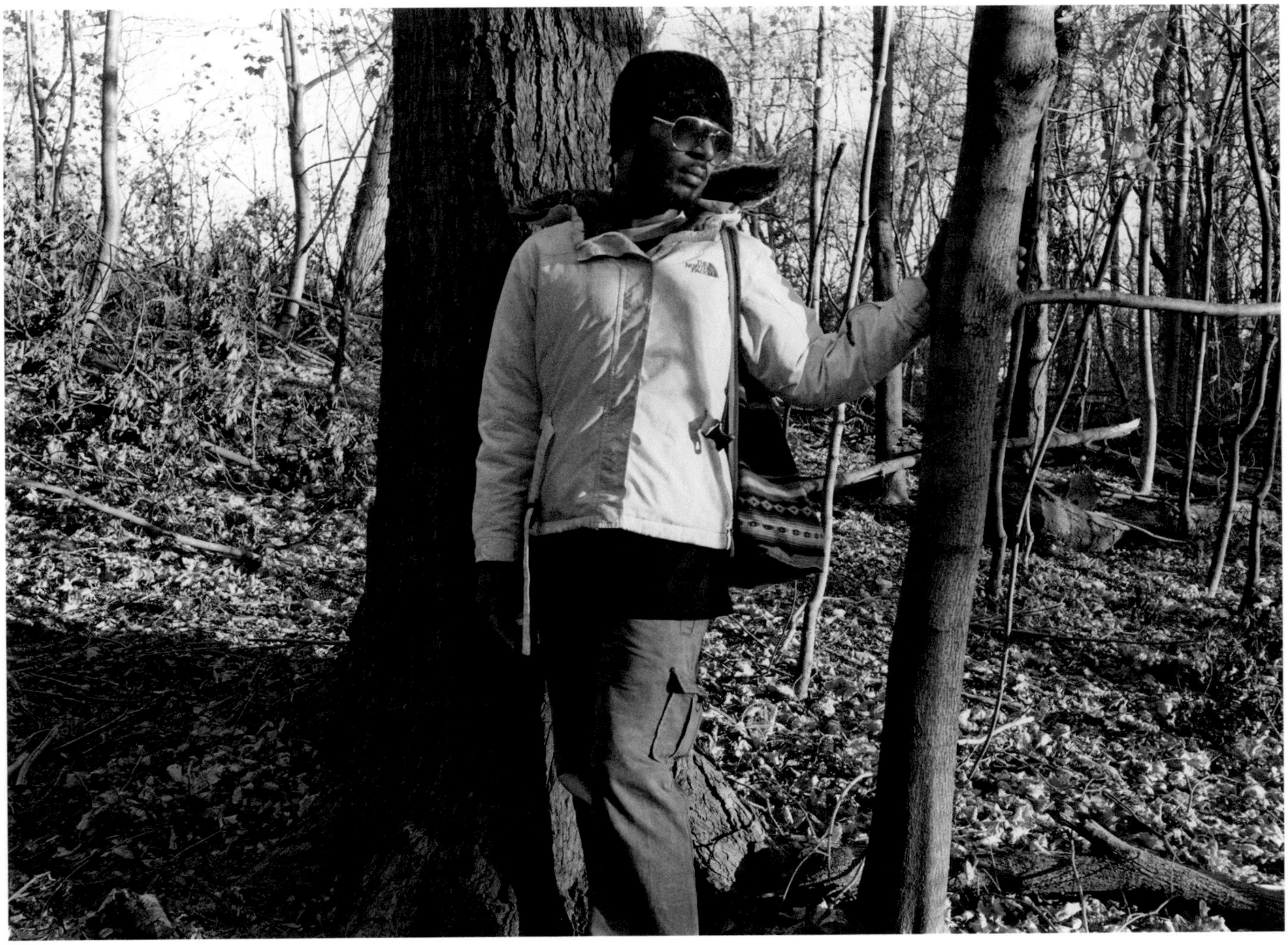

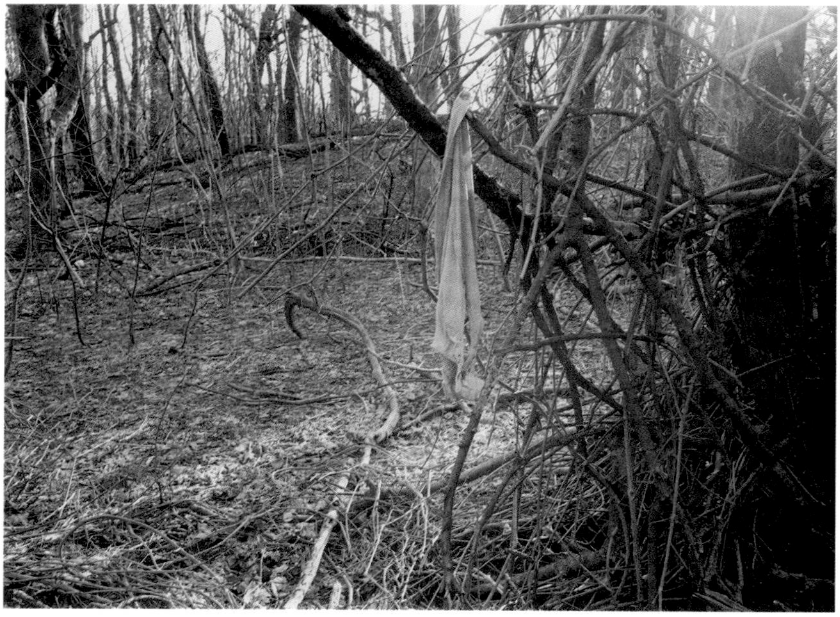

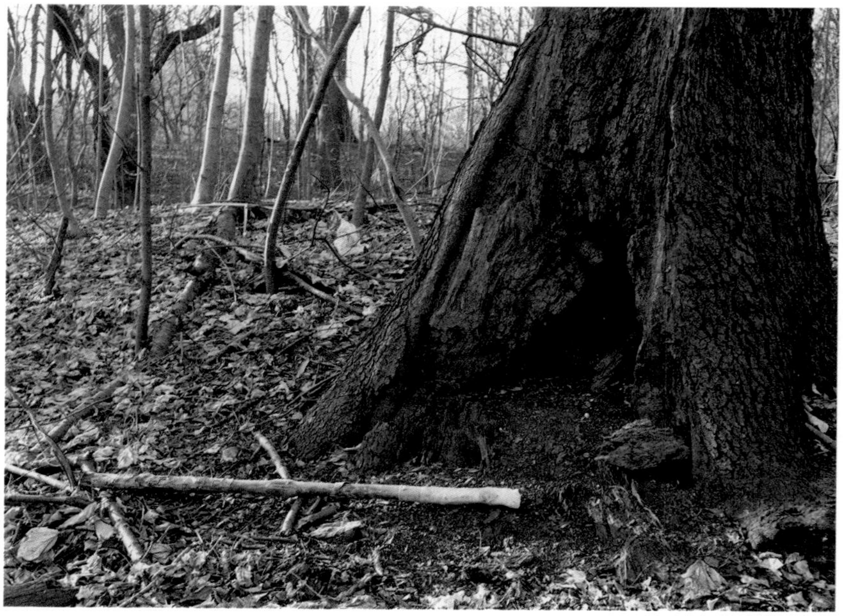

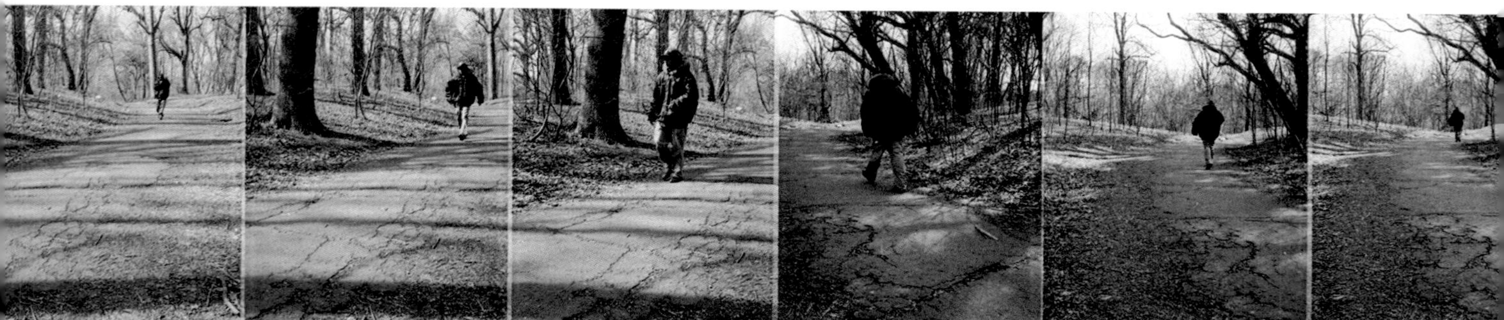

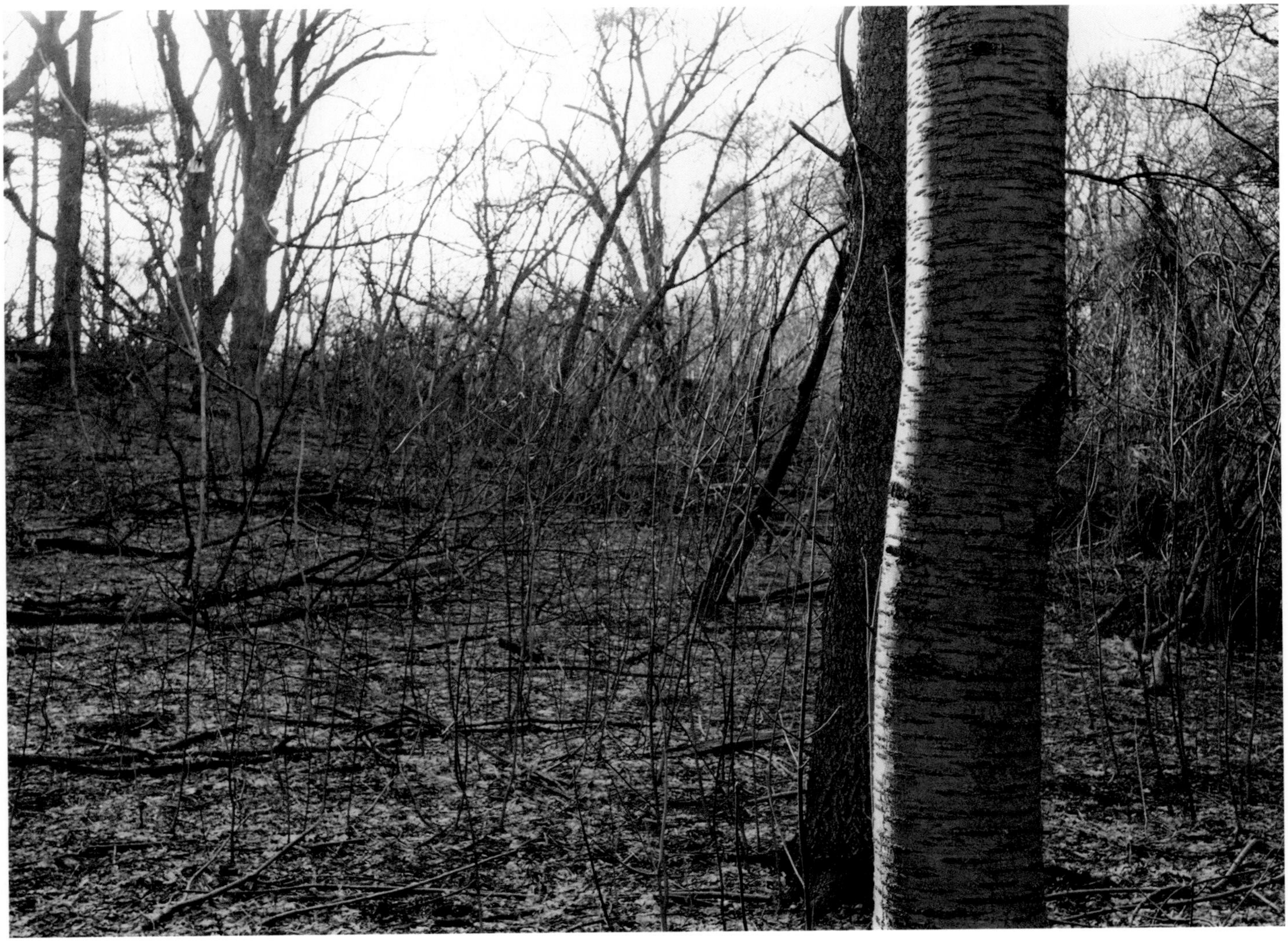

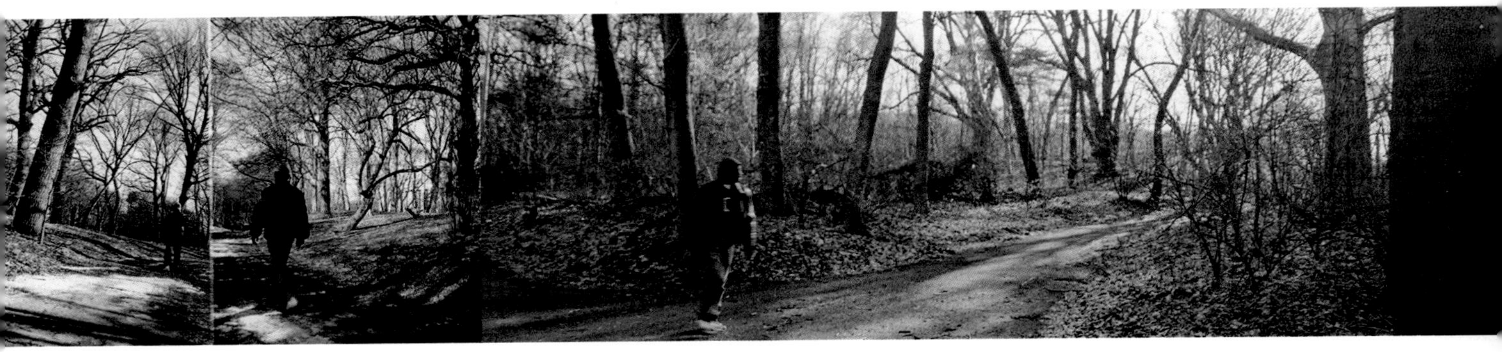

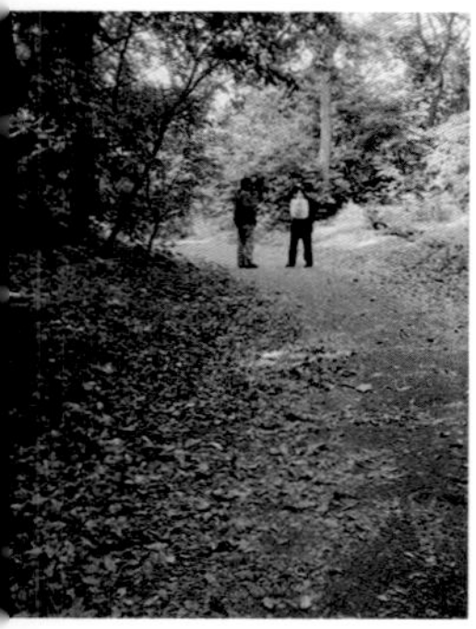

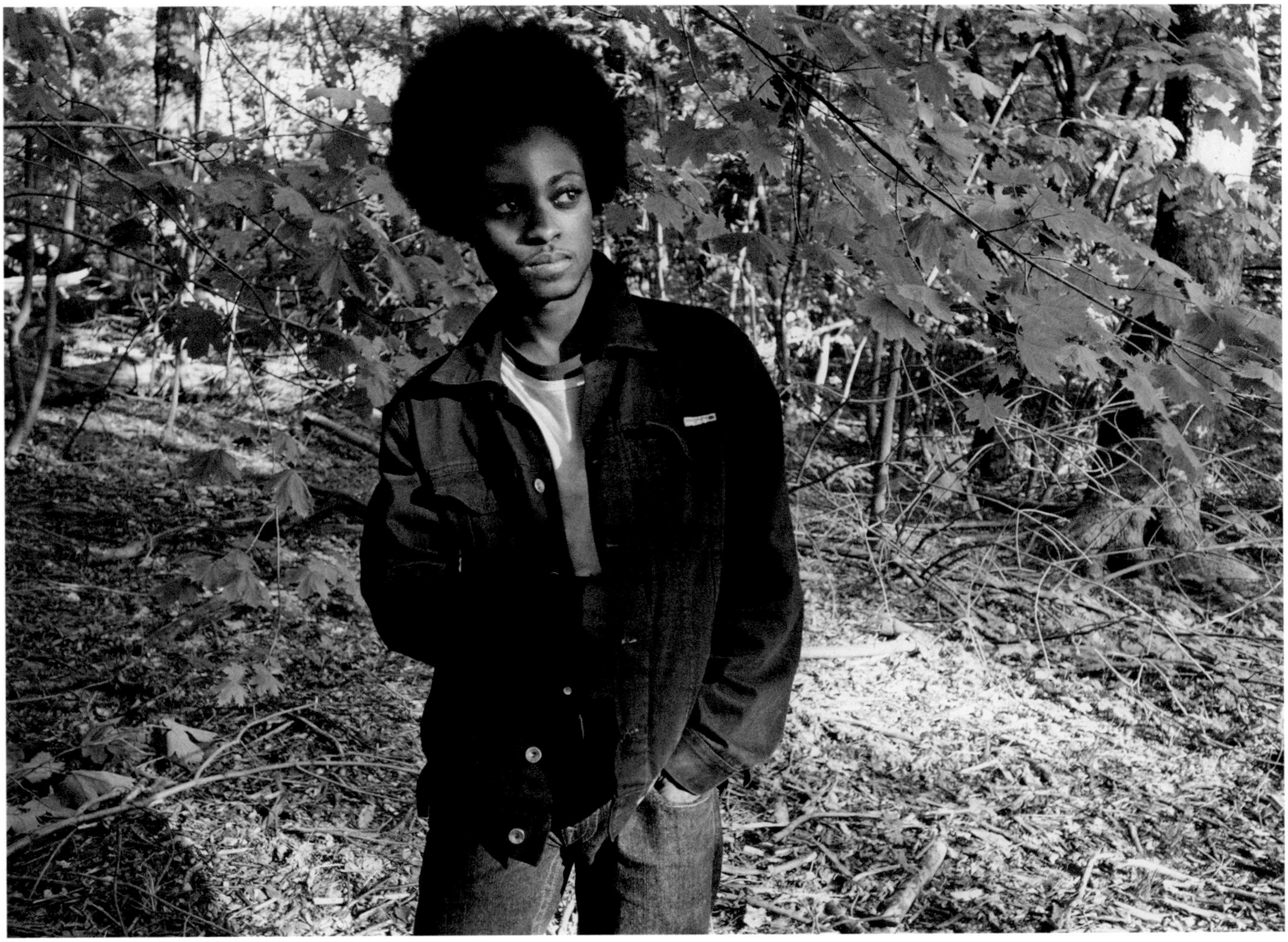

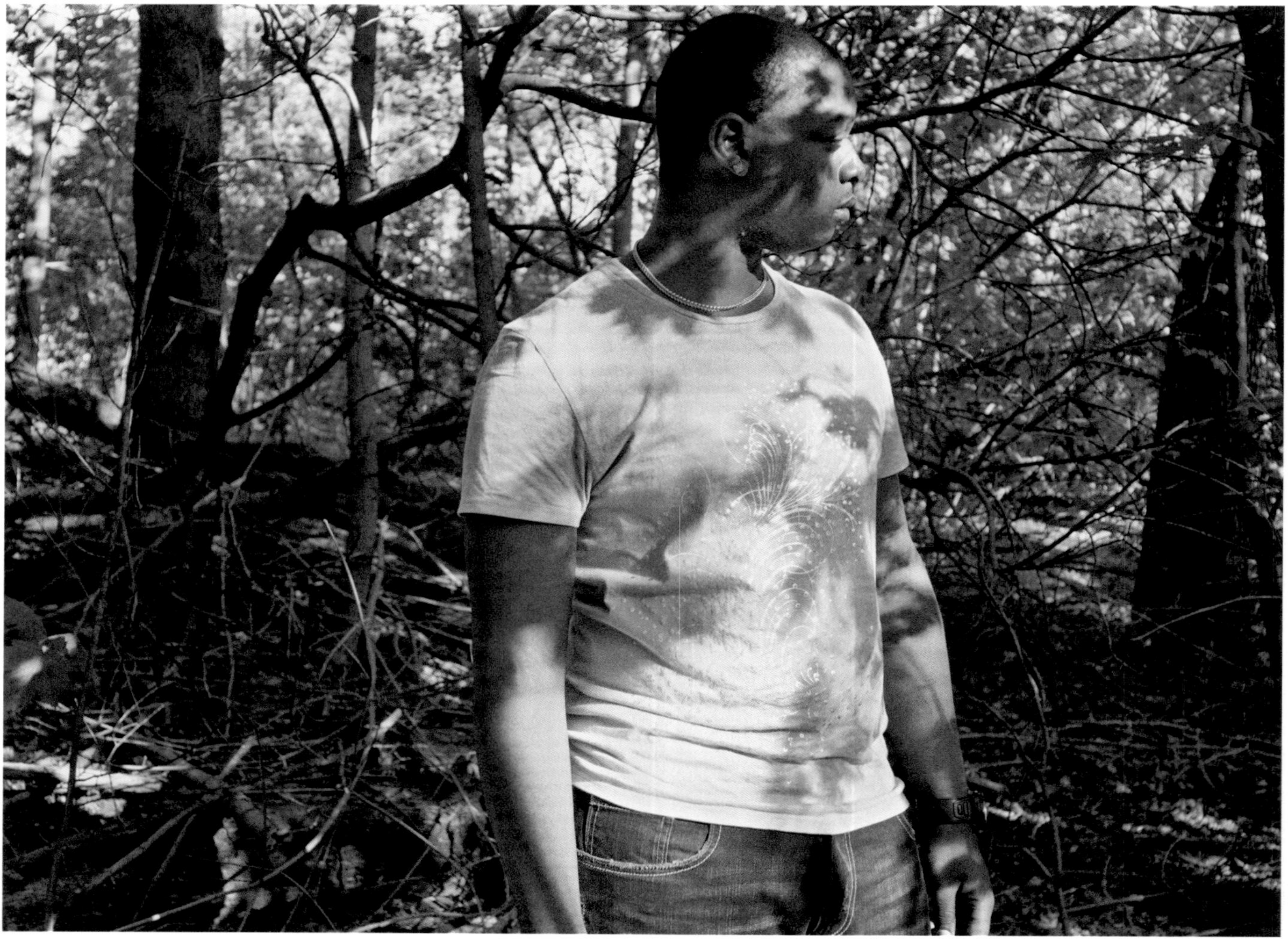

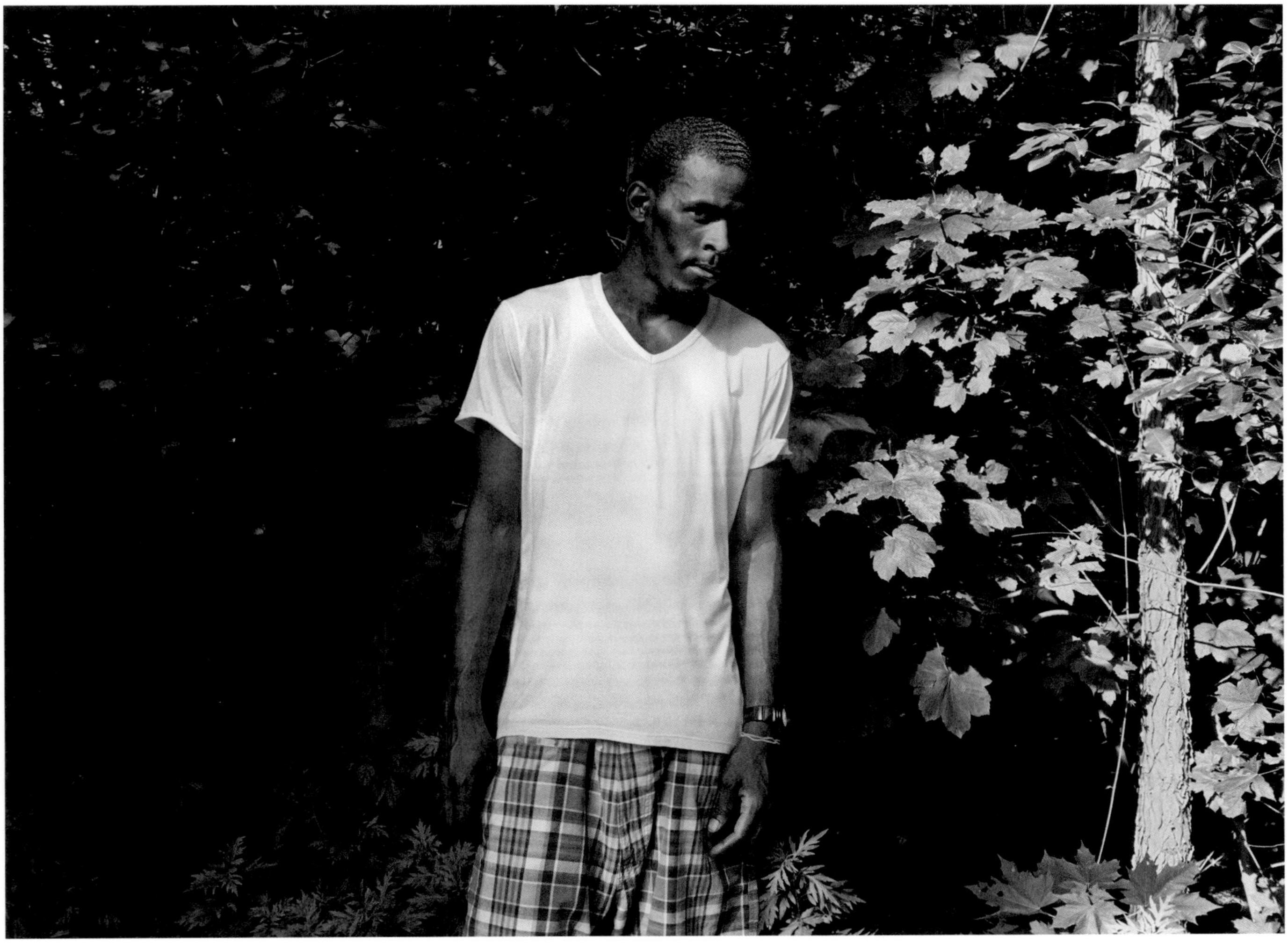

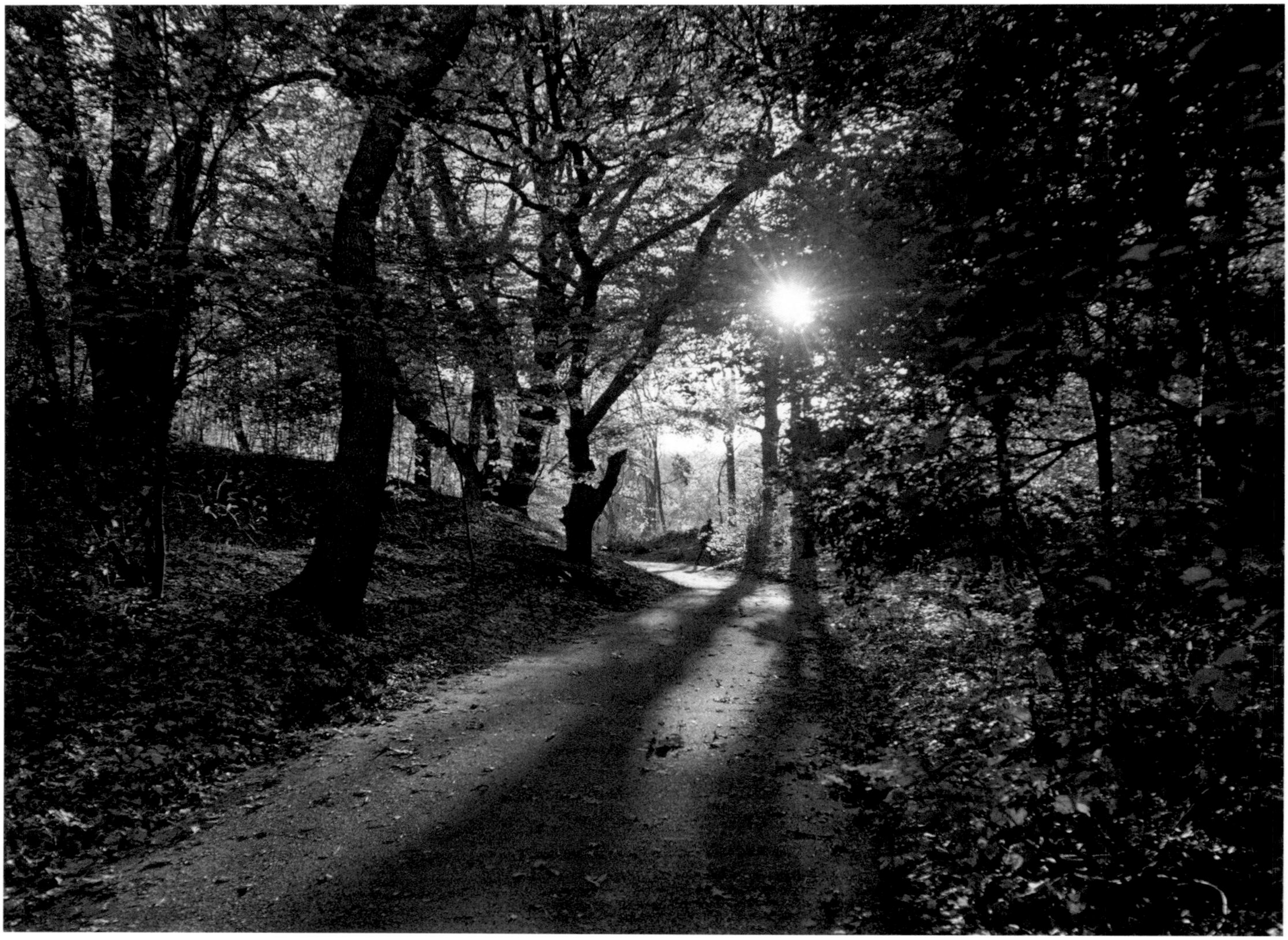

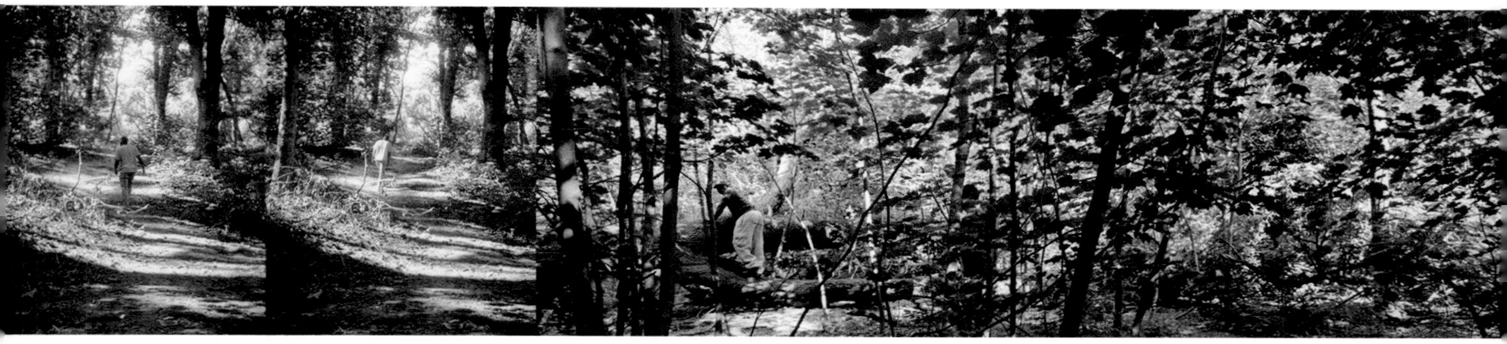

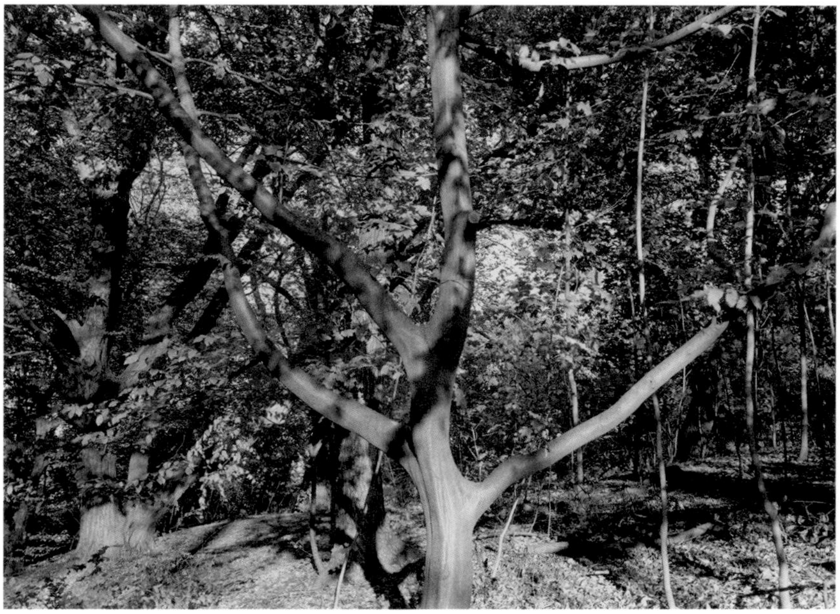

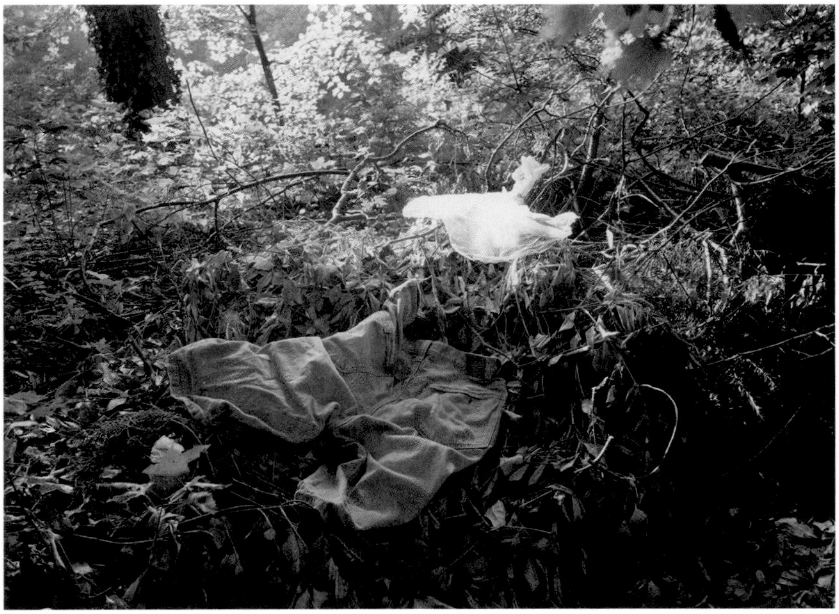

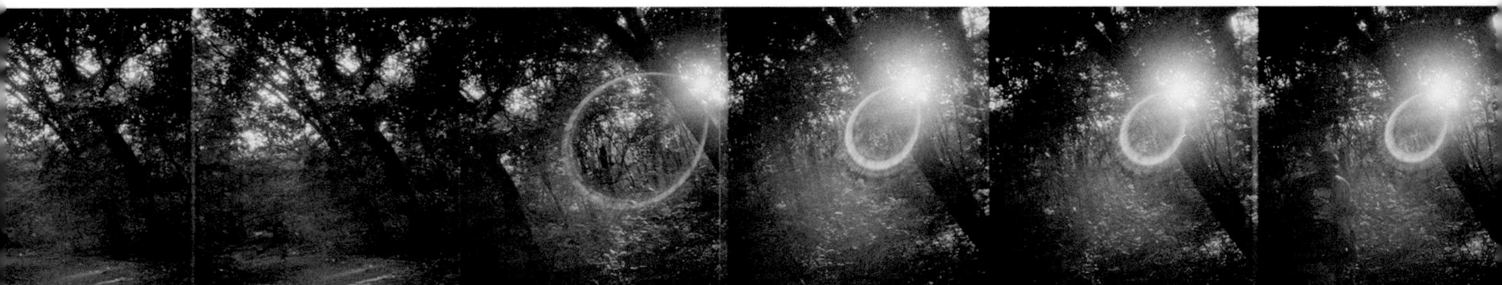

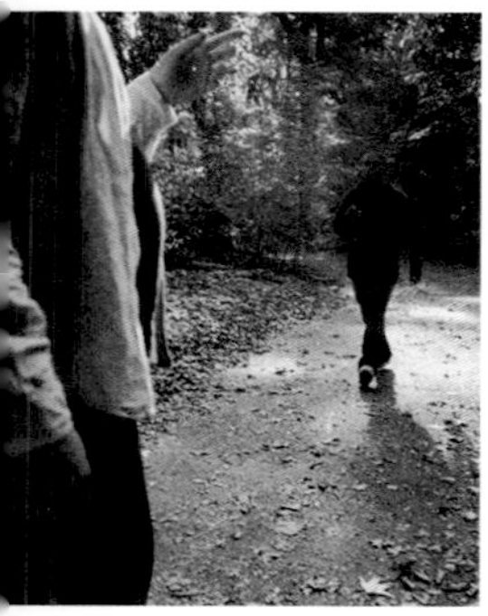

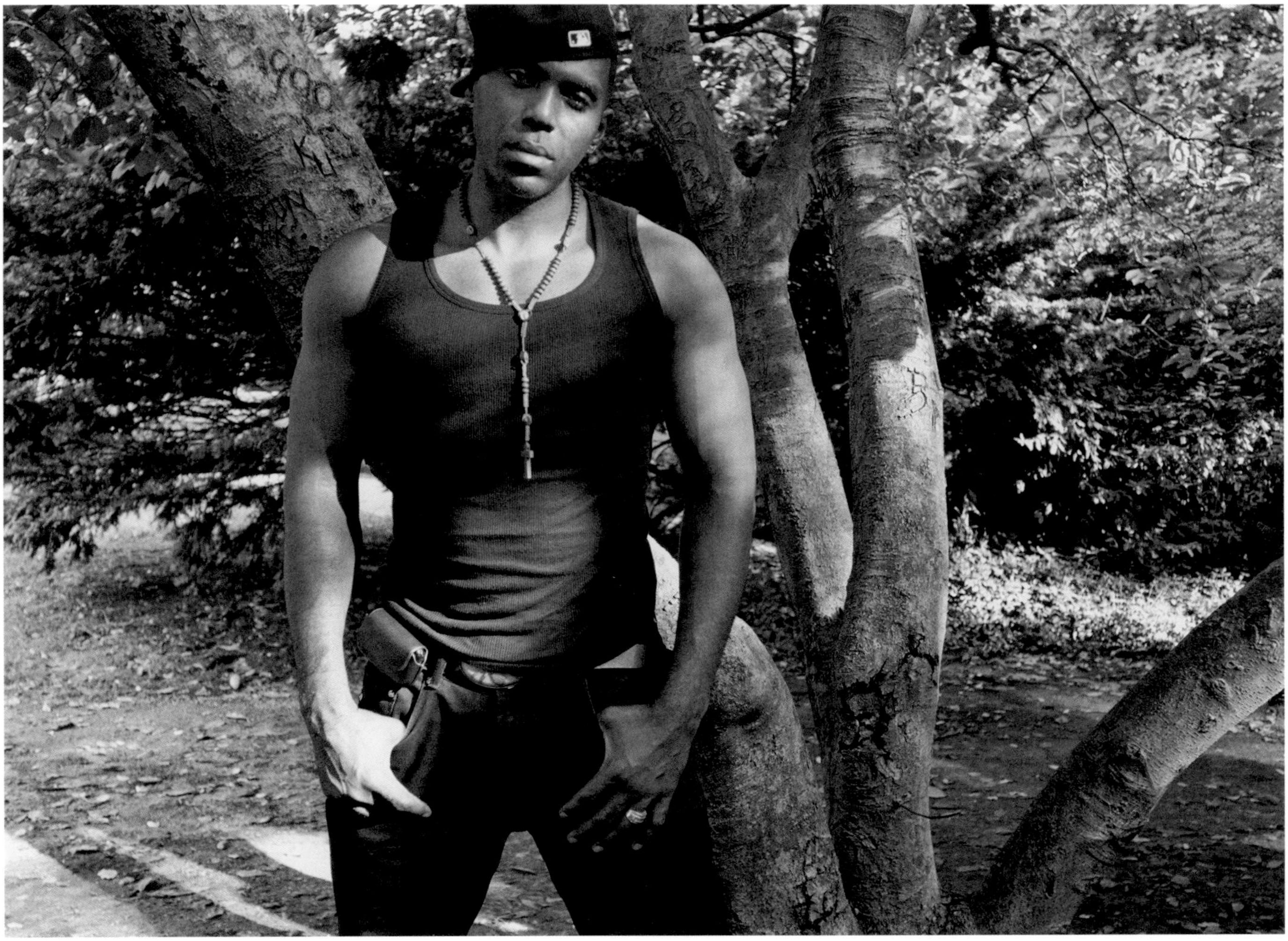

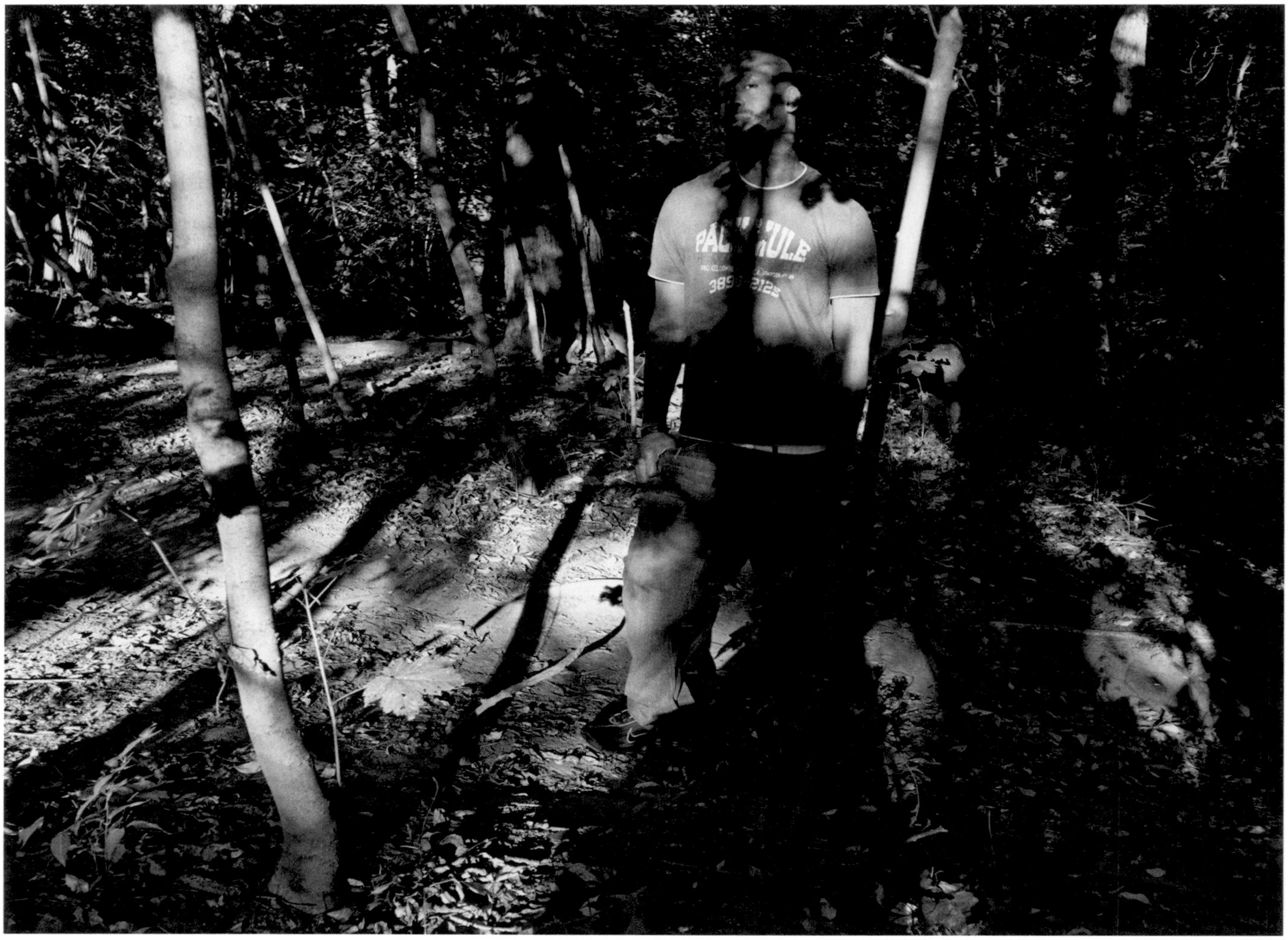

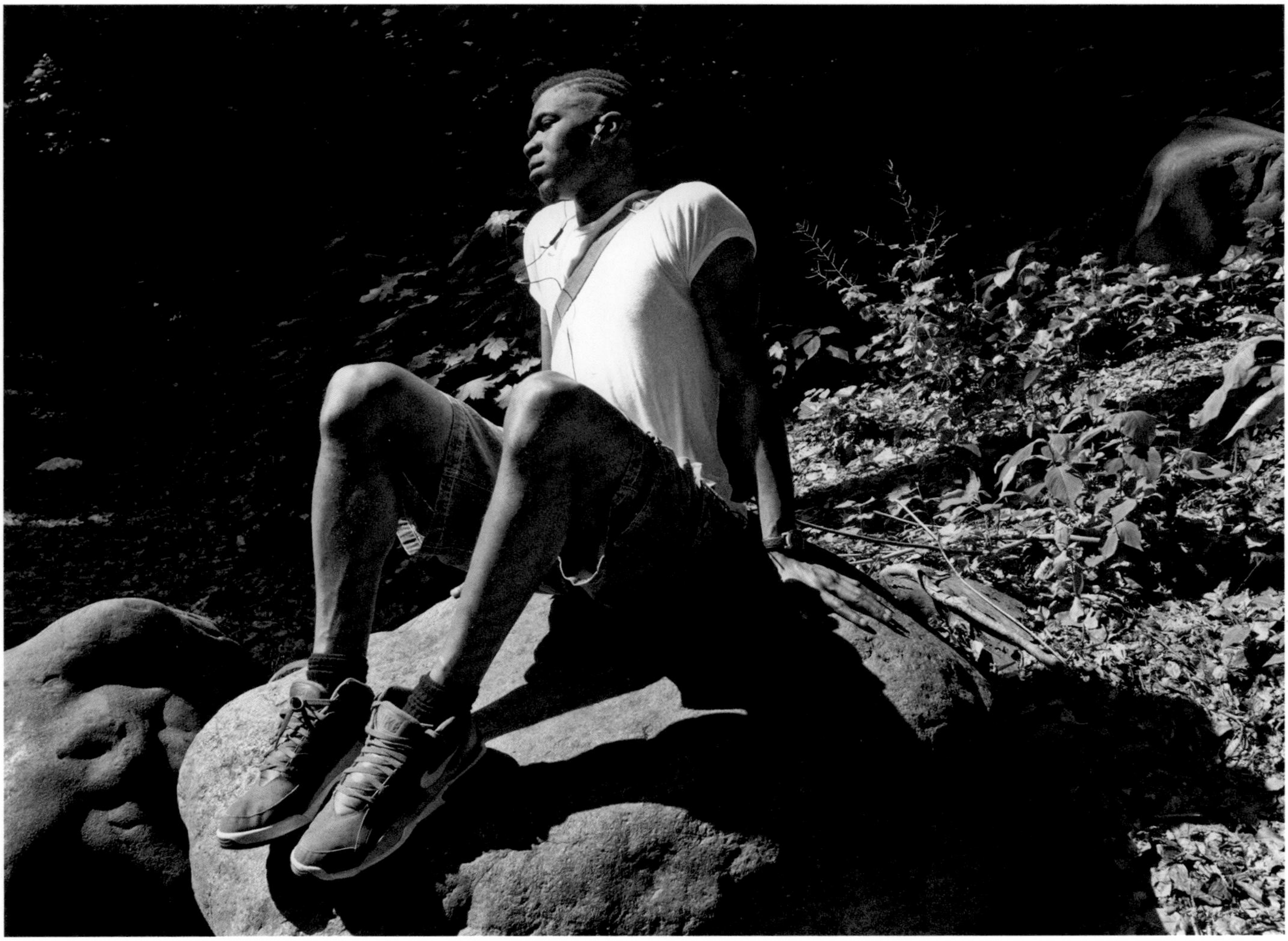

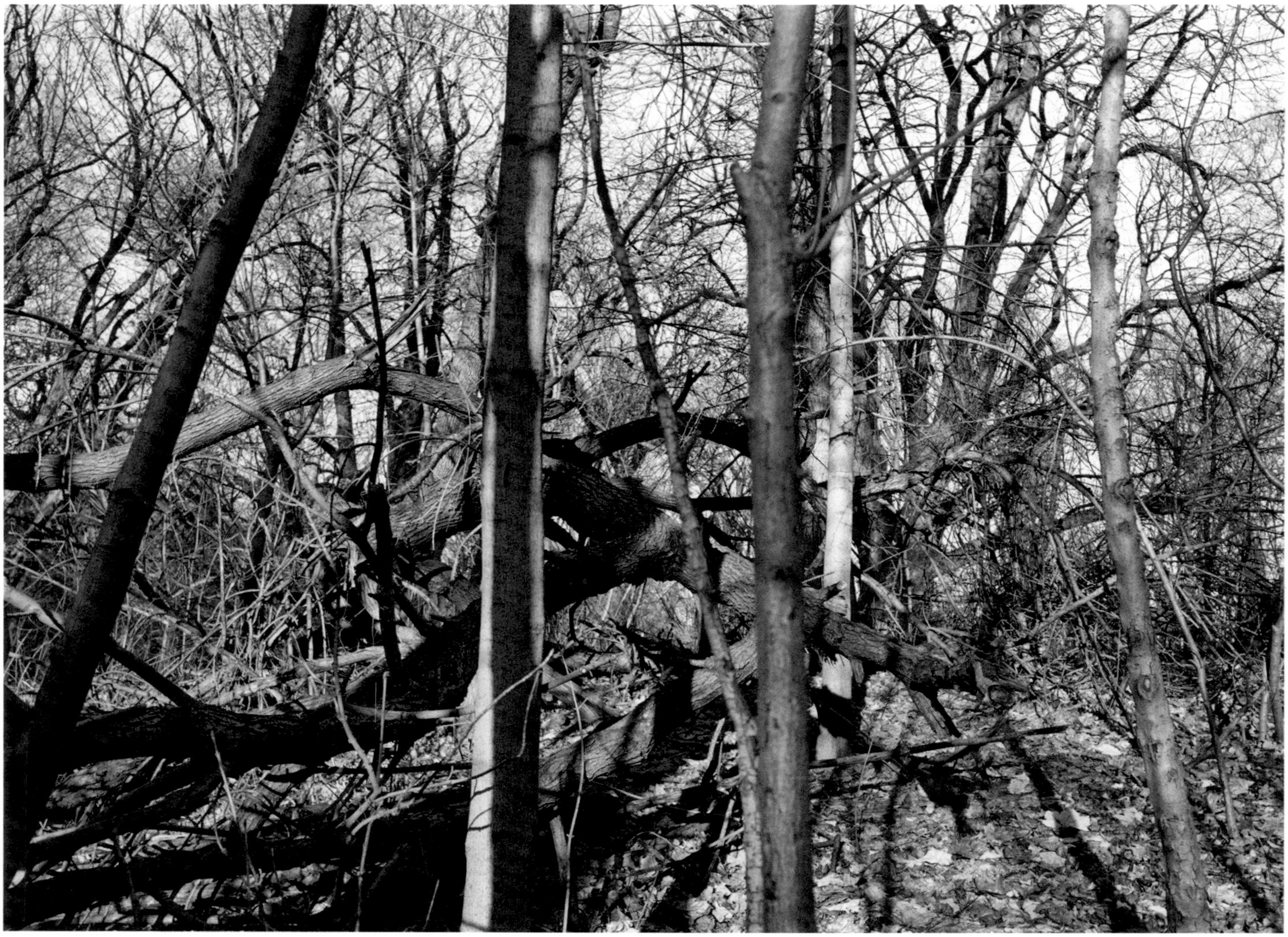

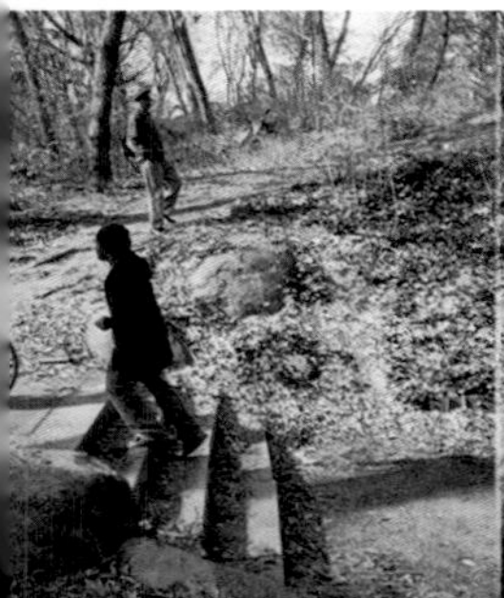

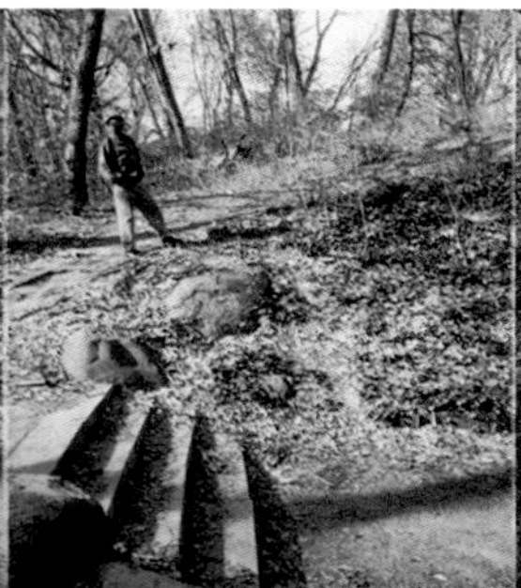

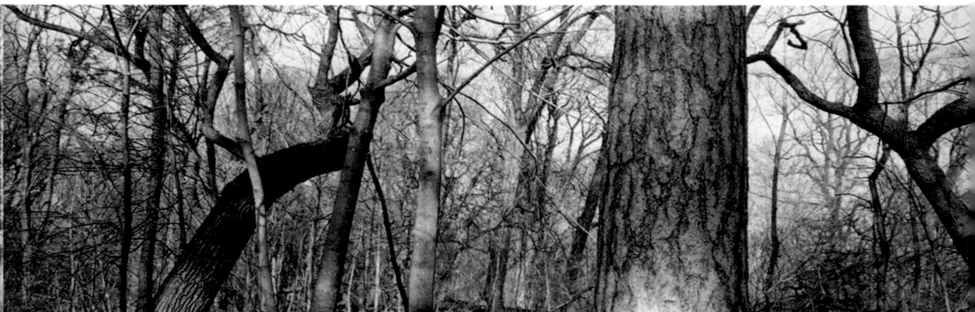

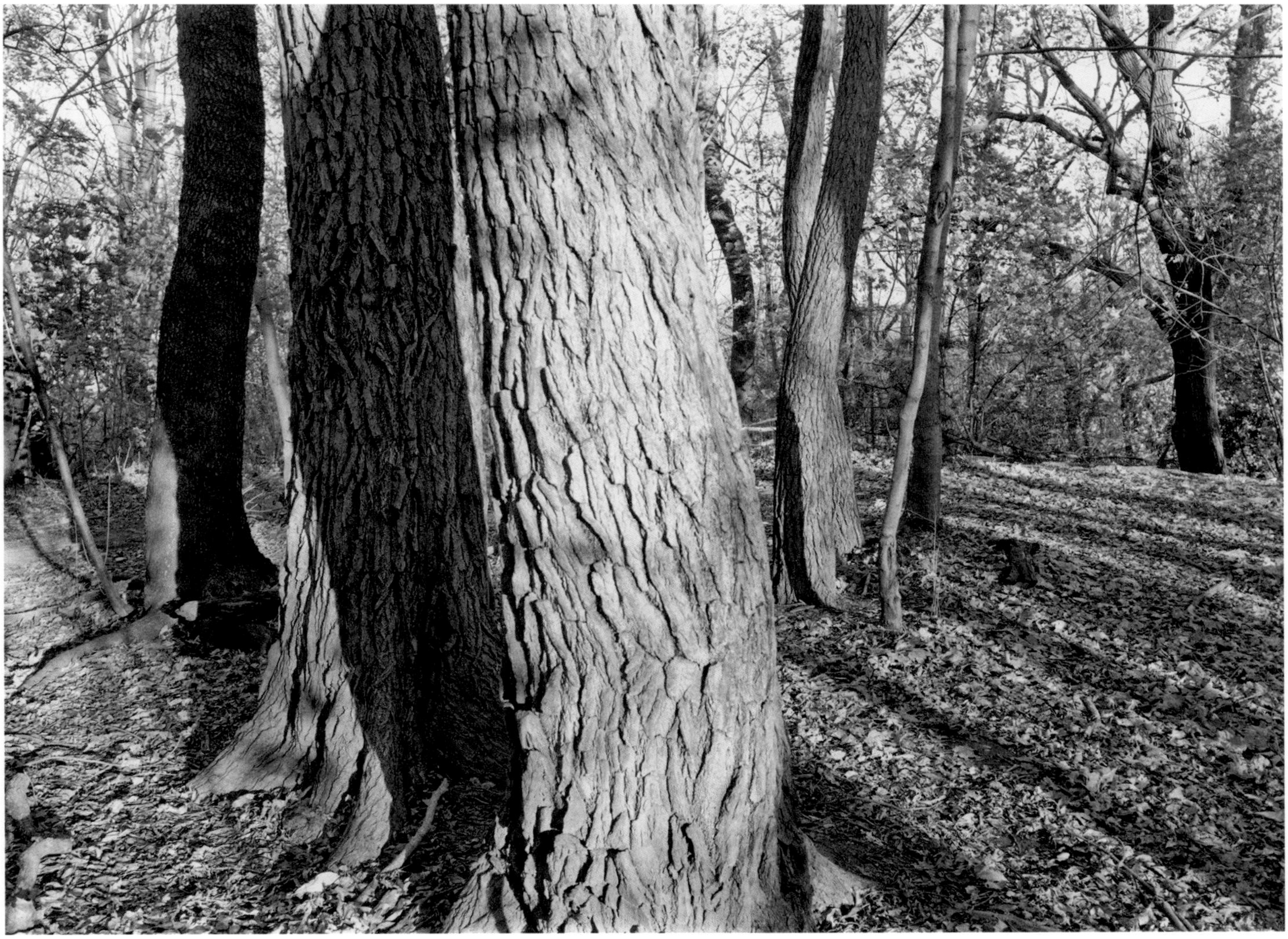

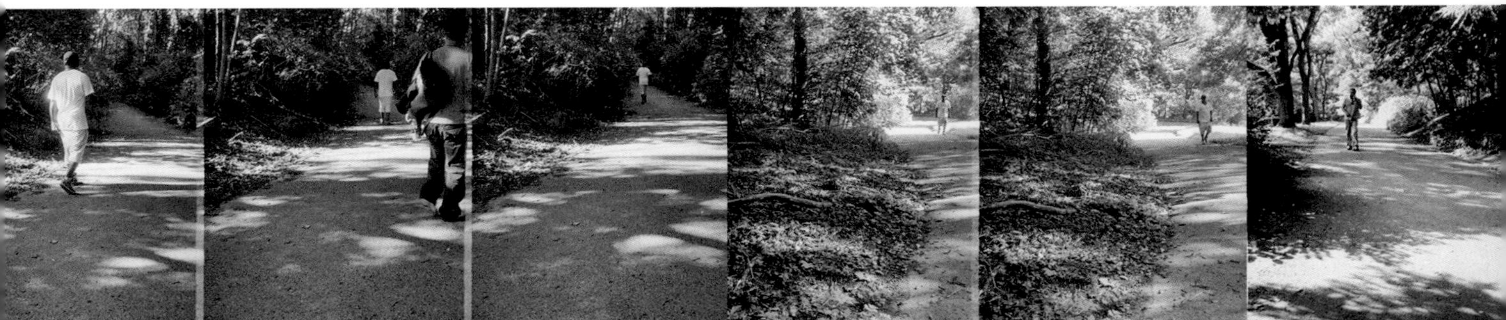

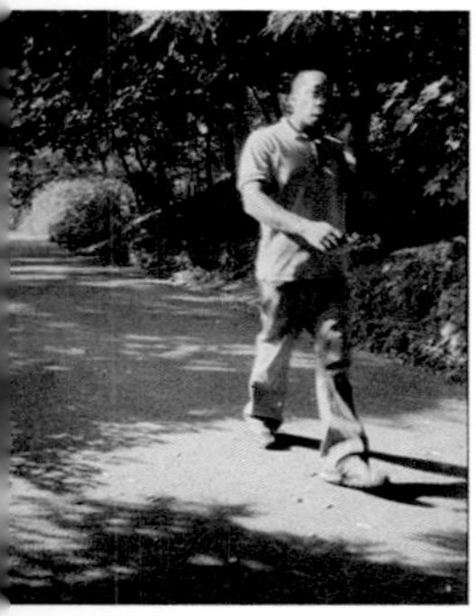

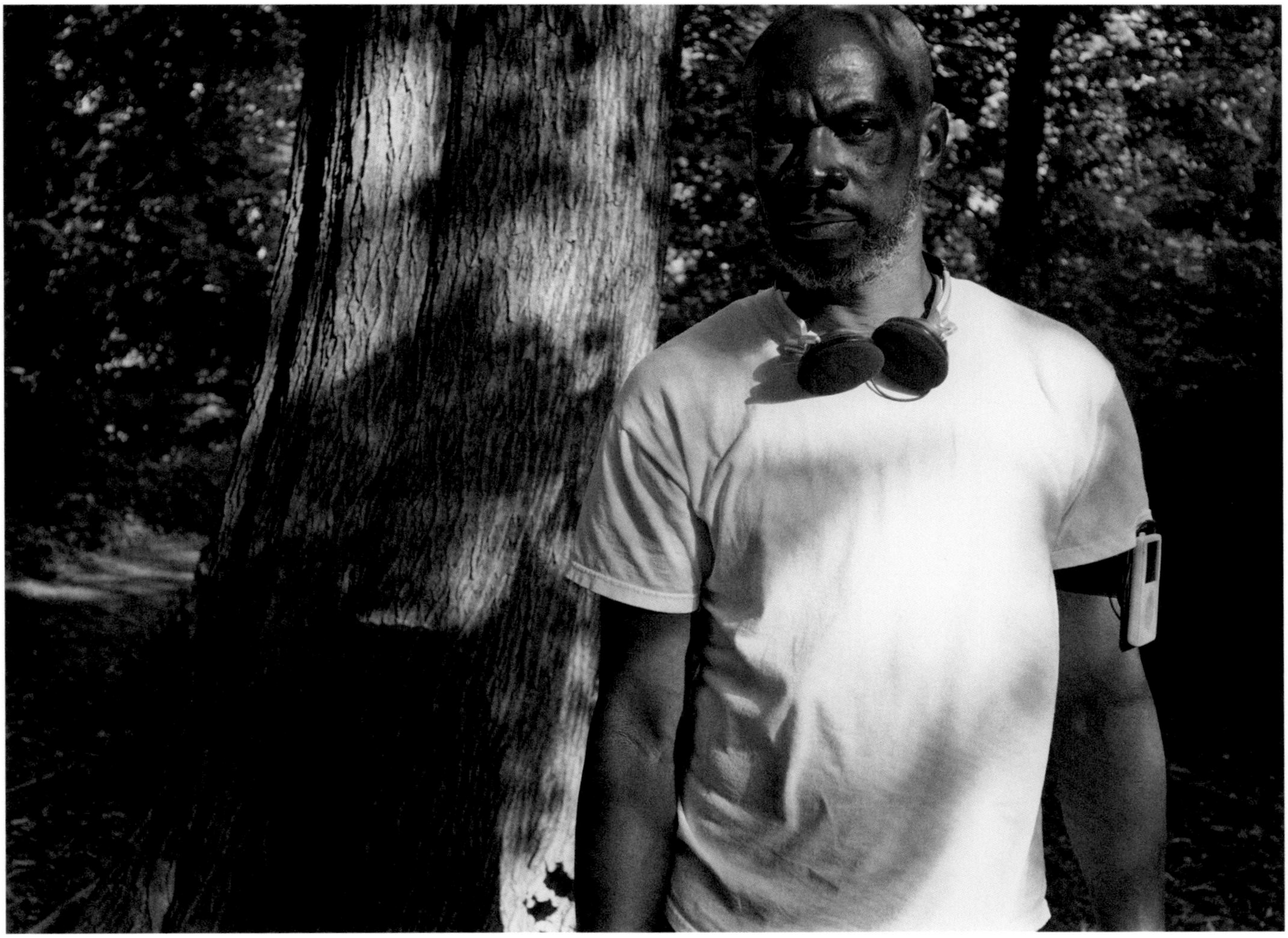

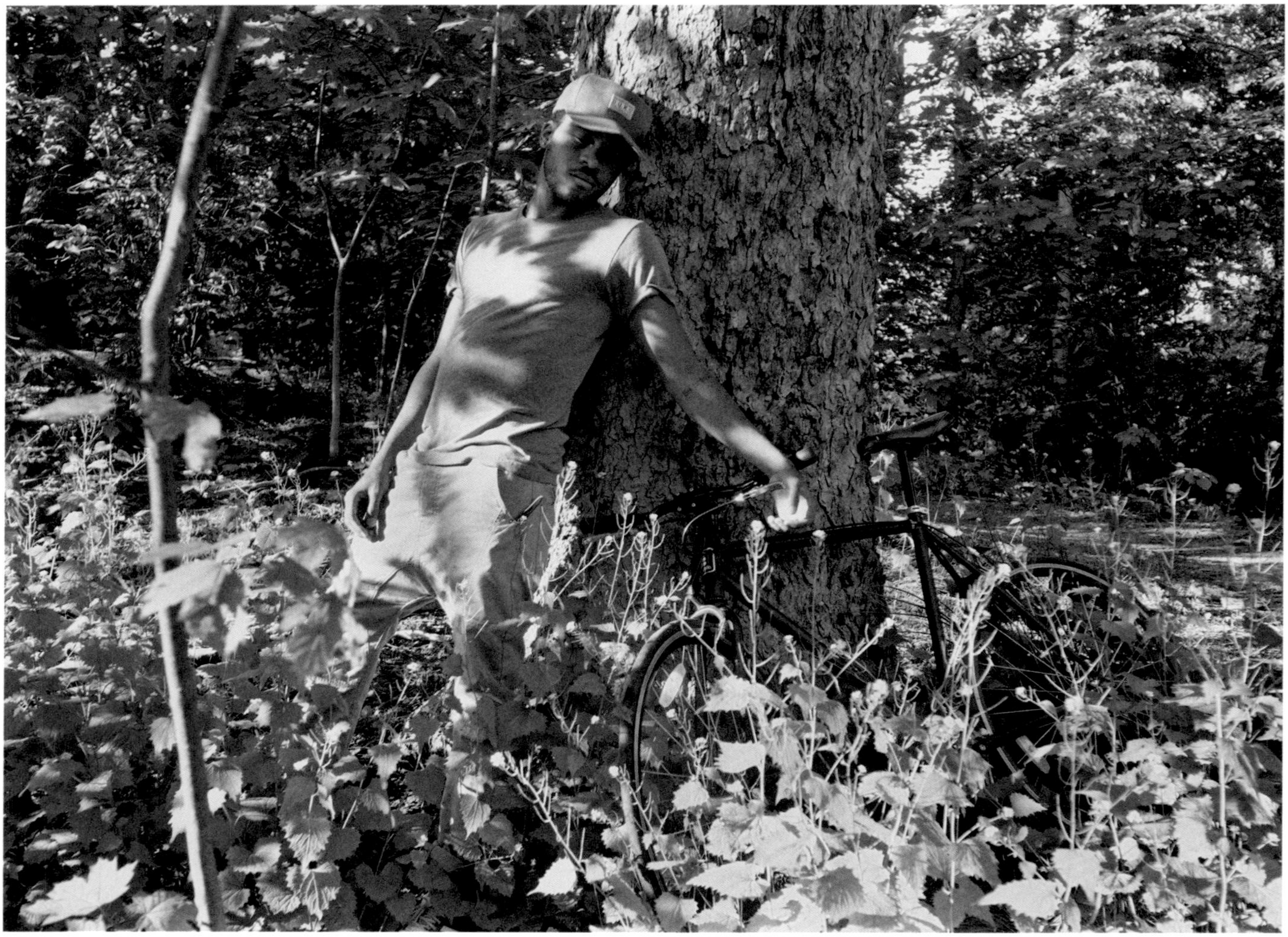

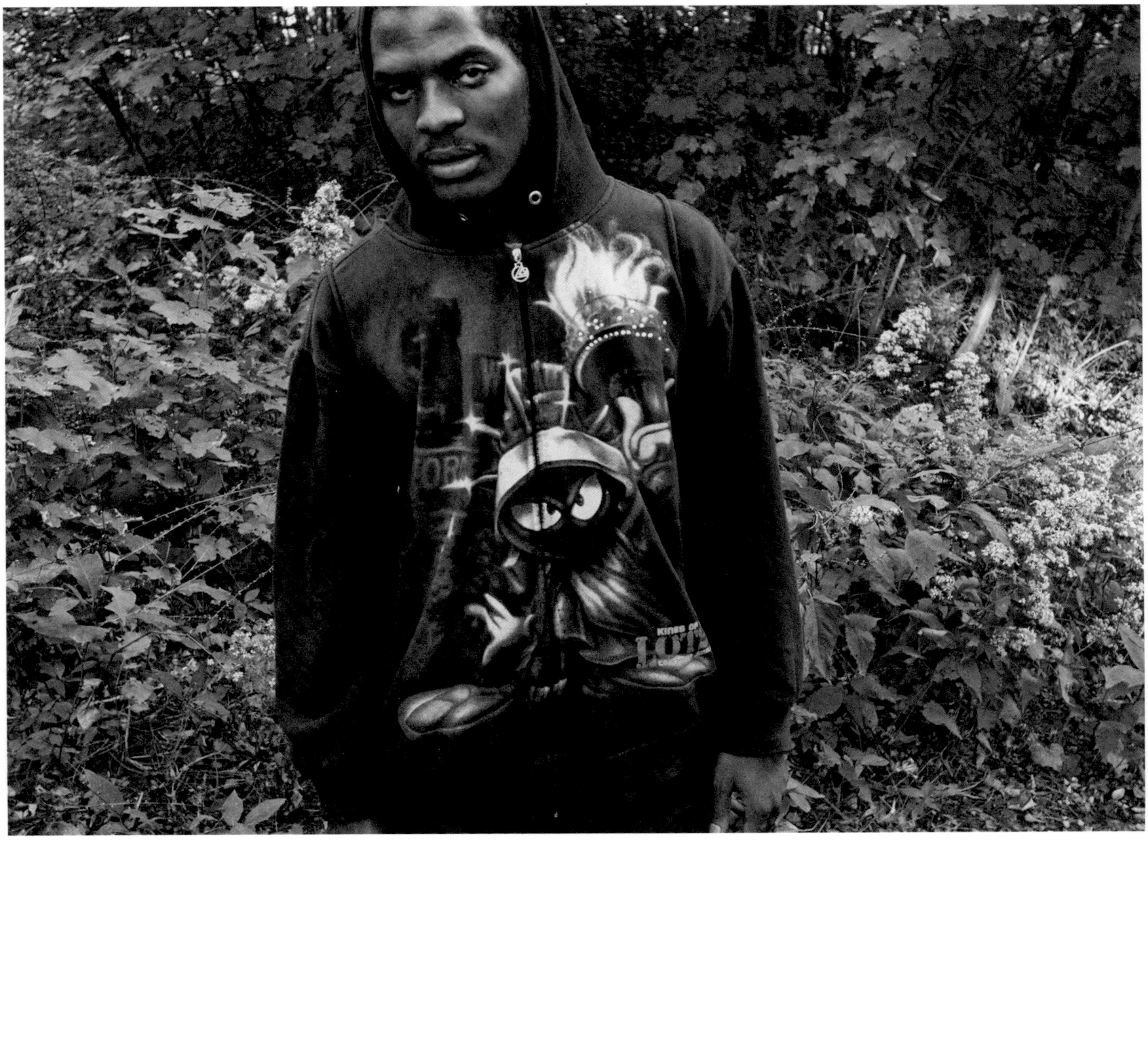
Kings of

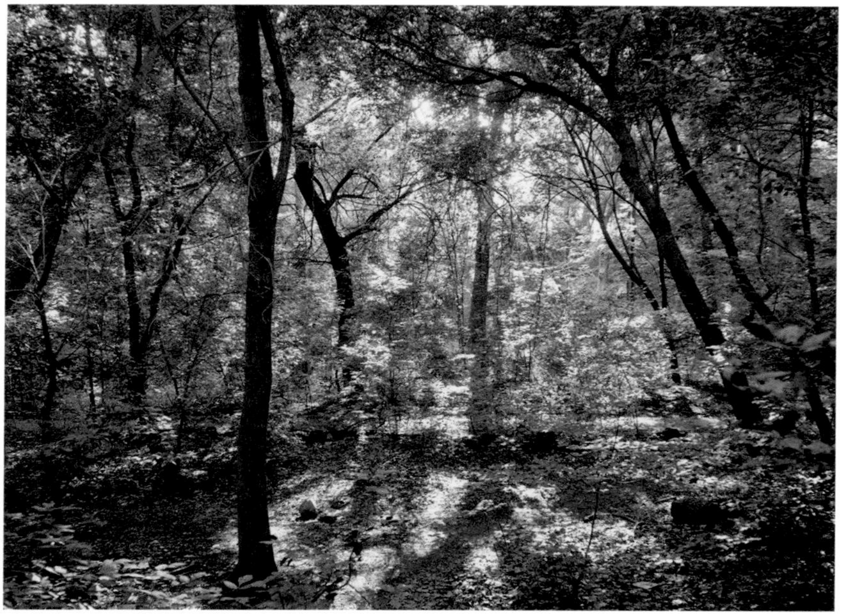

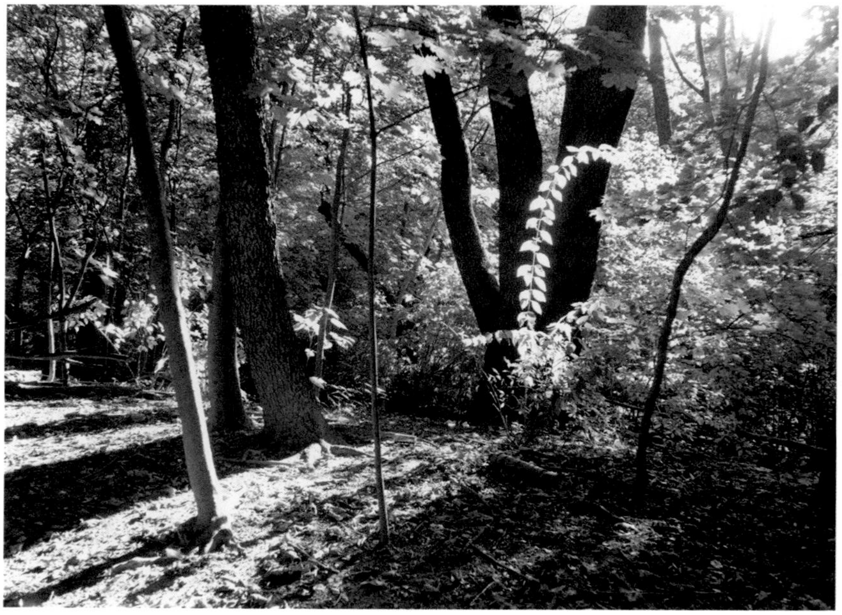

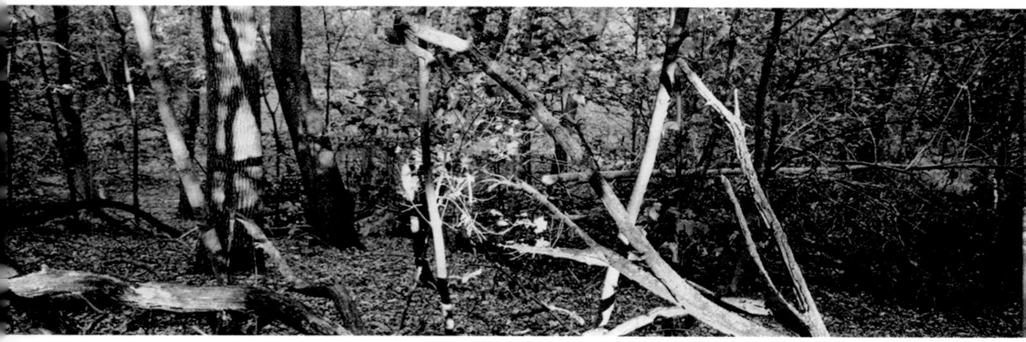

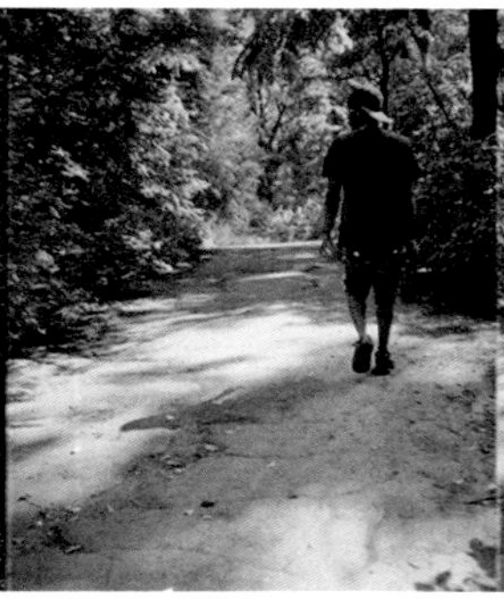

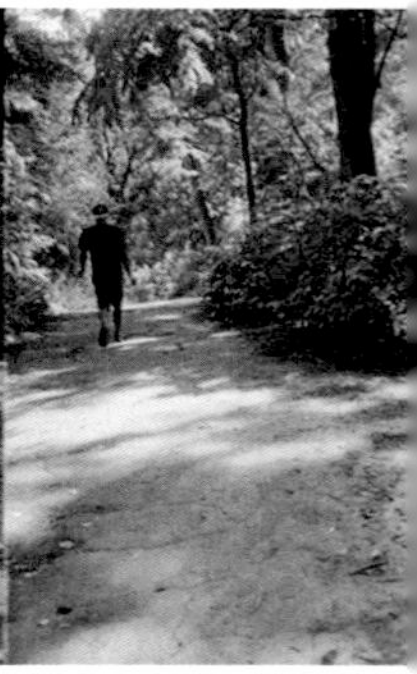

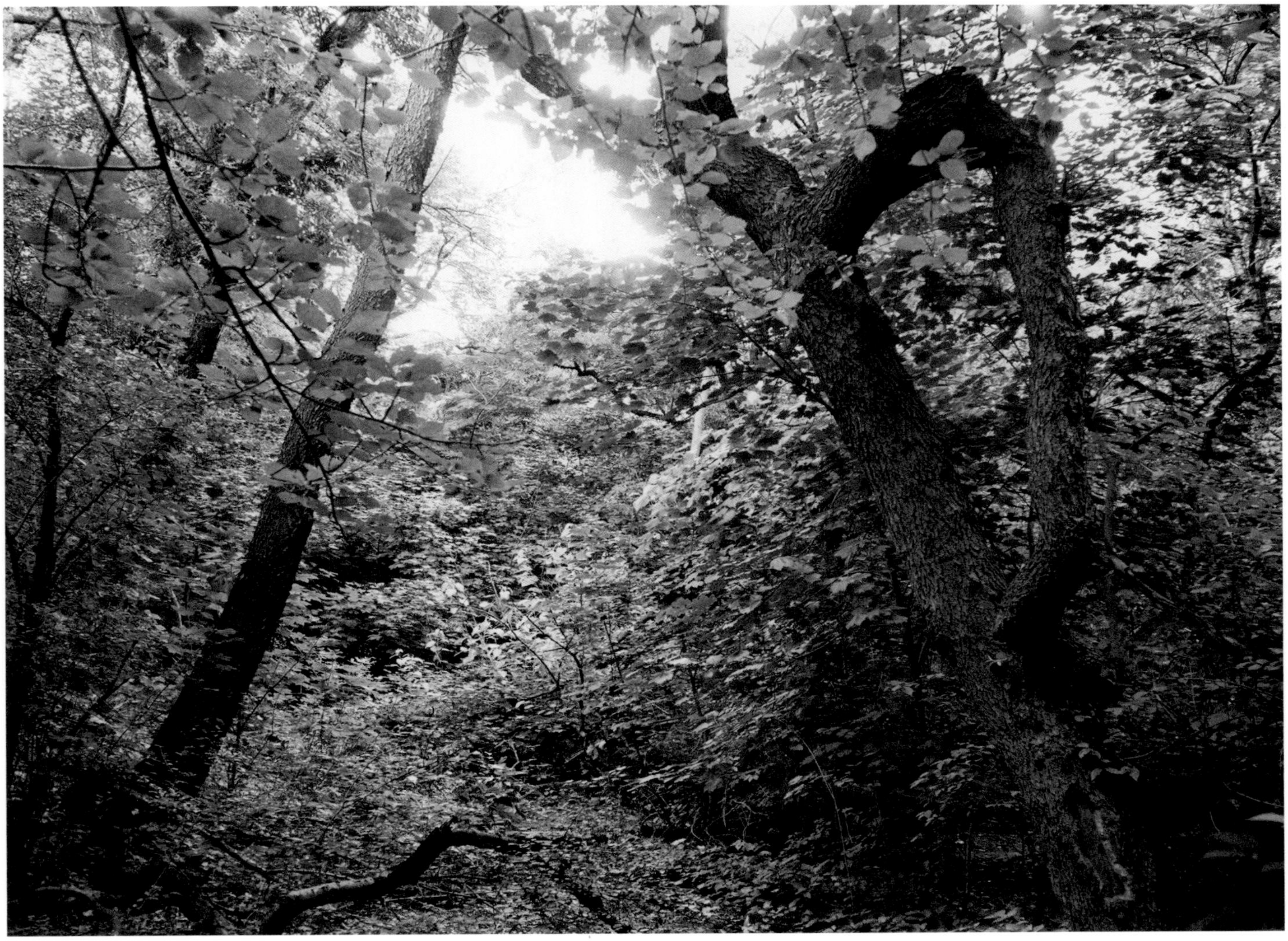

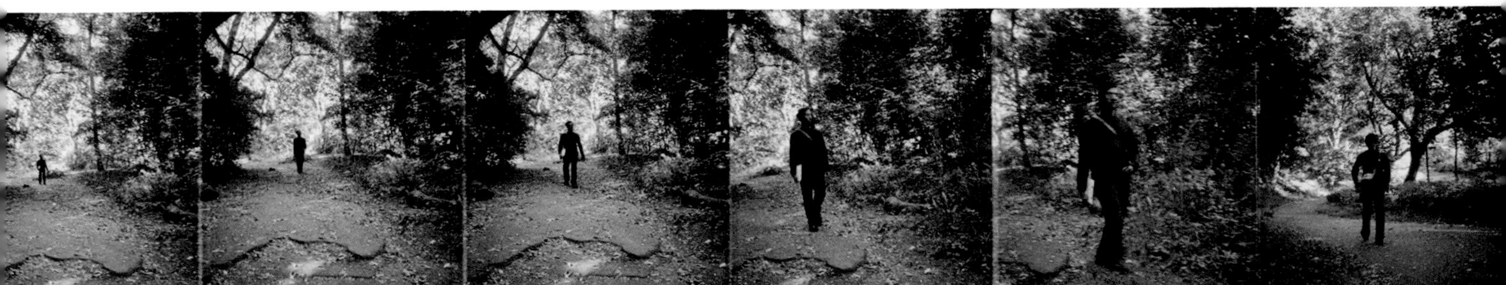

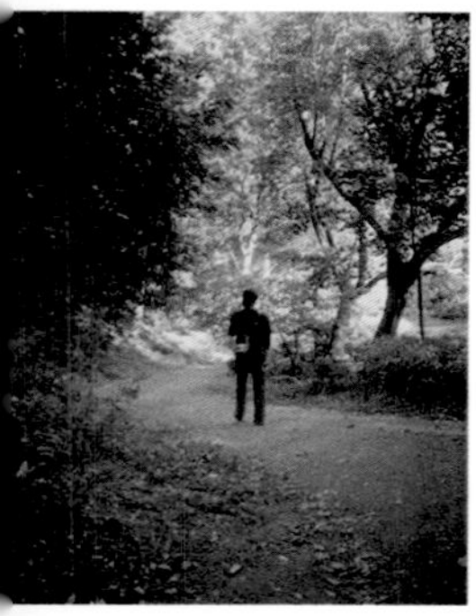

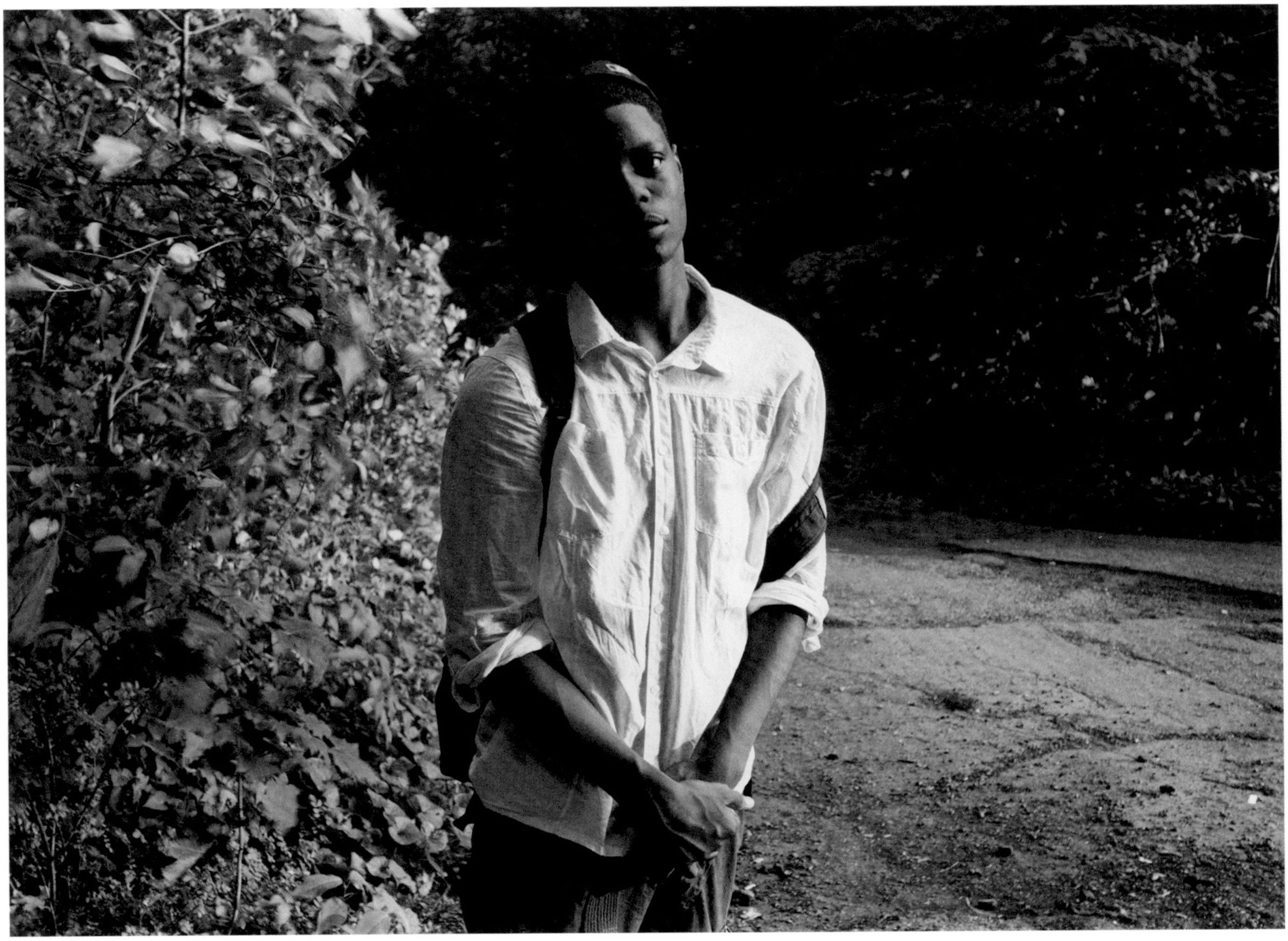

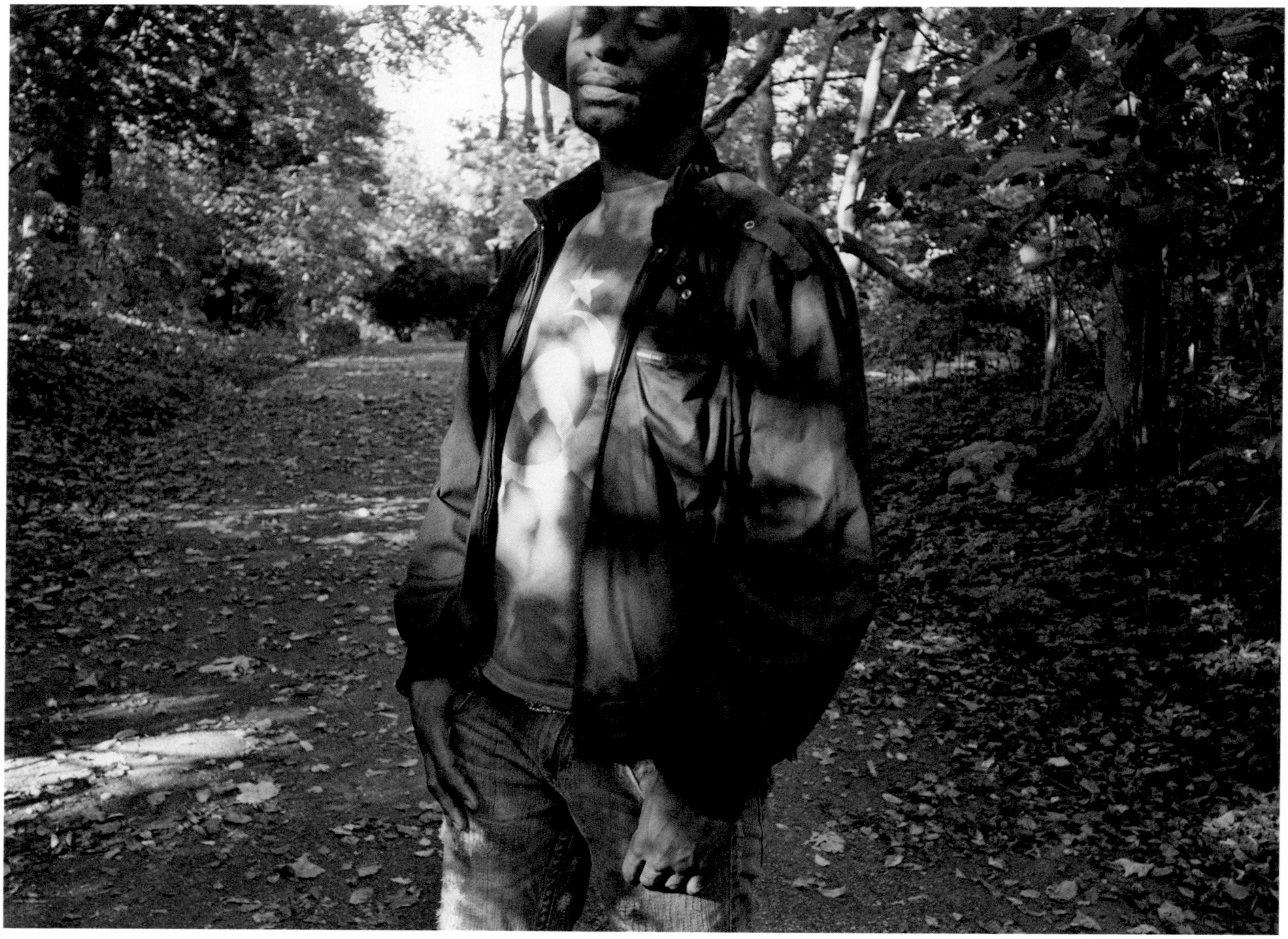

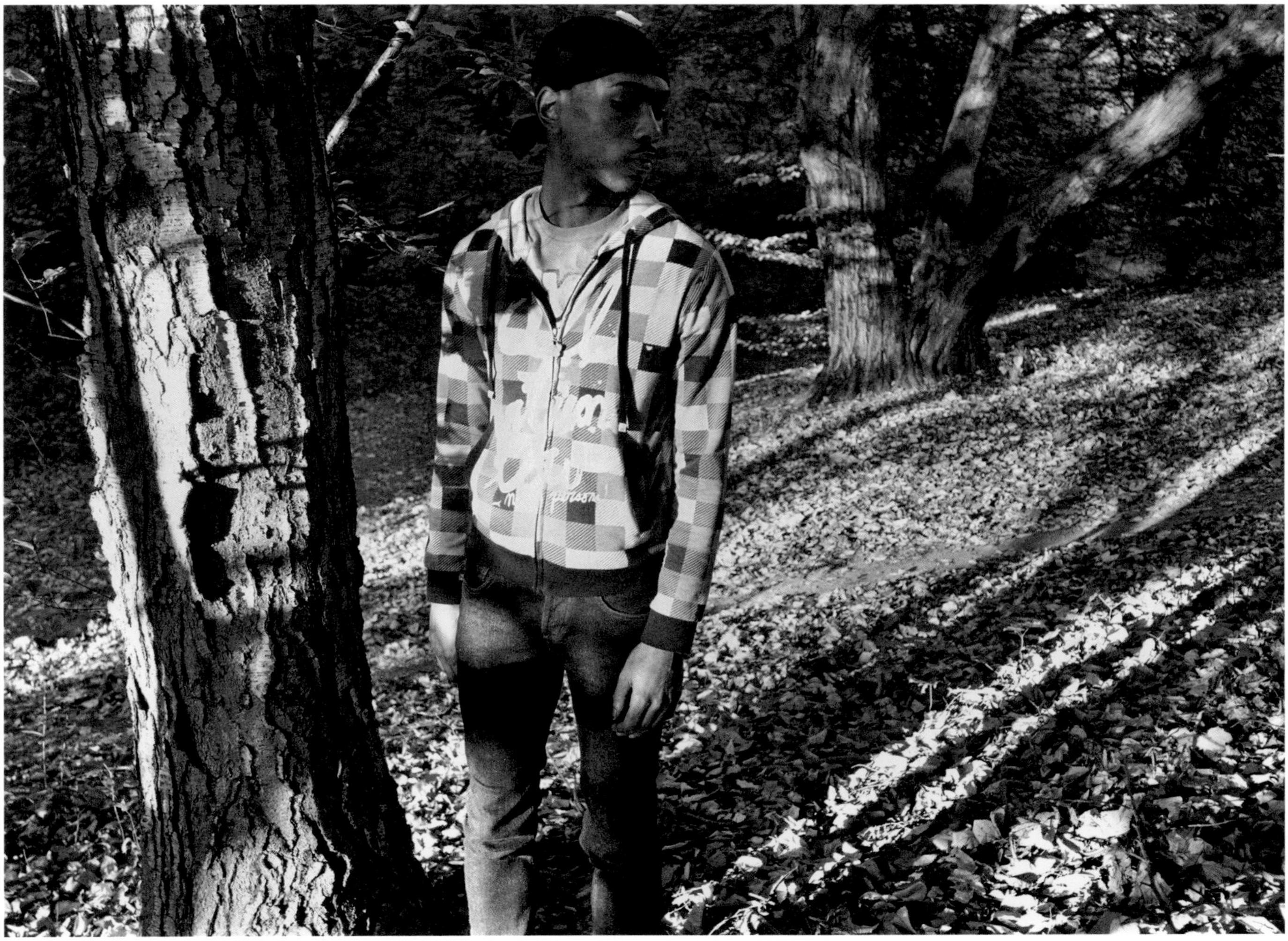

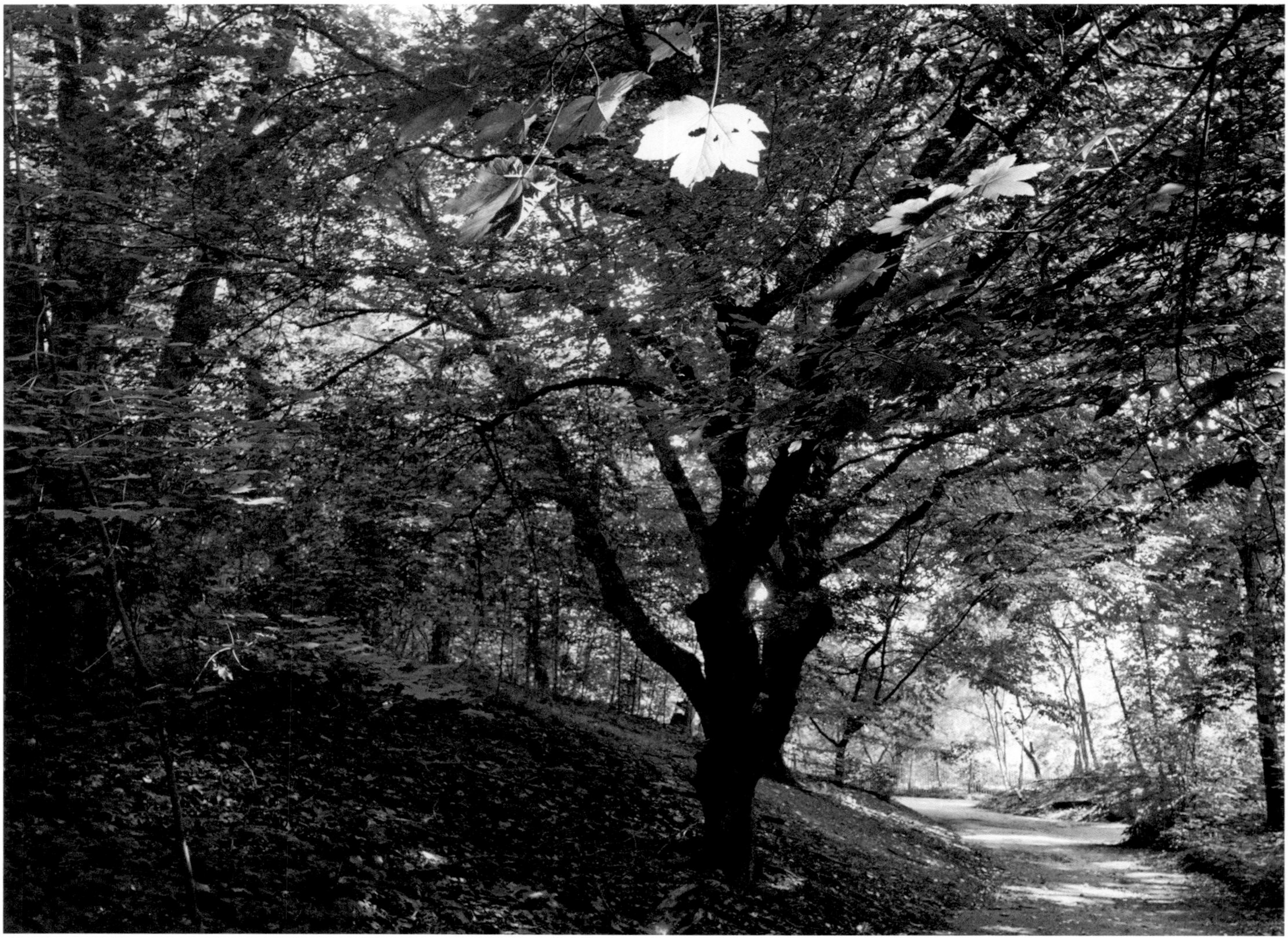

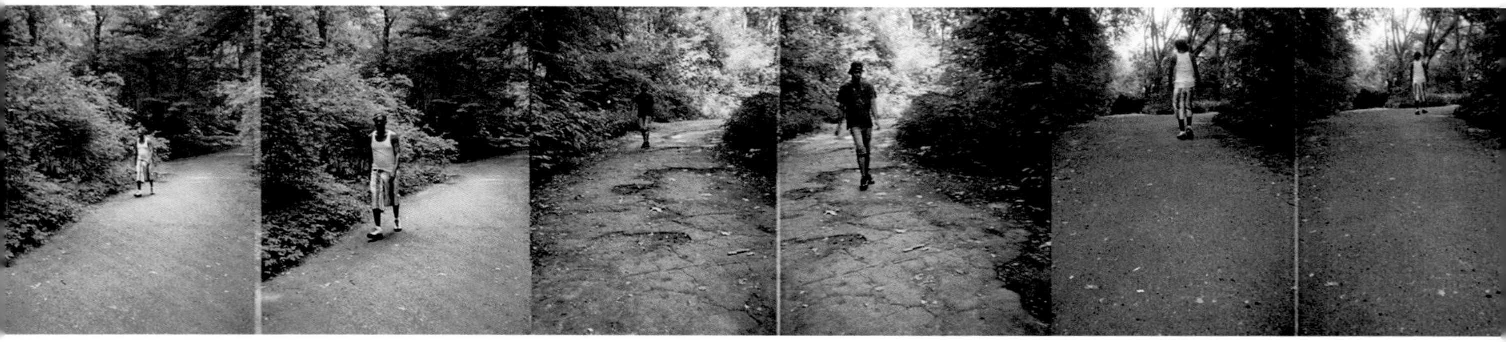

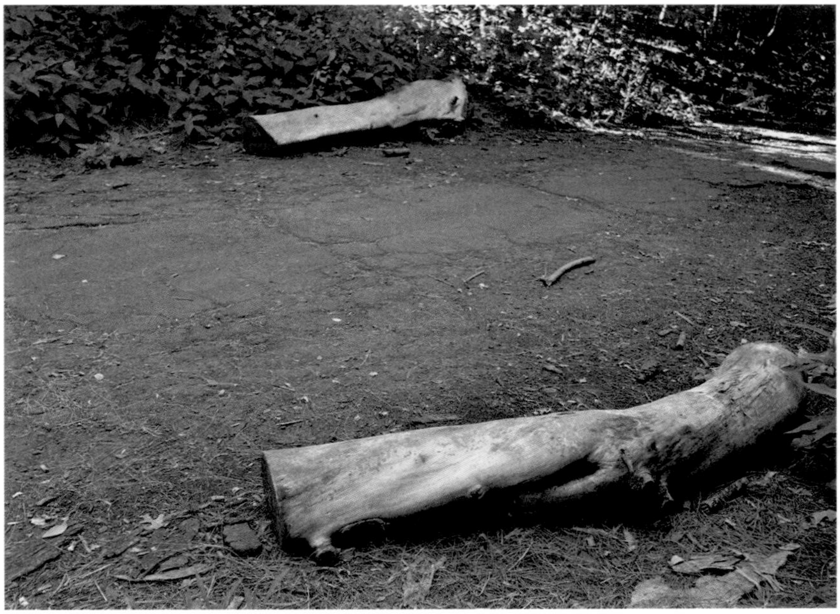

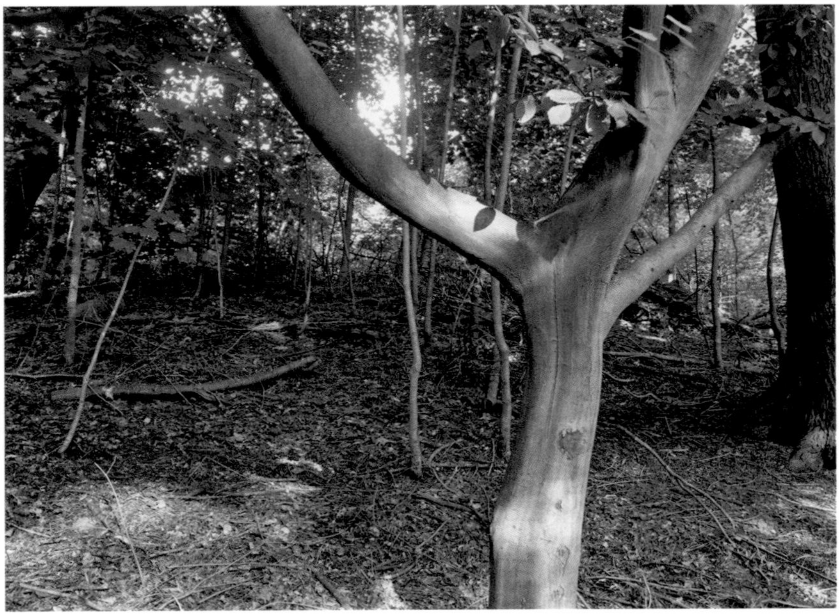

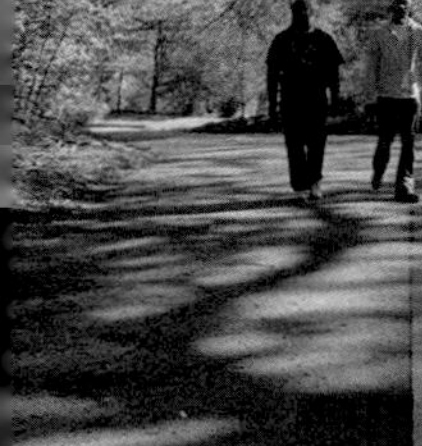

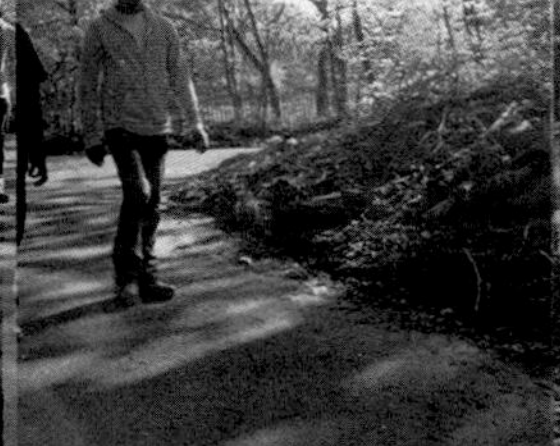

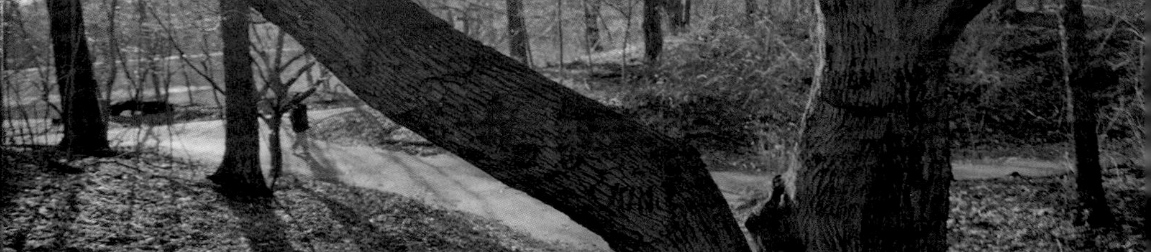

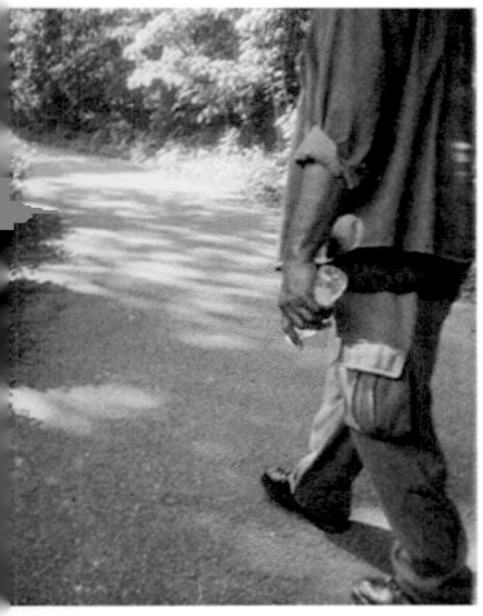

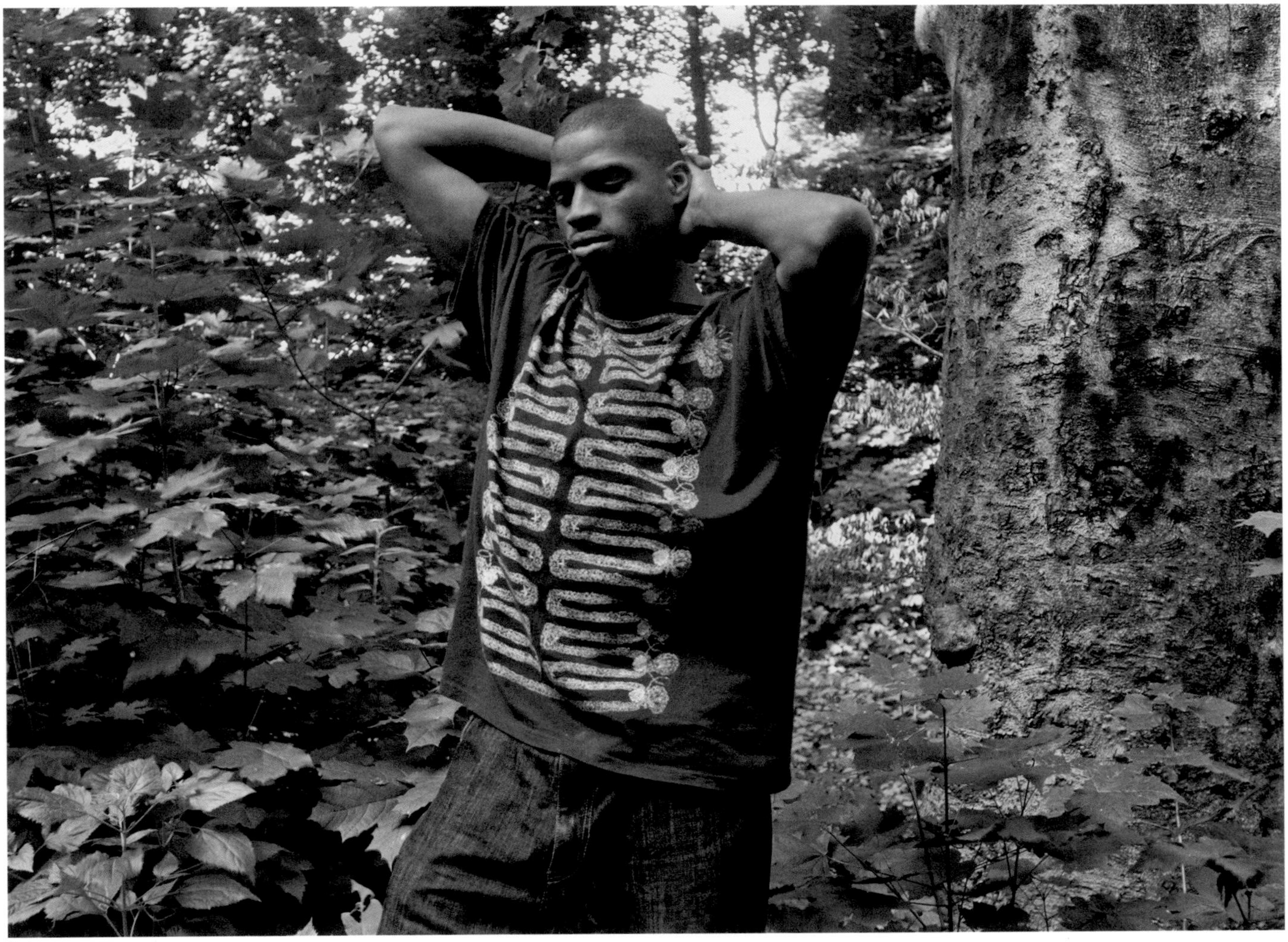

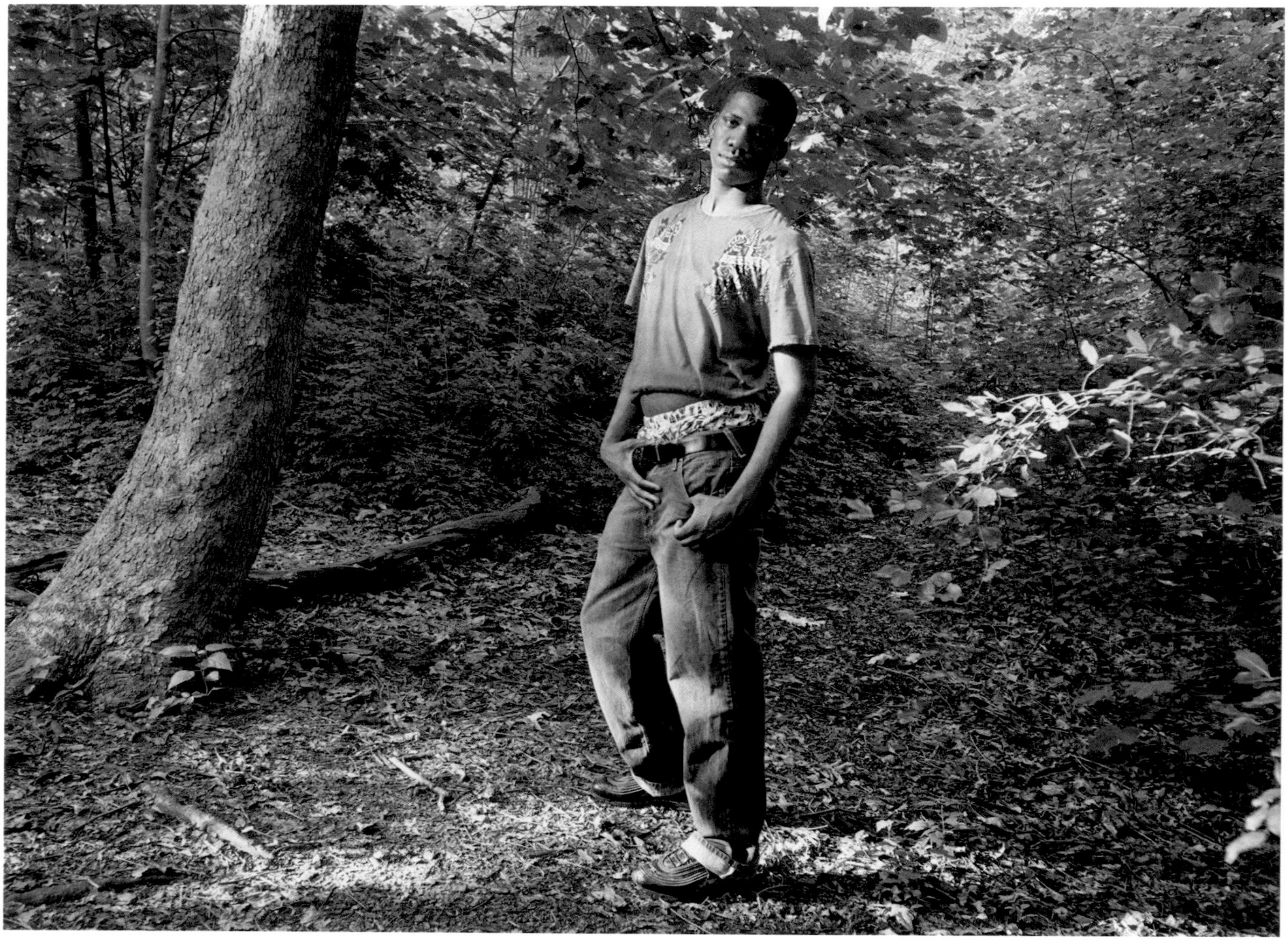

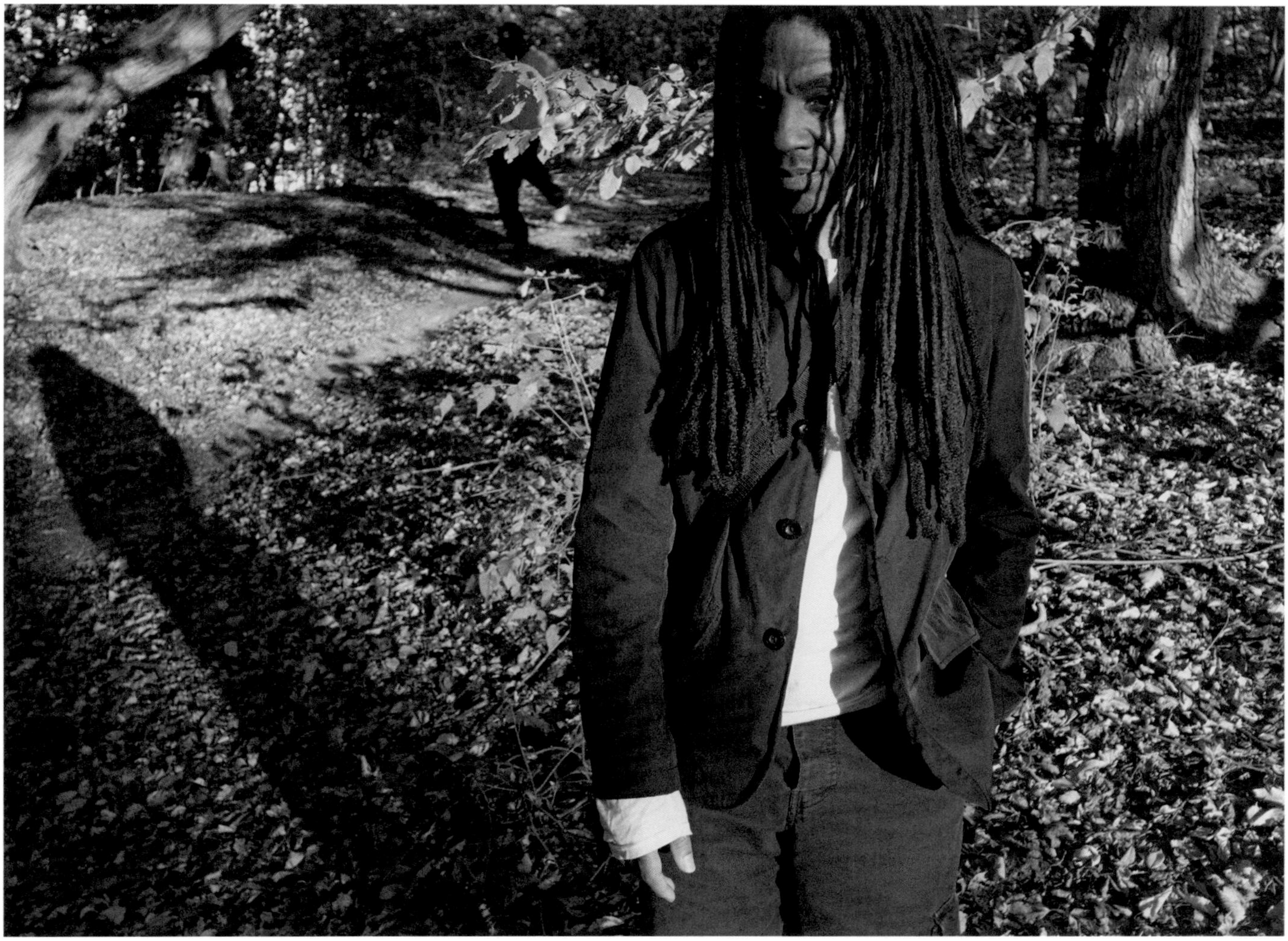

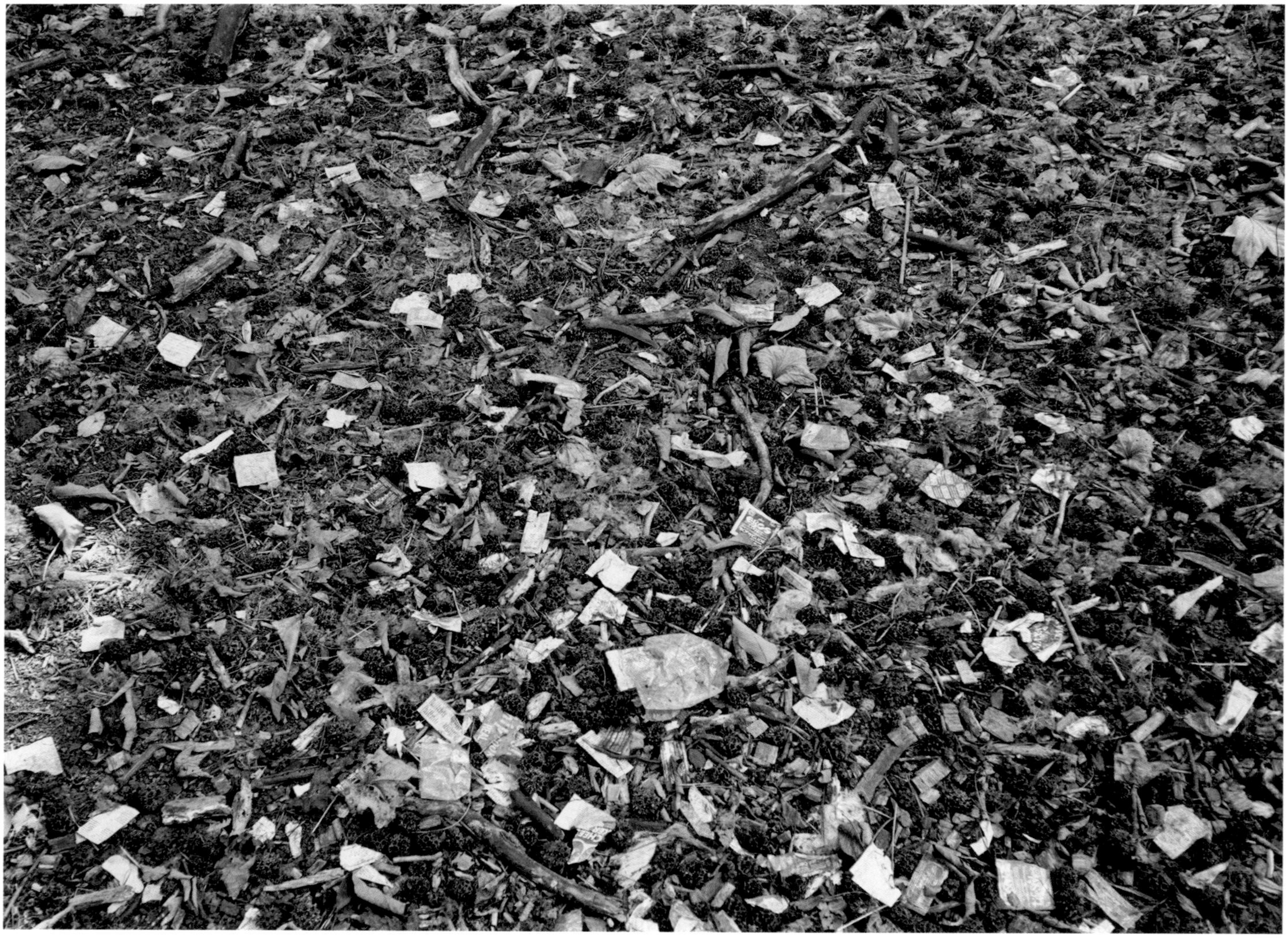

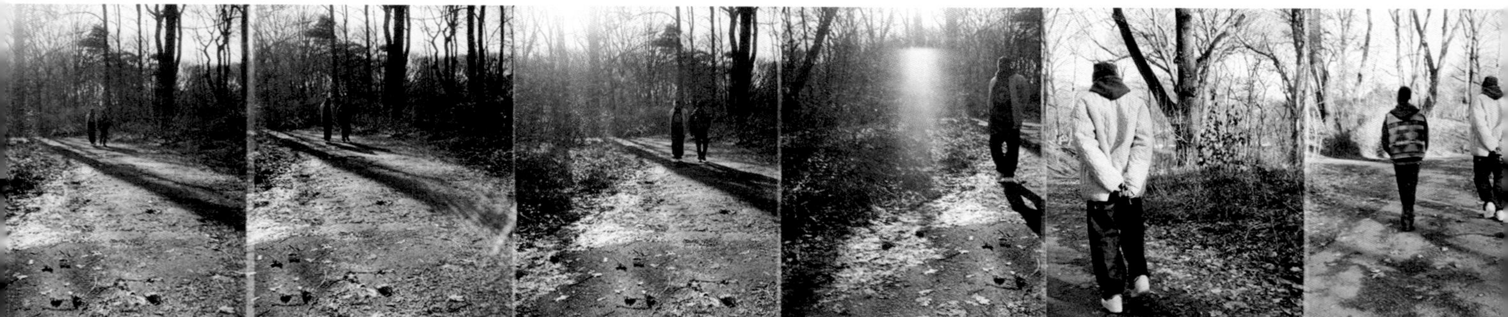

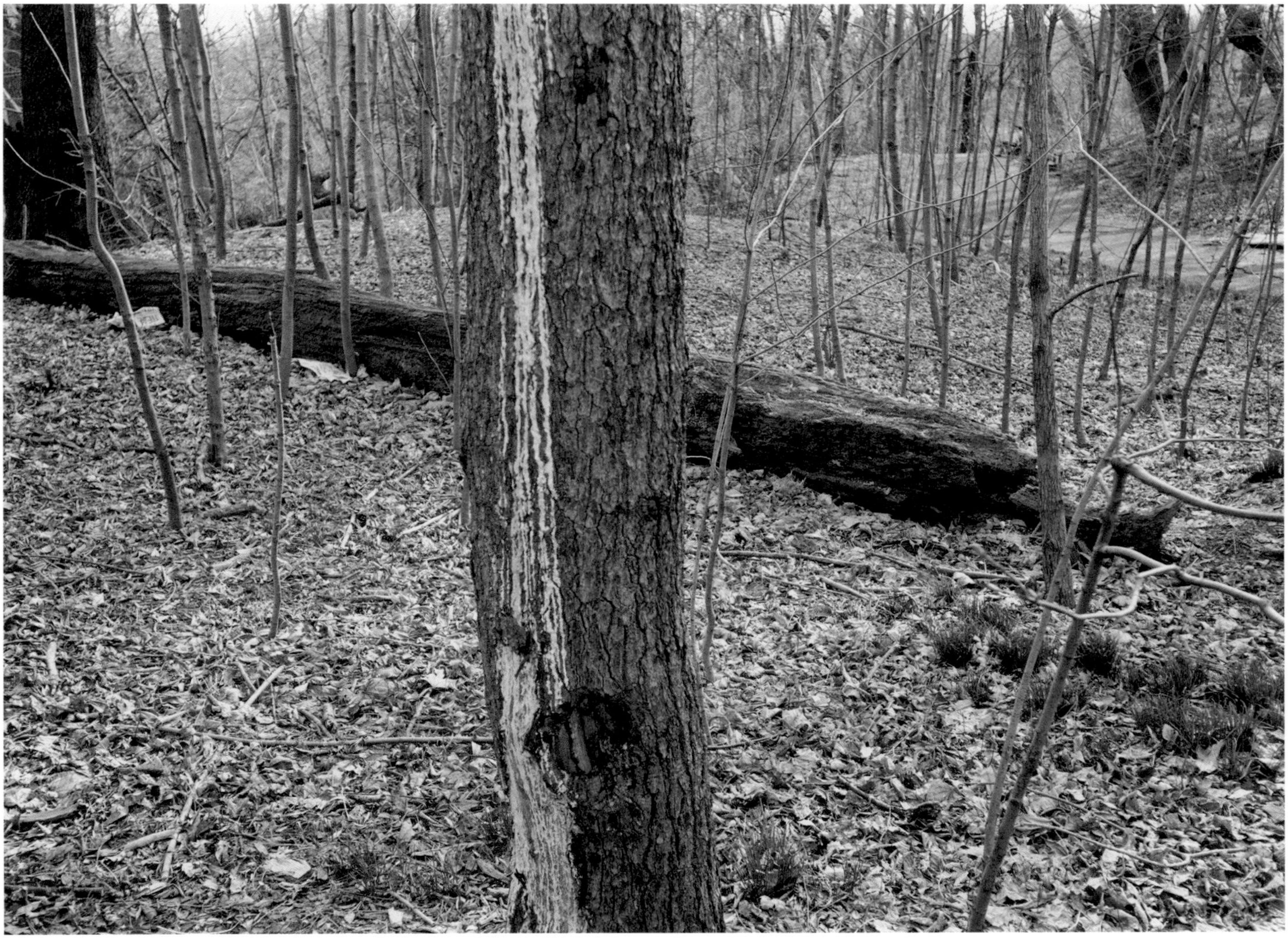

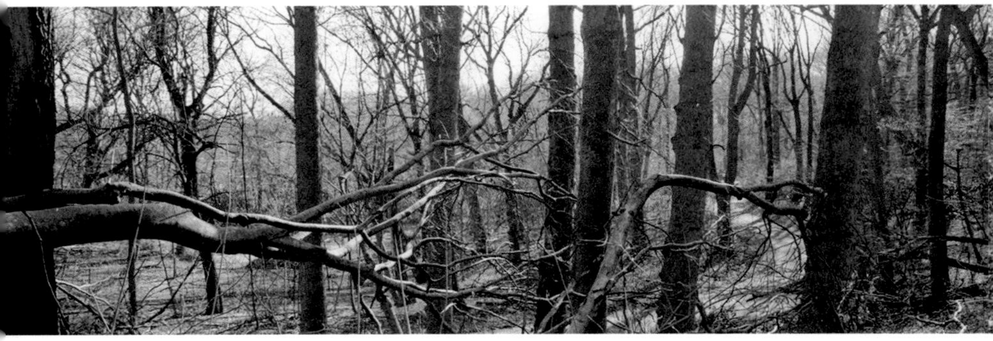

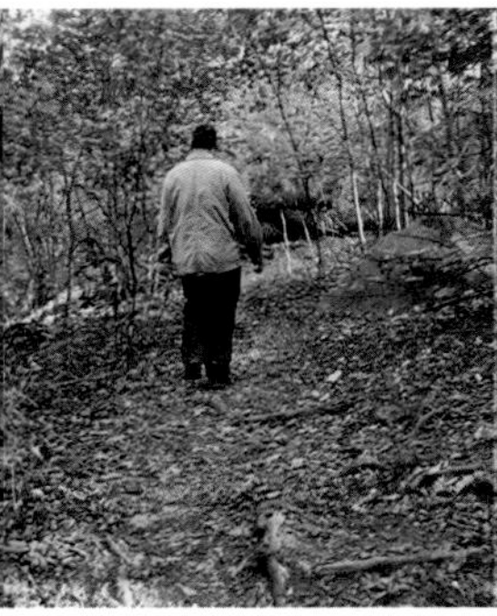

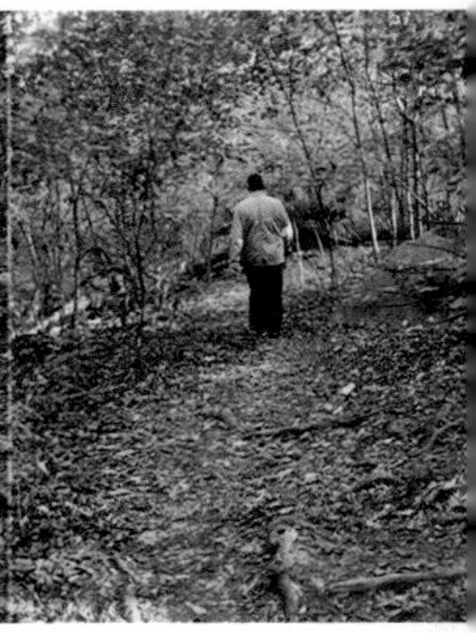

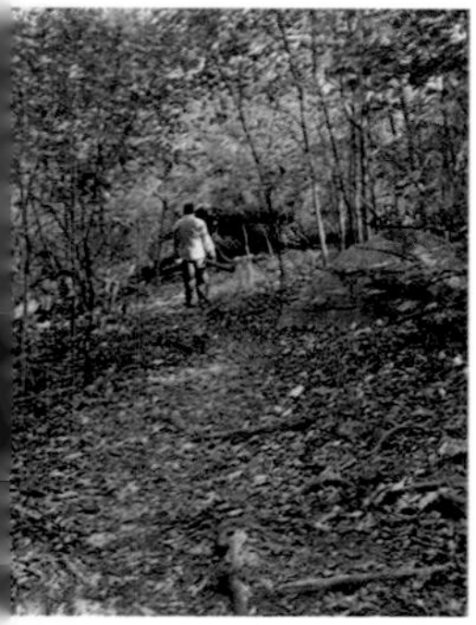

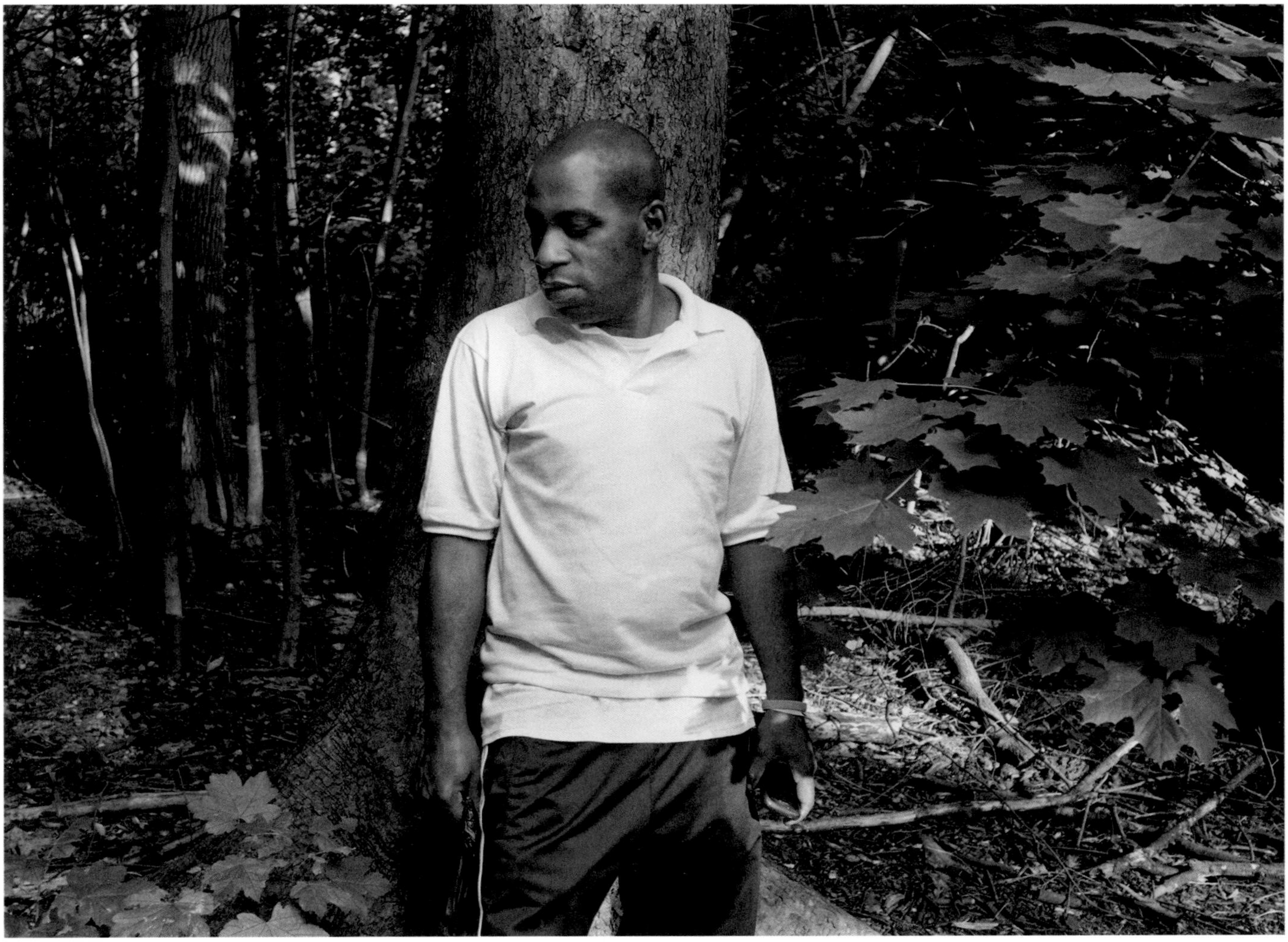

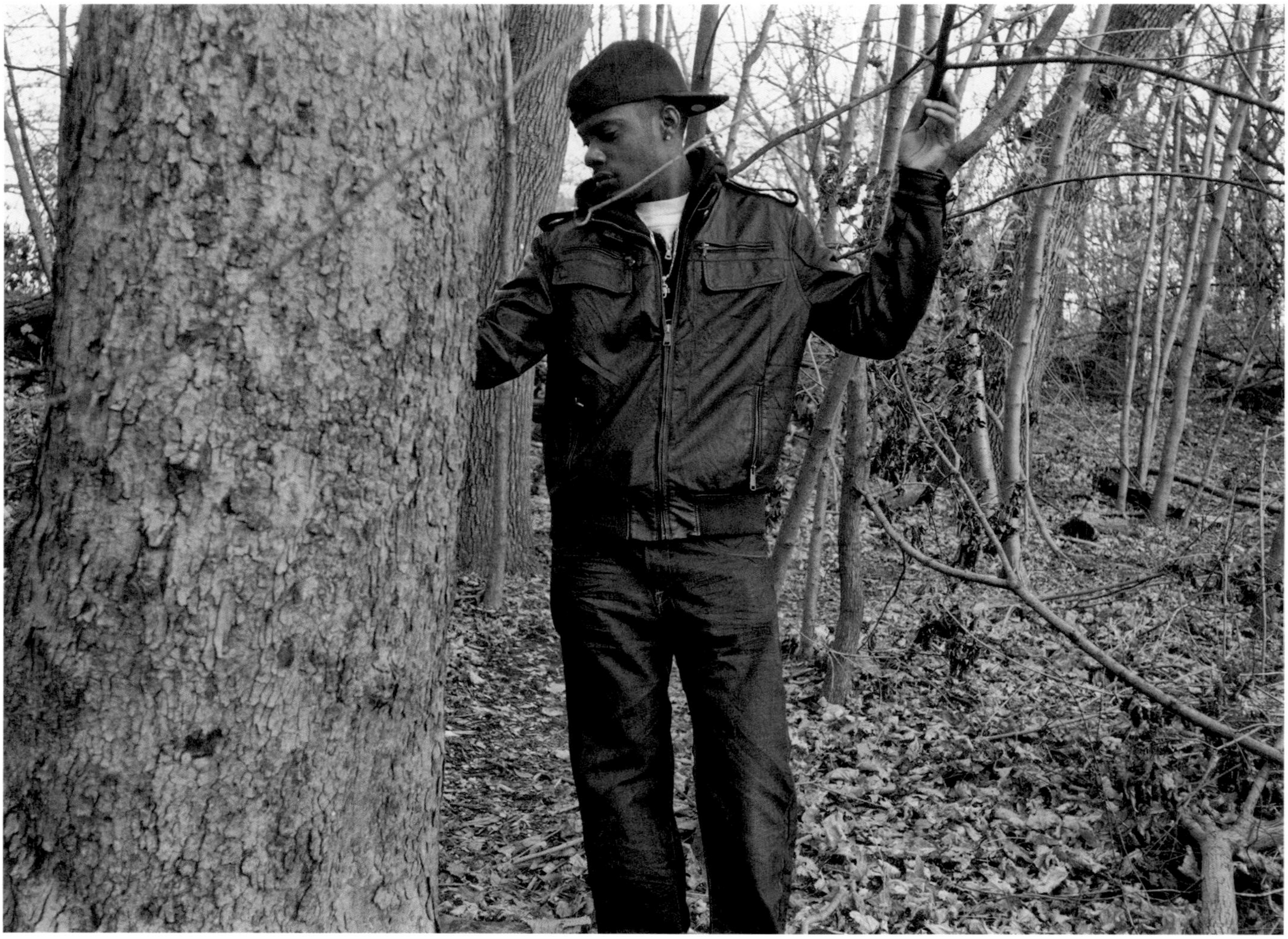

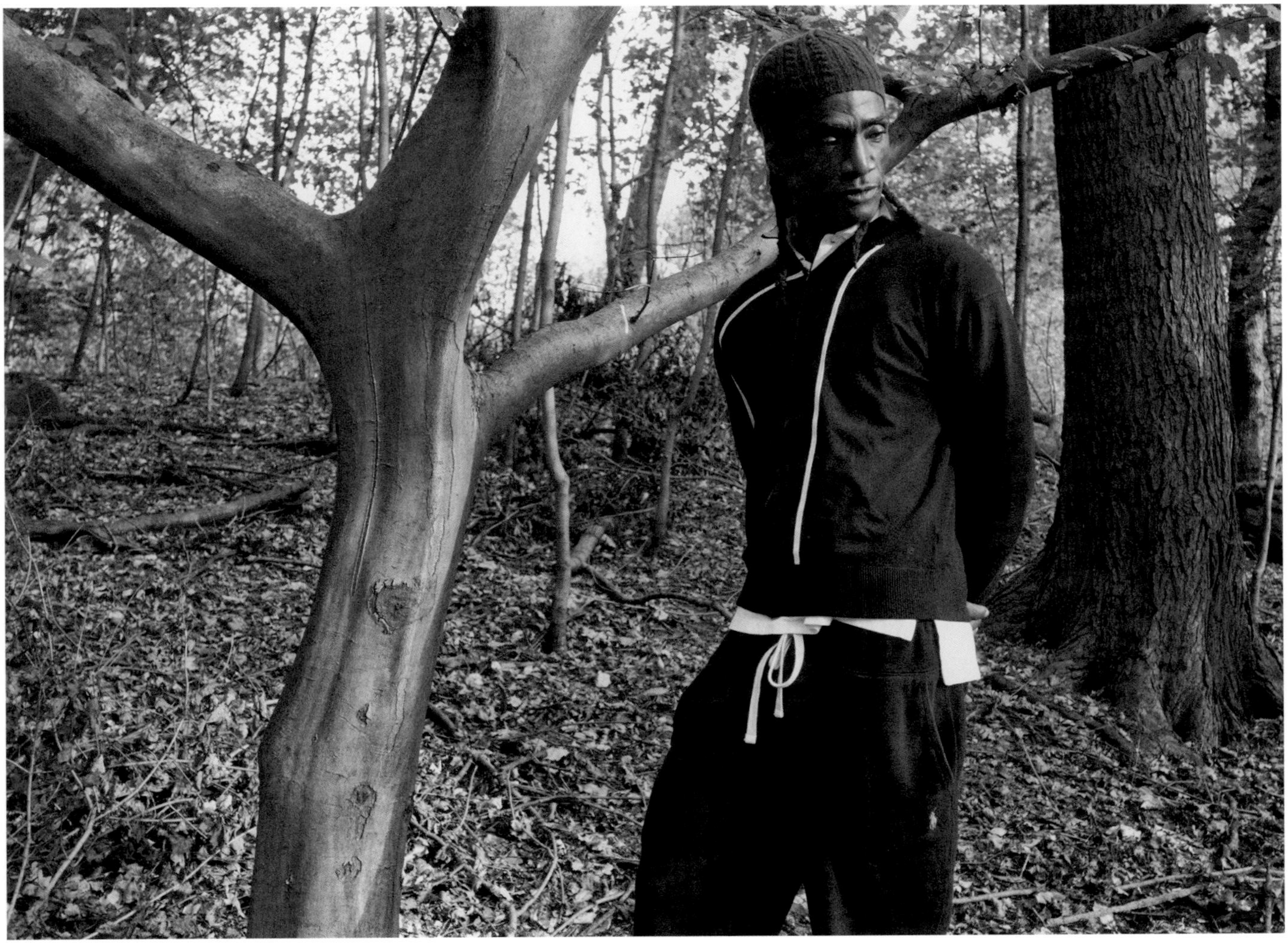

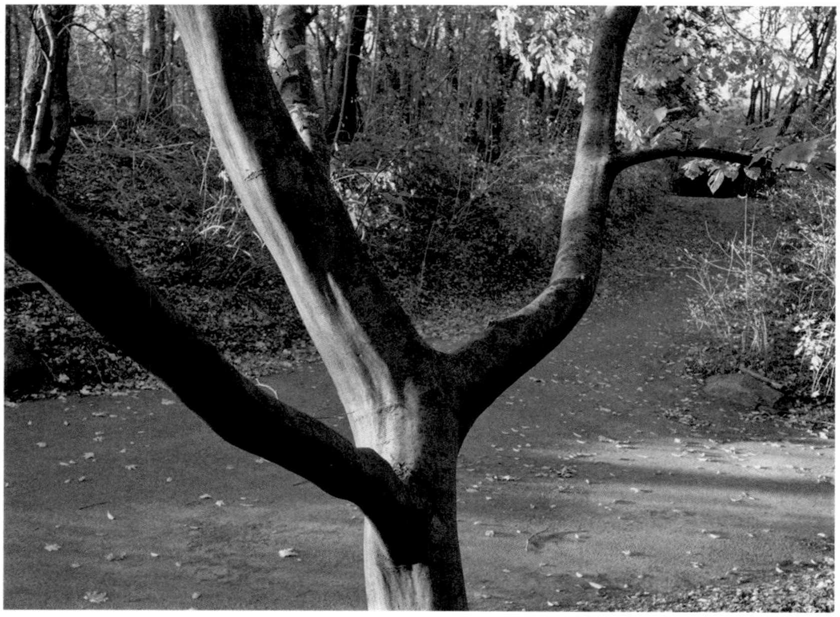

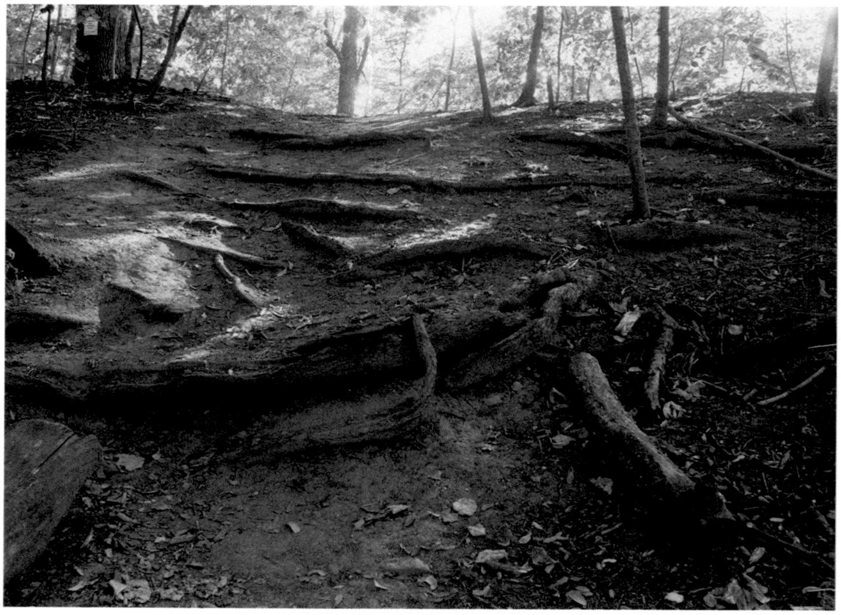

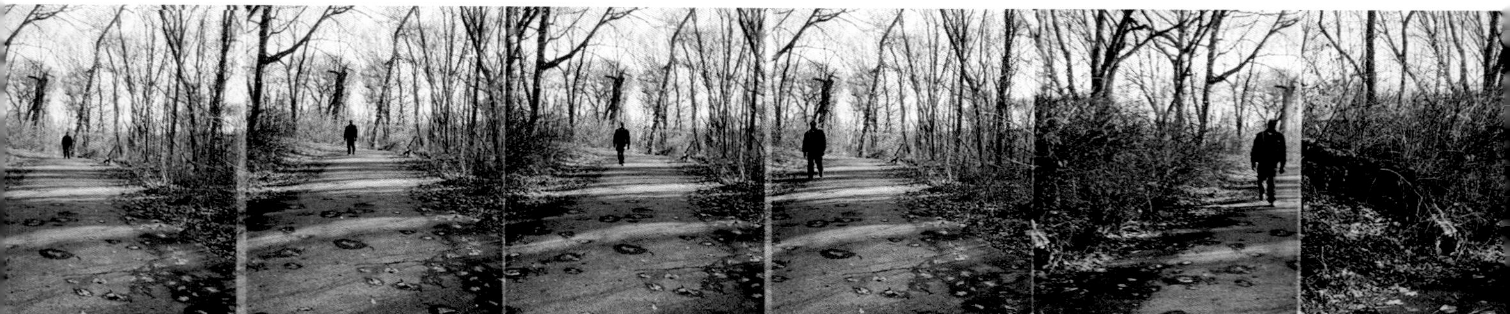

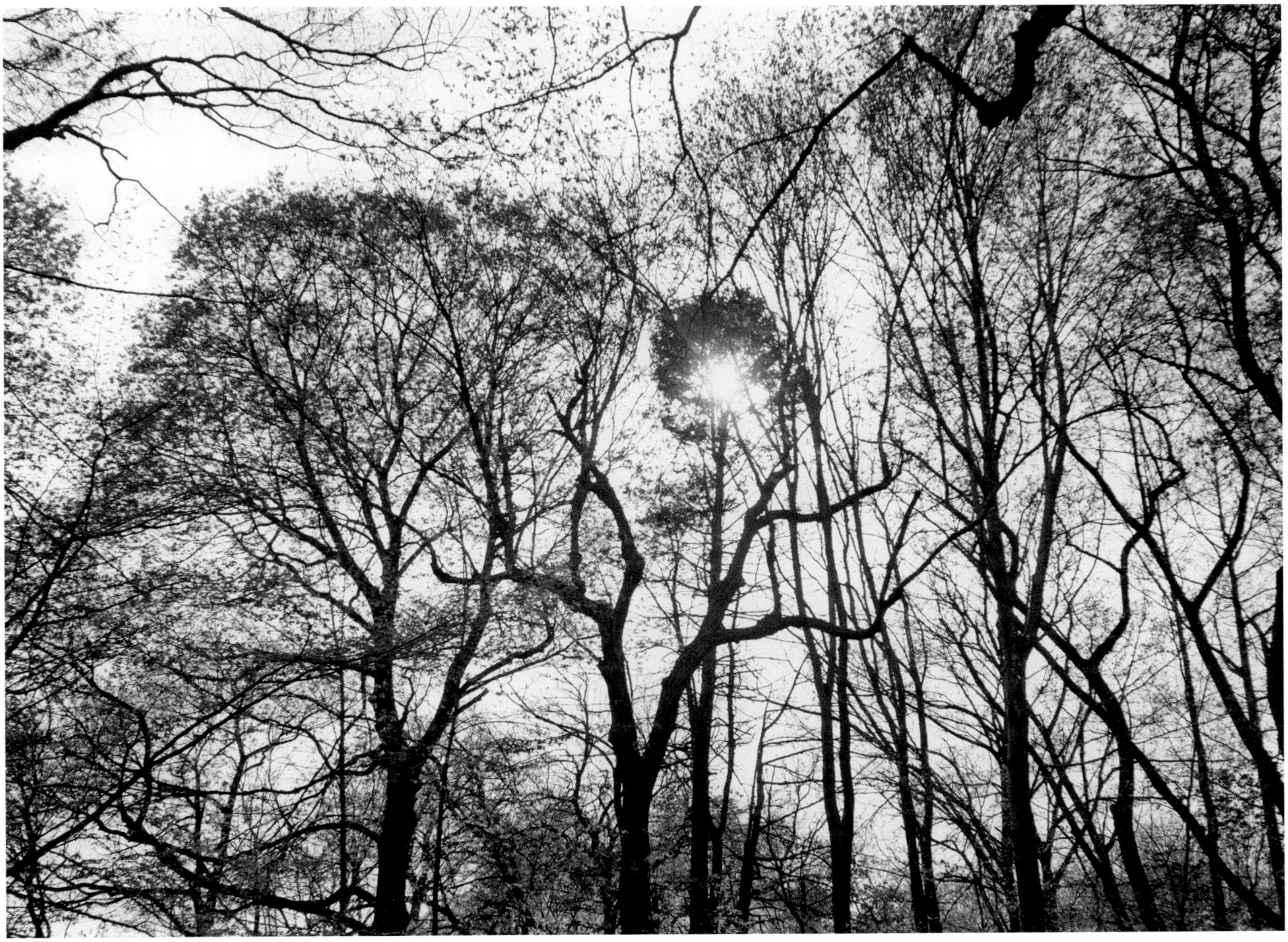

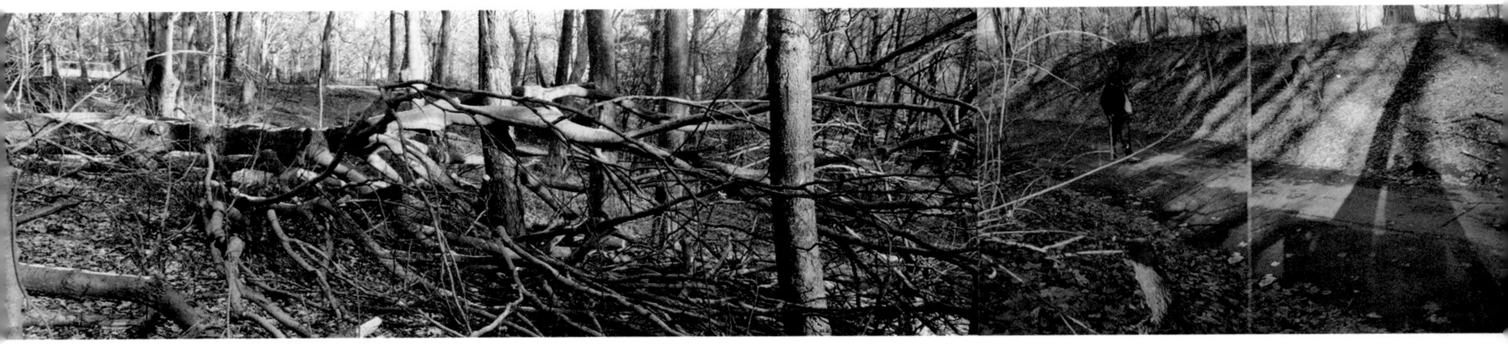

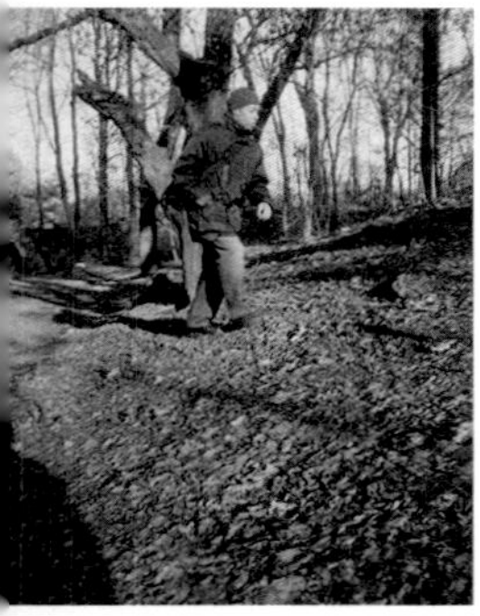

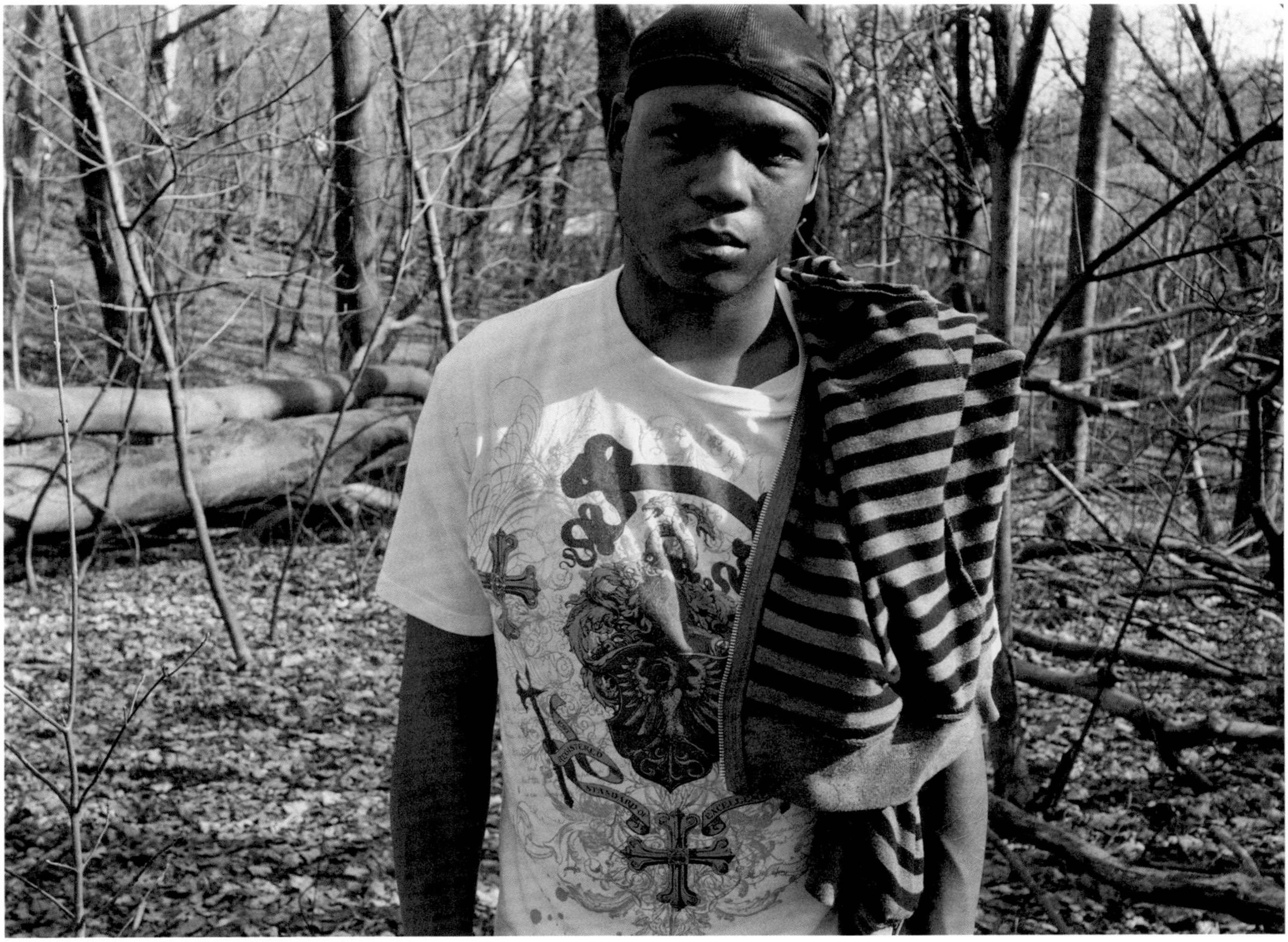

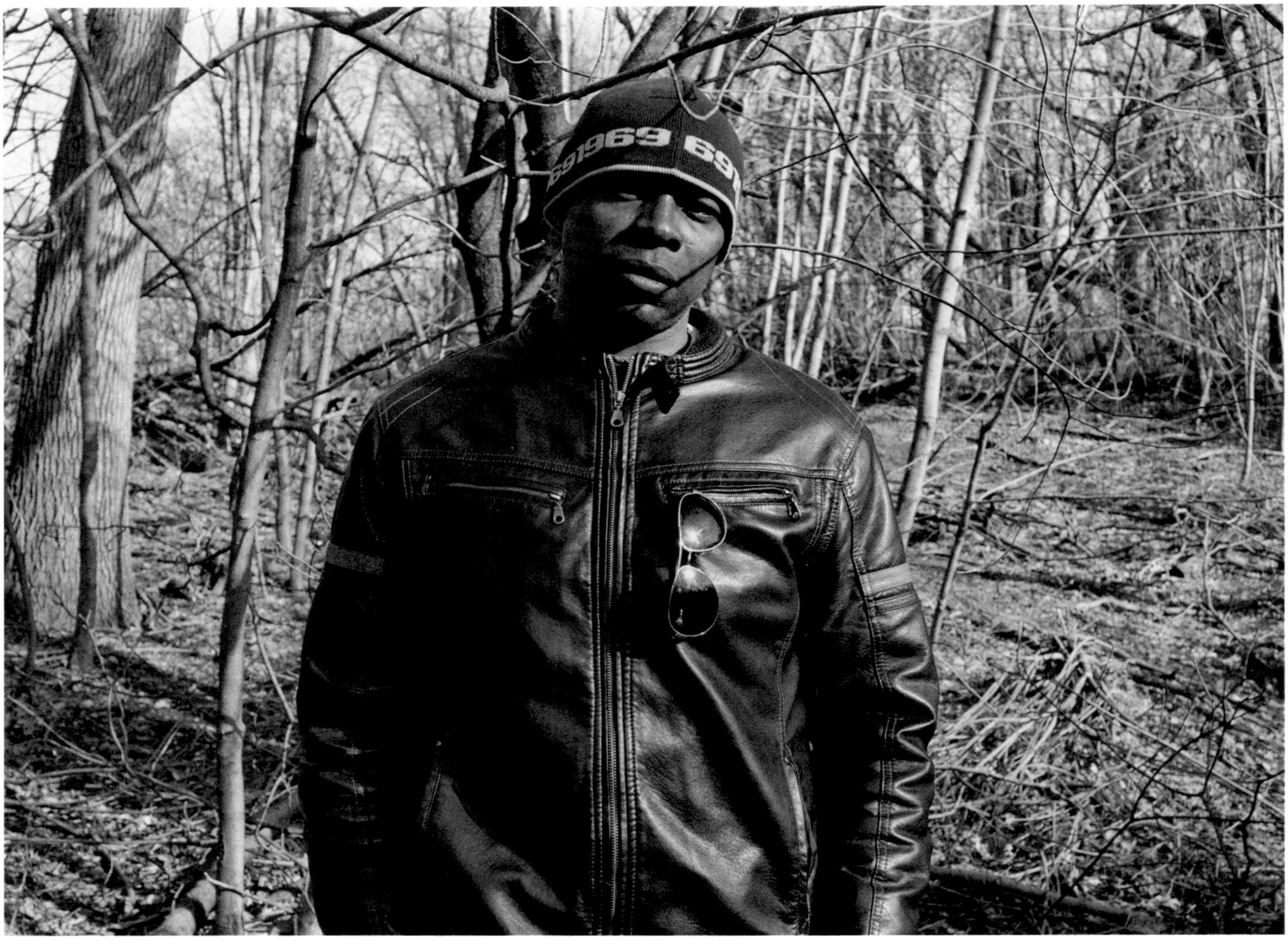

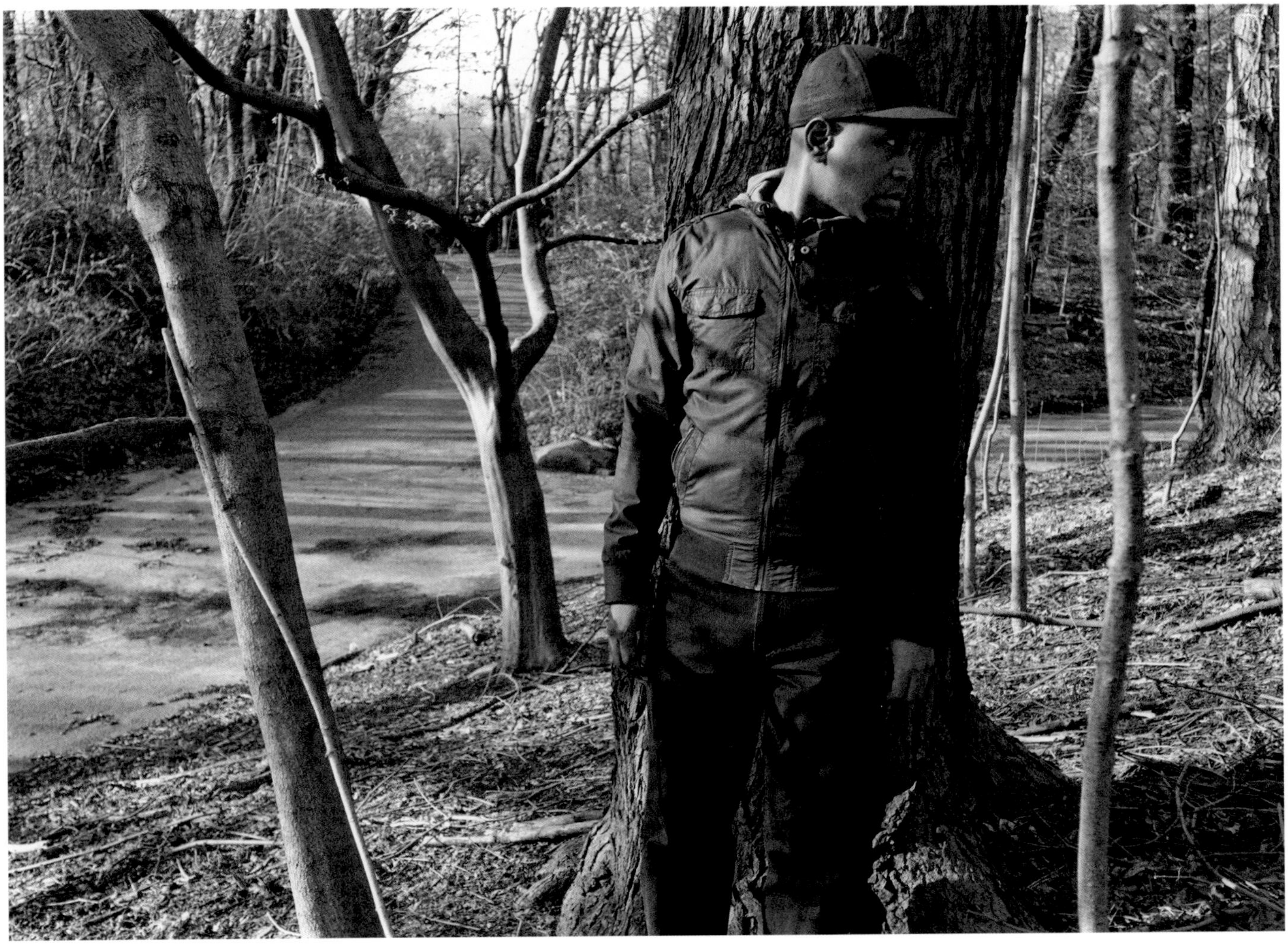

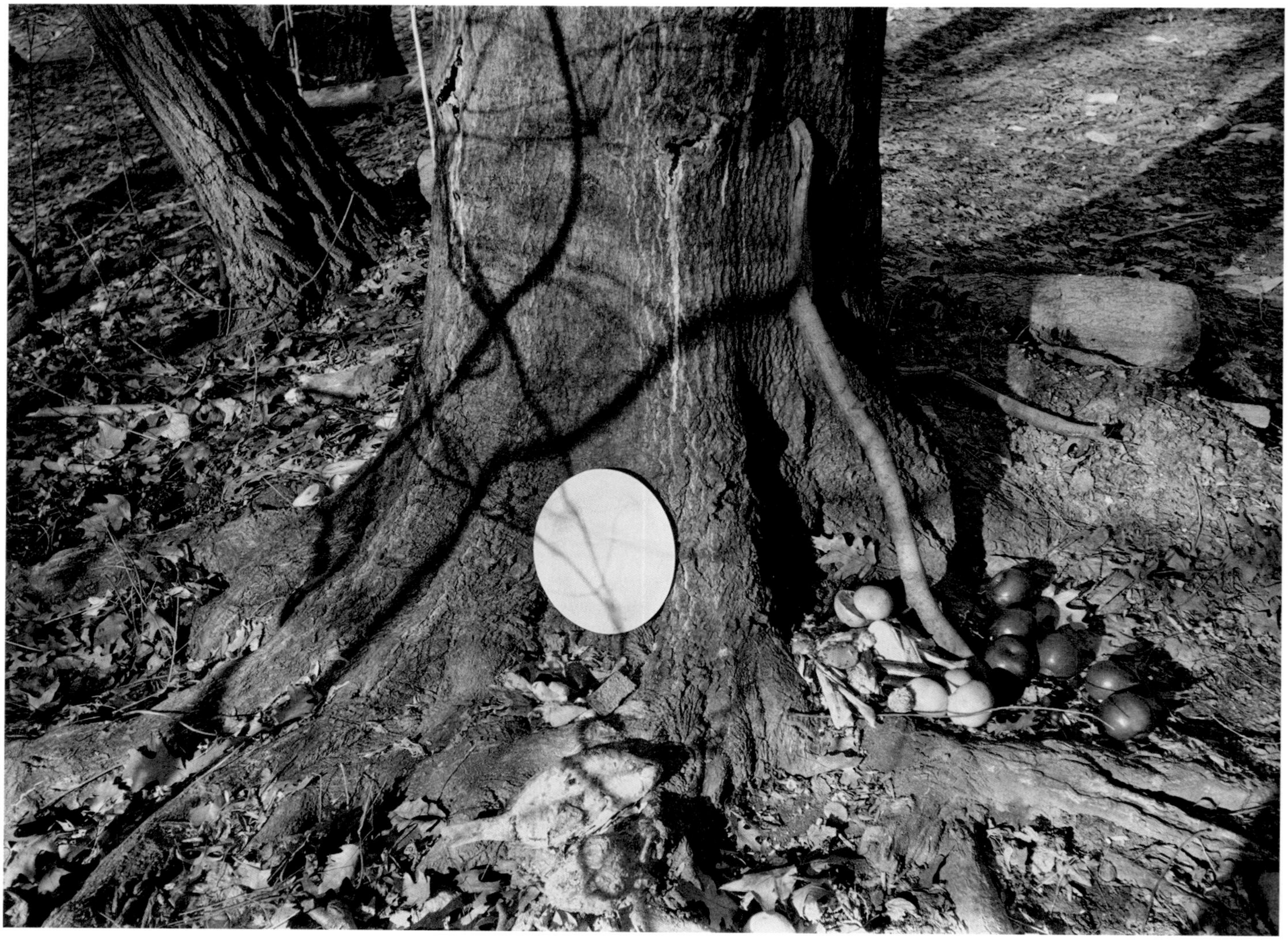

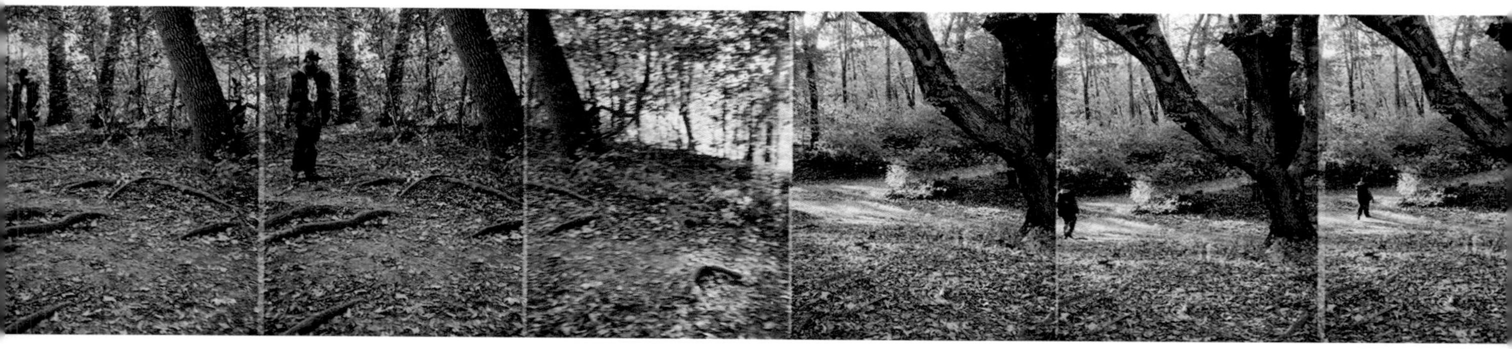

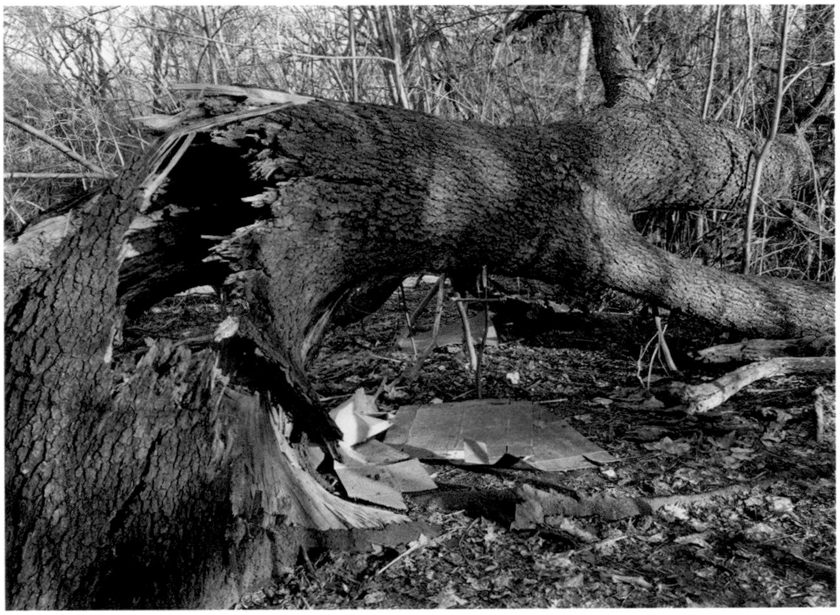

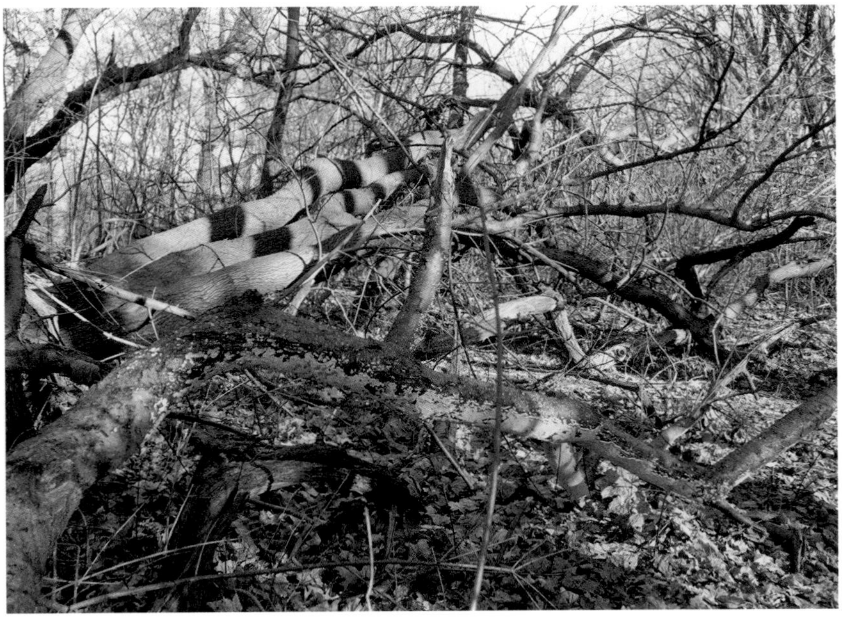

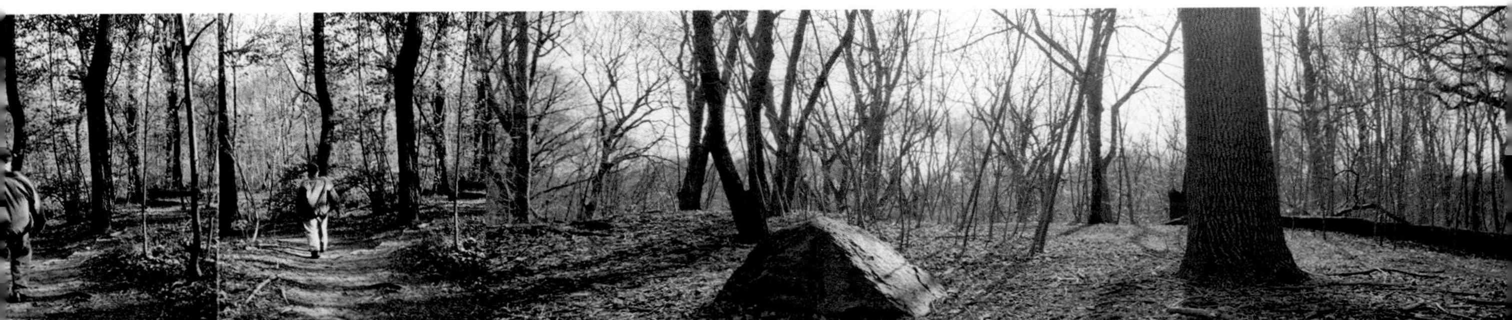

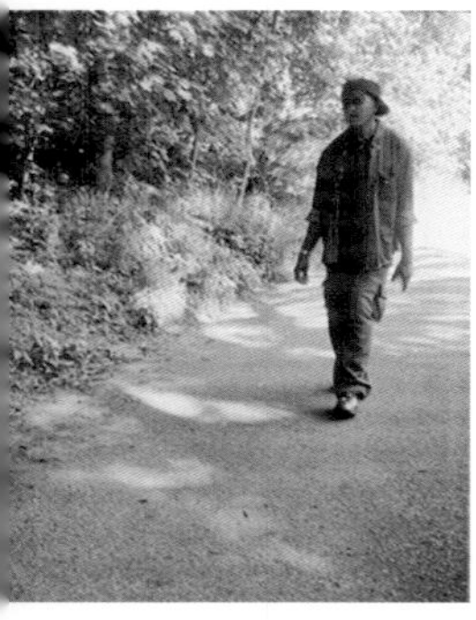

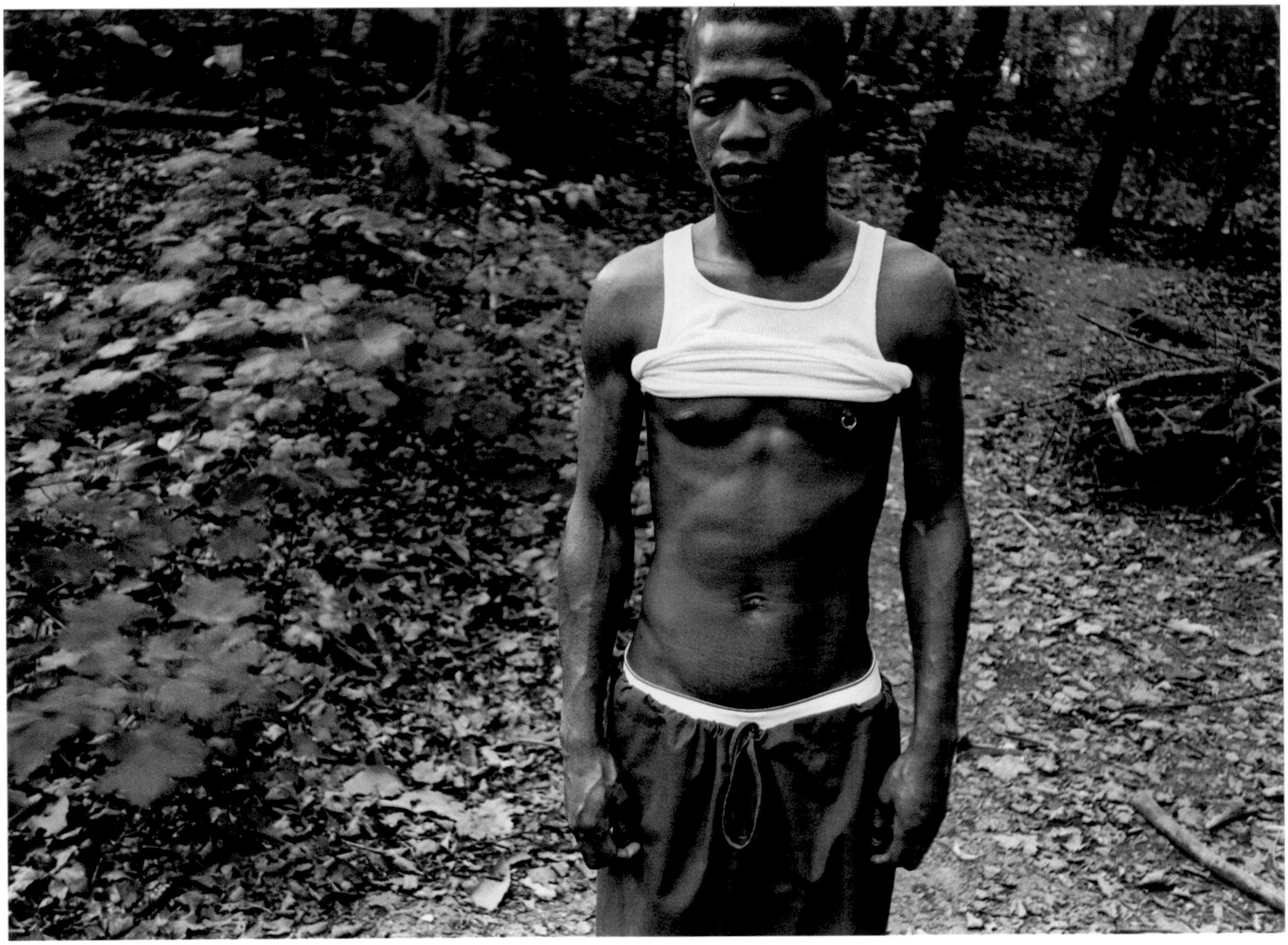

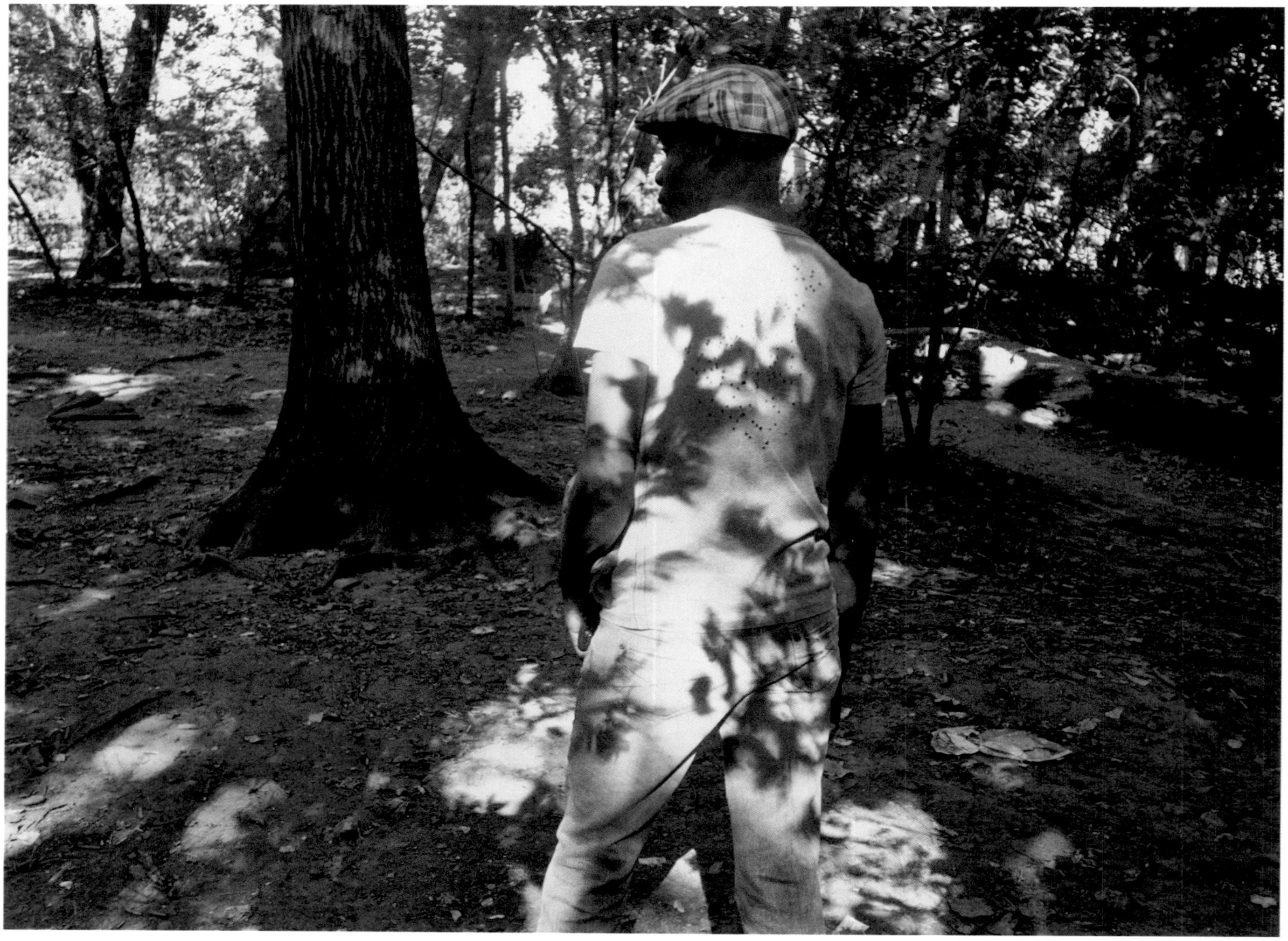

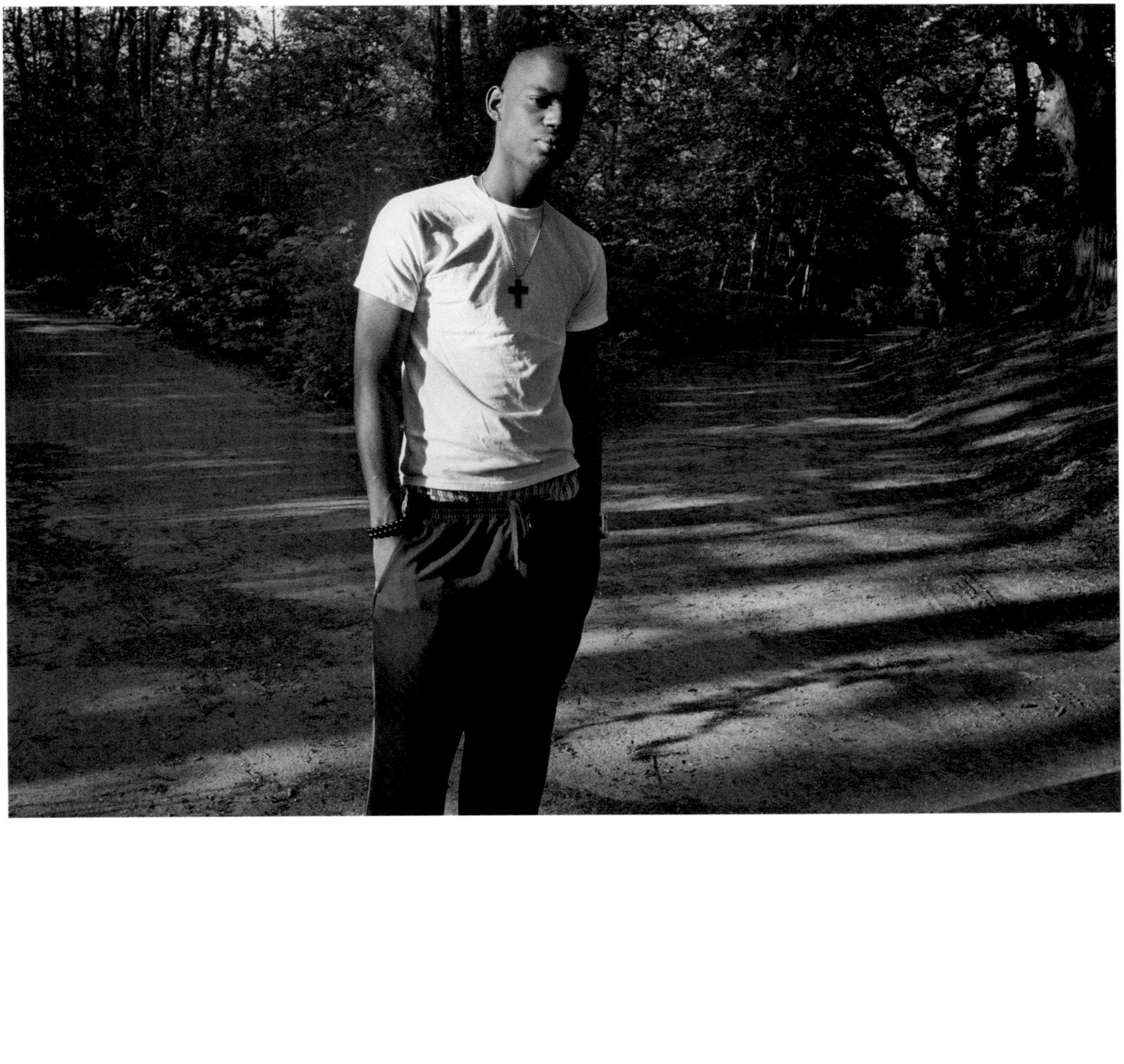

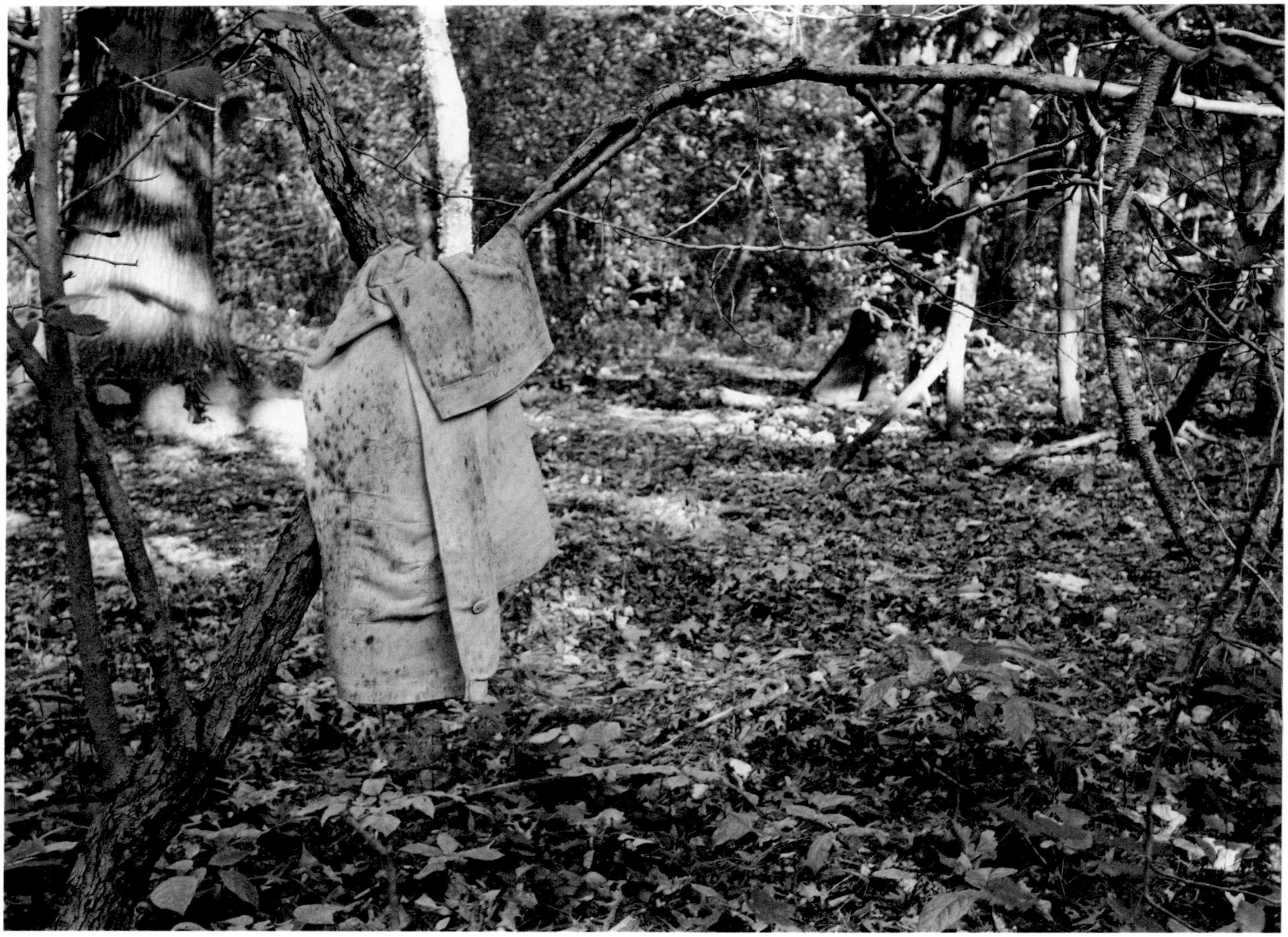

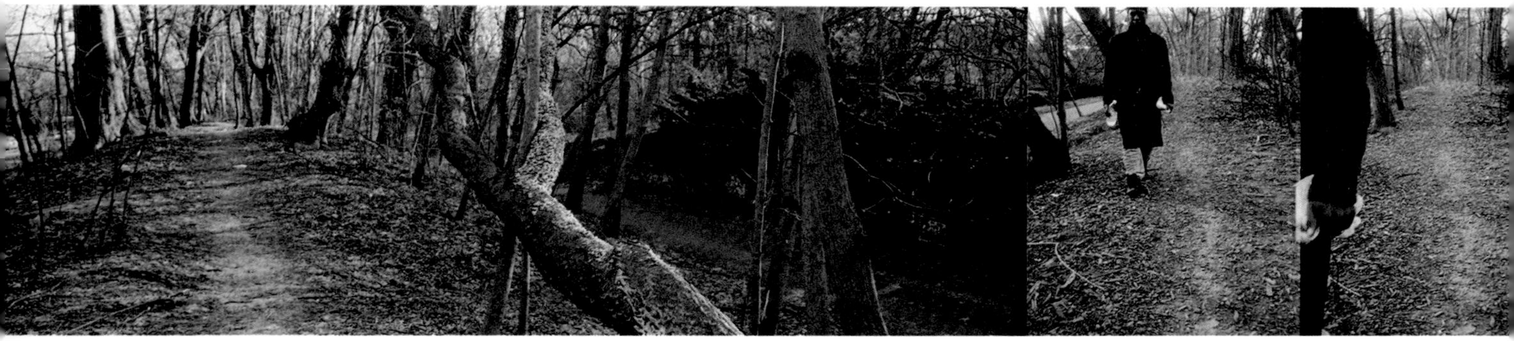

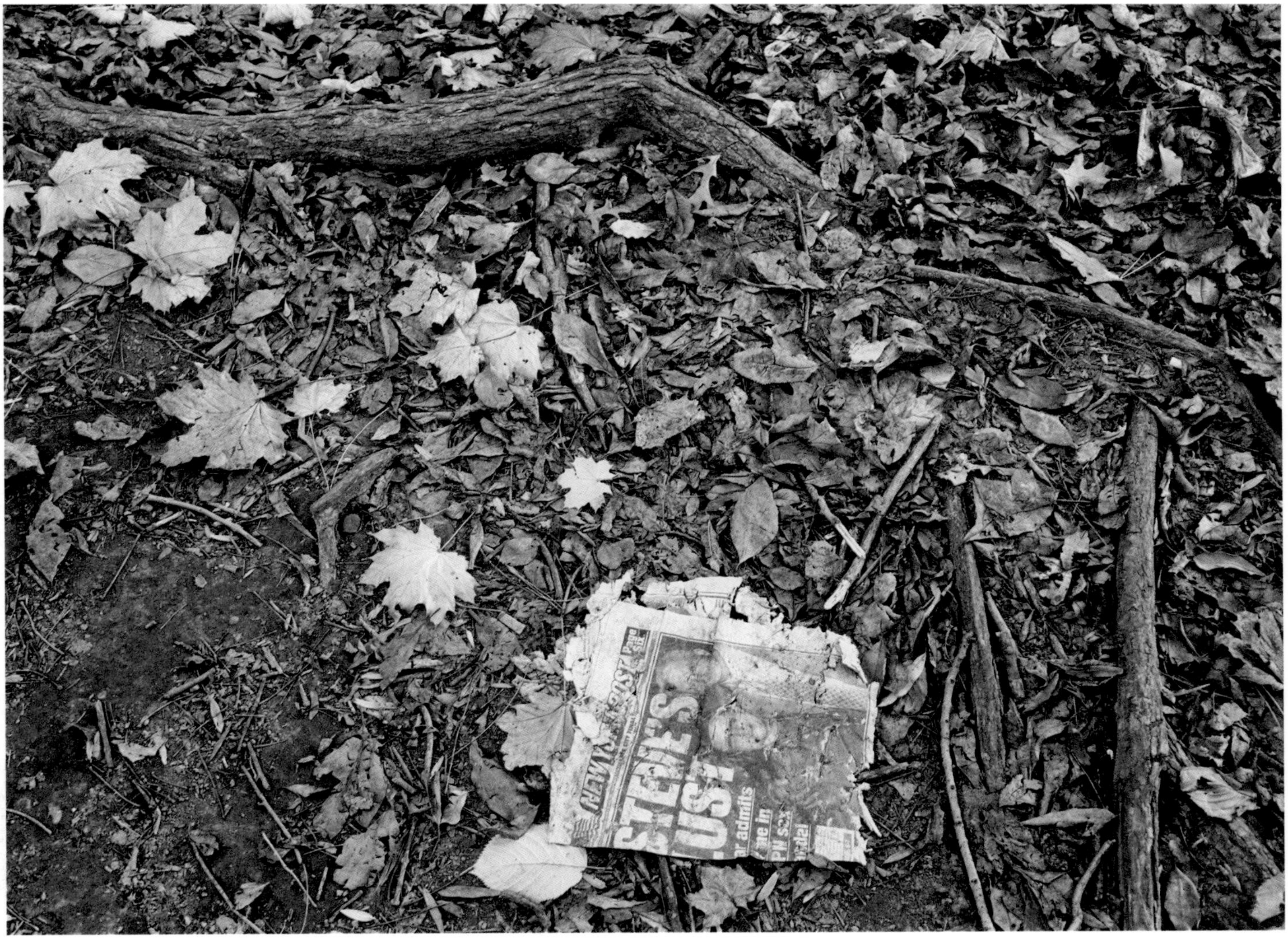
NEW YORK POST
Page Six
STEVE'S LUST
admits

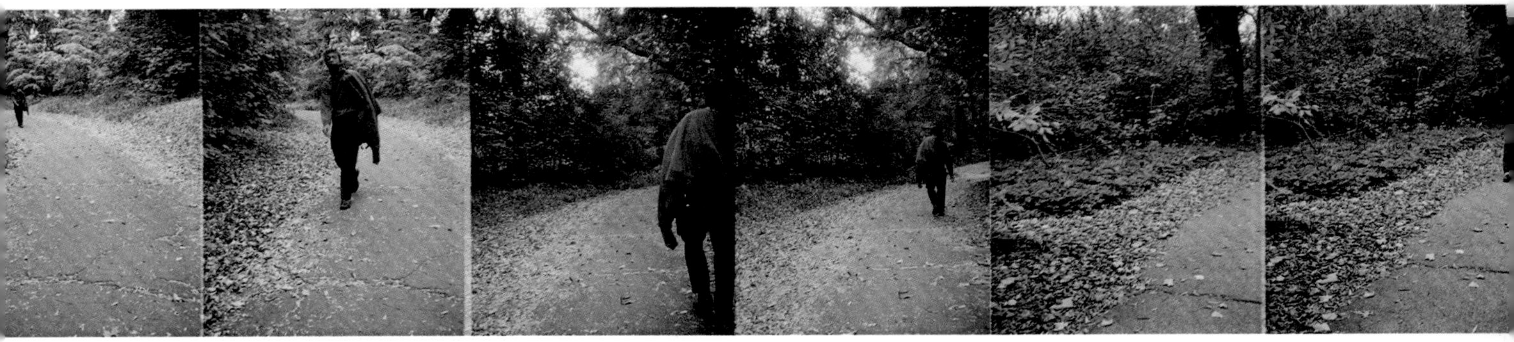

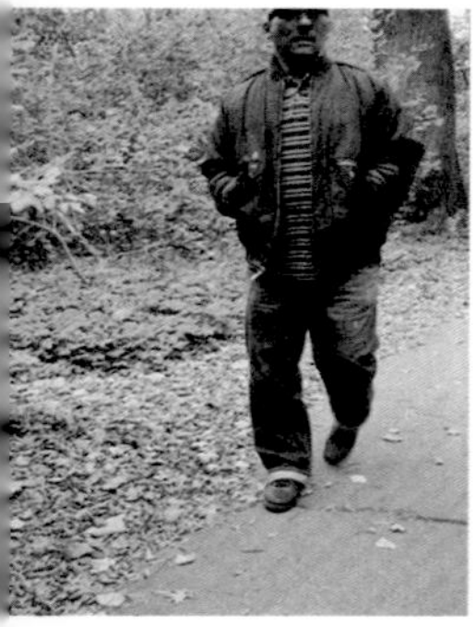

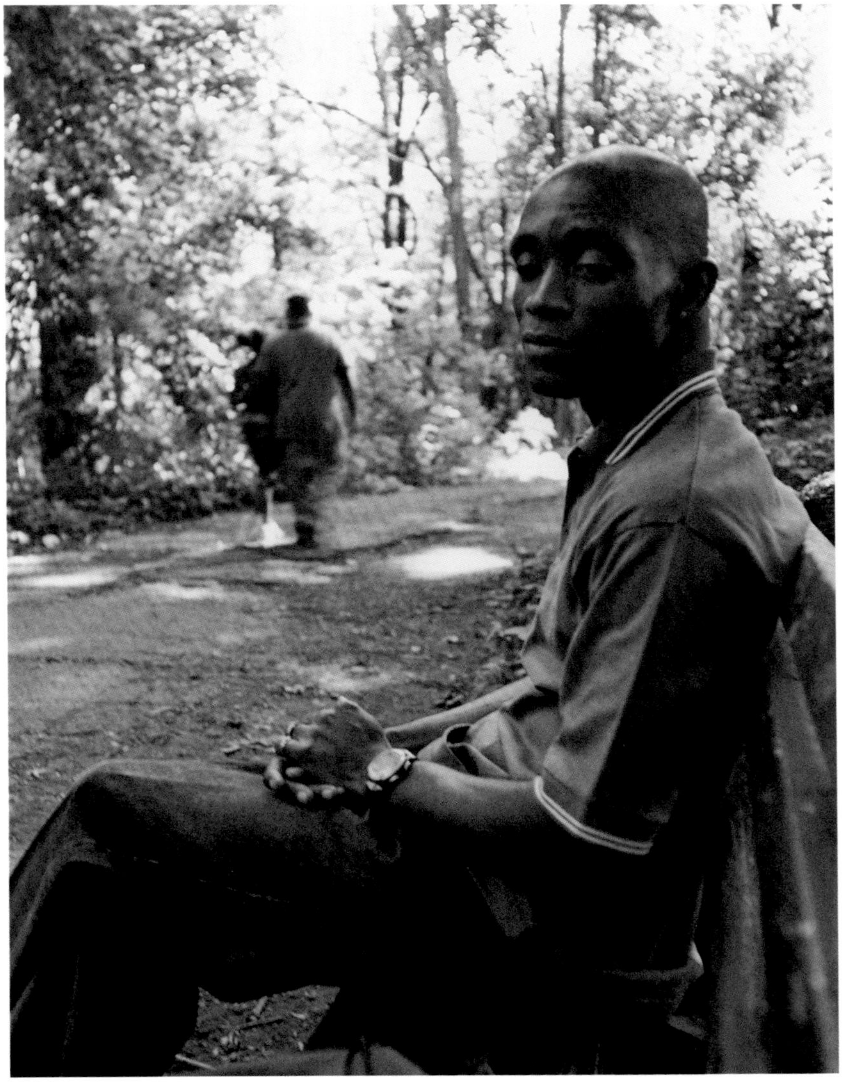

My thanks to Craig Cohen, Marvin Hoshino, G. Winston James,
Kai McBride, Daniel Power, and Anna and Giancarlo Roma.
T. R.

Published in the United States by powerHouse Books,
a division of powerHouse Cultural Entertainment, Inc.
37 Main Street, Brooklyn, NY 11201-1021
telephone: 212.604.9074
fax: 212.366.5247
e-mail: info@powerHouseBooks.com
website: www.powerHouseBooks.com

First edition, 2015
Library of Congress Control Number: 2015933682
ISBN: 978-1-57687-715-9

Printing and binding by EBS, Verona, Italy
Design by Marvin Hoshino

10 9 8 7 6 5 4 3 2 1

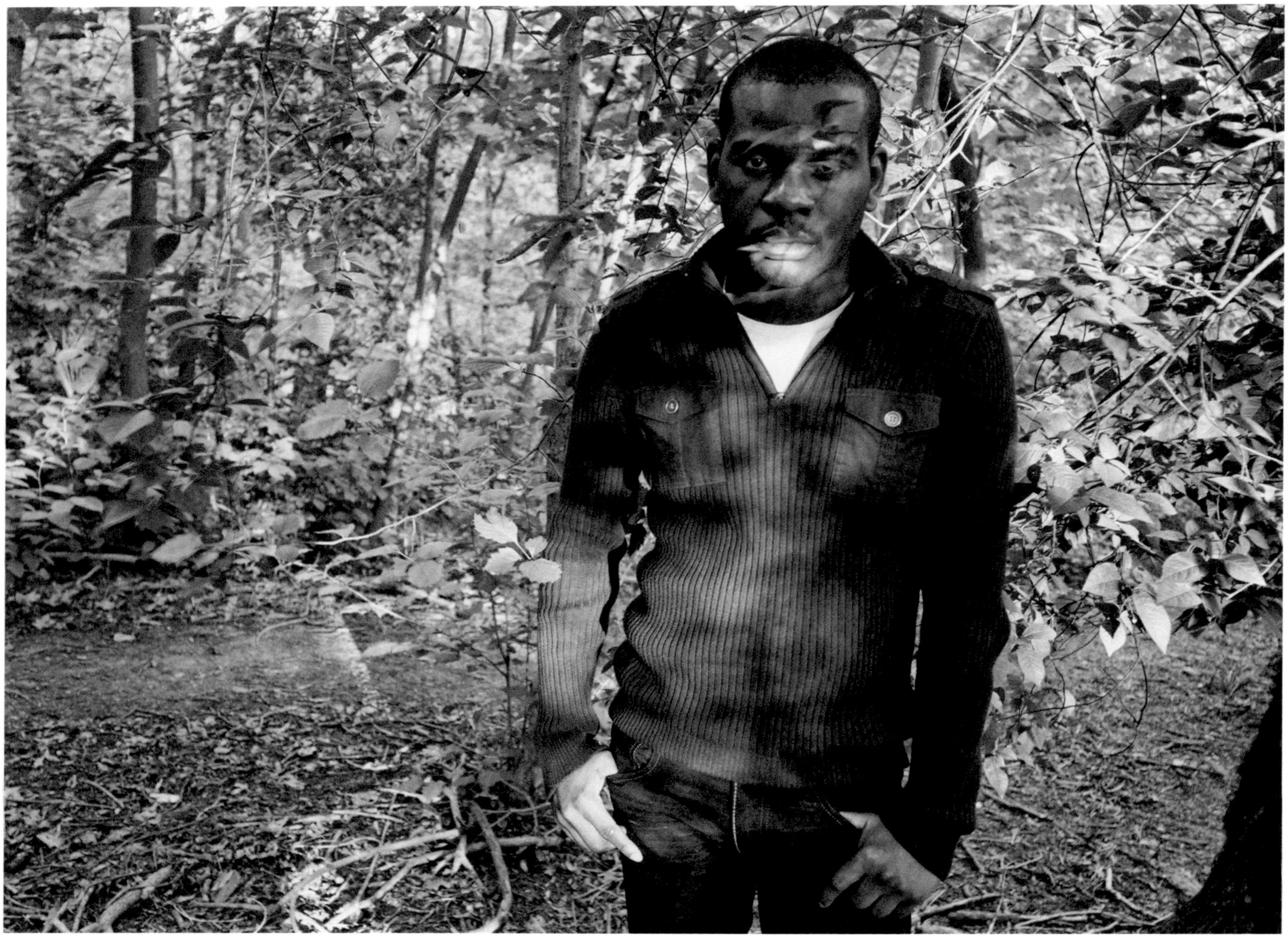